# Entertaining

## FROM AN ETHNIC INDIAN KITCHEN

# Entertaining

## FROM AN ETHNIC INDIAN KITCHEN

# KOMALI NUNNA

## Dedicated To

# Amma

Katiki Lakshmi Narasamma

*For her patience, hard work, love, strength, and inspiration*

## Thanks

**To my father, Late Katiki Venkata Subbaiah**

*Who gave me confidence and made me feel like a princess in his kingdom*

**To my brother, Katiki Ramakoteswara Rao**

*Who is responsible for the woman I am today*

**To all my brothers and sisters**

*For their unconditional love and support*

**To my children, Naveen and Silpa**

*Who made me realize that no other job in this world is more rewarding than being **Amma***

Most of all

**To my husband, Mal**
*For being patient with all my hobbies, collections, ventures and making my dream a reality*

# Contents

# Introduction

If you ask me what my passions are, my immediate response will be cooking and entertaining. And yet the word "entertaining" was not even part of my vocabulary while growing up in a small village called Swarna in the state of Andhra Pradesh, India.

I was born into a farming family, one of ten children. And I am not an exception to the rule; like every girl in the world, I received my cooking lessons while watching my mother in the kitchen. She was the backbone of our family structure, always attending to our needs, the household chores, sending workers to the field with designated responsibilities and cooking and taking care of guests. Whenever people visited (which was very frequent in my village), my mother would graciously invite them to join the family for a meal. It was not the beautiful flowers on the table or the elegant table settings and gourmet meals, but her hospitality that made people feel at home. Our day-to-day family meals were a simple affair, usually consisting of dal, one or two vegetable curries, chutney, yogurt and rice.

There was no television in those days. My mother would listen to the radio occasionally. If she heard a good recipe she would try to make it for the family. At times when the ingredients were not available, she would use her imagination to replace them, and would come up with her own variation. I paid little attention to all this and she often worried about my lack of interest in cooking, although my father had a lot of confidence in my potential to cook when the necessity arose.

In my village, a woman's role was limited to being a wife and a mother. Higher education and career advancement were not a part of a woman's agenda. It was my revolutionary older brother, Ramakoteswara Rao, with his strong belief in social reform and equal opportunities for women, who stood behind me in my choice to apply for college.

I enrolled in Maris Stella College in Vijayawada, in 1973. Here, I was fascinated by the beautifully decorated dorm dining room, with its walls painted a beautiful bluish green and decorated with tastefully chosen paintings. Even though I was born a Hindu, I would attend mass just to get a peek of the well-kept and beautifully adorned church on campus. I used to visit the convent to get a glimpse of the simple but elegant Ikebana flower arrangement (I didn't know that's what it was called at that time). Our college campus had beautiful manicured gardens where I would often go and daydream about having a garden of my own someday.

Like many women in India, mine was an arranged marriage. In 1980, I landed at the New York airport wearing a sari and sandals, my long braid almost touching my knees, without a clue as to how cold New York was in December. I continued on my journey to Grand Forks, North Dakota, where my husband was a post-doctoral scientist. The cold was severe, particularly for a person who had never seen snow in her life. I missed my mother's curries and chutneys and started experimenting with food to recreate her specialties. At our first party for my husband's friends, I waited nervously to see what the guests thought of my food. To my relief, they thought the dinner was great and finished the entire meal. Some of them wanted to learn Indian cooking! I felt like I had made my father proud. With the success of my first party, I was hooked onto cooking. I wanted to learn all the world-famous cuisines. I learned North Indian cooking from some of my friends, and from my American friends I learned baklava, quiche and pies. Soon, experimenting with different ethnic cuisines became my favorite pastime.

We moved to Boston in 1983, where I was introduced to Shobha Kumar, somebody who would become my special friend. She introduced me to the concept of elegant entertaining. Her house always had beautiful fresh flower arrangements and the table was always set with fine china. Then there were our neighbors, Pat and Georgette Coniglio, who introduced me to mouth-watering delicious Italian food, and consequently I was able to add Italian cuisine to my repertoire. My interest in cooking, gardening, flower arranging, cake decorating and entertaining grew tremendously. We rented a community garden plot during the summer to grow fresh vegetables. I hosted elaborate birthday parties for kids and dinner parties for adults. As a stay-at-home mom taking care of two kids, I would religiously watch *Mastering the Art of French Cooking with Julia Child* every afternoon as the kids took their nap. I learned how to cook French food, including homemade puff pastry and pithiviers.

In 1989 we moved to Southern California, a land of abundant sunshine perfect for growing anything. We started looking for a house with plenty of planting space and after five years of vigorous searching, we found a house with enough land for a vegetable garden, a flower garden and an herb garden. My husband converted the slope on the outside into an orchard, digging inch by inch, collecting every fruit tree possible and planting passionately. Soon the garden was full of flowers, fruits and vegetables. I made jams, marmalades and pickles from my home-grown produce.

Over the years, outdoor entertaining has become my signature style and entertaining an even bigger part of my life. My collections of pots, pans, cook books, china and linens have mushroomed. Every time I entertain, I set the most beautiful table and cook the most elegant meal to complement it. And now that my children have left home to attend college, I have finally found time to pursue my dream of writing a book about cooking and entertaining. It is my cherished hope that this will be a book that every bride would love to receive as a wedding present. I hope you share my passion for entertaining and find this book a handy companion.

# Elements of Entertaining

This book has evolved from my passion for cooking, decorating and entertaining. I have had the opportunity to learn the art of entertaining and the privilege to host many parties over the past 25 years. You will see my love for cooking, entertaining and decorating throughout the book. For me, cooking is an art, decorating a craft and entertaining a passion. Whether it is creating a culinary feast or decorating a dazzling table, I do it with the same passion and zeal.

Entertaining is not just the act of serving food and wine, as food and wine are only a part of the whole process. Entertaining is also about creating an ambiance that people will remember. The food, china, linens, candles, flowers, music and accessories are all necessary components that make a perfect ambiance.

## STYLE AND DESIGN

Style is simply an expression of oneself. There is a saying in India that a home tells a lot about the hostess. Everybody's home is a reflection of their personality and the way people entertain reflects personal style.

When I was growing up I would constantly be surrounded by a stream of visitors, but we never got the feeling that we were "entertaining" them, since it was more a way of life back then.

One should learn the basic elements of entertaining first, then combine the basics with original ideas, and finally derive a style of entertaining with a personal and unique flair.

When I came to America, I learned the basic elements of entertaining and married them with the traditions and culture I grew up with. I embellished this style with vibrant fabrics and the aromas, flavors and colors of Indian cuisine. I call my style eclectic, since it is a fusion of Eastern philosophy and Western style.

As far as design is concerned, choosing the colors, pattern and accessories for the party is much like designing and decorating your living space. The same rules also apply for setting a table.

## THEME

You need an inspiration to create a theme. The inspiration comes mainly from the nature of the event. Whether it is a celebration of tradition, season or a festival or simply having people over for dinner, they all contribute to the inspiration for a theme. Start planning the event once the theme is finalized. My inspiration for the color scheme sometimes comes from nature, my garden, and from the spices I use. If you look at the photos in this book, you will see that every chapter has a different theme. Each theme is supported by many details with the common denominator being Indian cuisine. The theme you choose should flow cohesively from the beginning to the end of the event.

When we moved into our house, I celebrated a 50th birthday party for a very special friend. It was my favorite garden party theme. I sent invitations that looked liked seed pockets. I made picket fence planters with the help of a friend, decorated the planters with vines, flowers and fruits in keeping with the garden theme. I used simple geraniums with one or two bright blooms inside the painted planters as center pieces. Since the guest of honor was a vegetarian, the menu was planned around garden-fresh vegetables. I painted small terra-cotta pots and filled them with a bag of wild flower seeds attached to a small poem to give as party favors. When you plan a party, you should take into consideration the theme of the event.

Each element of the design collectively creates the overall theme of the party.

## PREPARATION AND PLANNING

Proper planning and organization are keys to successful entertaining. Any party, whether small or big, requires planning. It is a good idea to read all the recipes you are planning to cook and make a list of the ingredients you need. Most of the spices can be found at regular supermarkets. You can get the specialty spices at Indian stores.

1. Plan the menu.
2. Check for the ingredients and spices.
3. Come up with a check list.
4. Prepare the time line.

Once you come up with the time line, it is important to stick to it.

## PANTRY

I keep a well-stocked pantry with spices, dry legumes, different kinds of flours and of course a variety of rice. Coming from South India, rice is a staple in every meal in my household. You can entertain people with ease for any last-minute get-togethers if you have a well-stocked pantry.

## INVITATIONS

I send invitations for special occasions and formal entertaining. Usually I end up picking up the phone and inviting the guests. I stay away from E-vites, though. I feel it is impersonal to invite people with electronic mail.

## MENU

If you're an amateur cook, I suggest you try the recipes first before including them in your party menu.

Almost all types of Indian food can be made in advance with the exception of the breads. Most of the dishes taste better after they sit in the refrigerator for a day, allowing you to plan and cook in advance for the party. I often plan my menu around the seasonal ingredients. When you choose the menu with seasonal vegetables and fruits, they not only taste better but you can also find them at lower prices (for example, in holiday entertaining, seasonal pomegranates play an important role in the menu planning).

When you are entertaining, keep in mind that some people are vegetarians and that many people are turning to vegetarianism. In this book, all the menus are designed to accommodate both vegetarians and non-vegetarians.

The menus provided in this book are my suggestions. You can mix and match in any way that you choose. It is important to create a menu with a combination of texture, flavor, color and balance in nutrition.

Aesthetics are very important to me when I plan a menu. I don't serve all dishes with a similar texture or color. Unlike Western menus, Indian menus do not have one main dish. All dishes complement one another. For example, you don't serve two dishes that are similar in taste and texture, such as two types of dals or two soupy dishes. If you are serving one curry with gravy, complement it with a dry curry, that is a curry without gravy. Usually curries with lot of gravy are served with chappatis or parathas. Soupy vegetables, such as sambar, are served with plain rice accompanied by one or two dry vegetable curries.

Some menus in this book may seem elaborate. It is not my intention to make them complicated, but it is my desire to give you options to choose when you entertain. You don't have to cook the entire menu. You can cook part of a meal, buy ready made food and put it all together to complete the meal. For instance, naan is readily available at some super markets such as Trader Joe's.

# TABLE SETTING

Setting the table is an art in itself. It is an expression of the host's personal style to create an atmosphere that makes guests feel special the moment they walk in. Your table setting need not be grand and expensive, but it should be appropriate for the occasion that you are celebrating. Proper table setting will enhance the food and the mood around the table.

# CHINA

My interest for dishes goes back to my college days. Whenever I would go to exhibitions and fairs, I would spend my pocket money on plates and nice coffee mugs for my mother's kitchen back in the village. Here in America, I have been collecting china ever since I got married. Not all china is expensive. Sometimes I collect things for their color or shape. I like Japanese pottery for its artistry and elegance.

I have to admit that I have enough plates to serve at least a hundred people. I collected the basic white Corningware plates many years ago. I still get a lot of use out of them. I don't like to use disposables while entertaining at home. You can keep the paper plates aside for picnics. Even then, choose something biodegradable to save the planet.

My advice for any host or hostess is to buy basic china to serve eight. If your collection is of the same color, you can add an accent piece or change the napkins to create an entirely different look. Oftentimes I see people using their china as show pieces and not ever using them. There is no point in owning something if you don't use it with the people you love. I like to engage my kids in setting the table for the family meals. They come up with a new design every time.

# SILVERWARE

If you are entertaining with Indian food, you cannot avoid using your fingers to eat parathas or naan (check page 26, about eating with your fingers). In Indian cuisine, almost all curries are made up of bite-sized pieces of meat or vegetables, which makes it easy to eliminate the use of the dinner knife. It is also a common practice in India to use two spoons to eat. One spoon to eat the food and the other to push the food into the first.

There are numerous ways to arrange the silverware on the table. I stick with the classic method. You set the silverware in such a way that you work your way in. Silverware should be placed along the side of the plate in the order that you will be using it. Forks go on the left and knife and spoons on the right. The serrated edge of the knife faces the plate. The dessert fork and/or spoon rest horizontally on the table directly above the dinner plate. The outermost silverware are used first and the innermost in the end. For example, if you are serving soup as the first course, the soup spoon should be at the outer edge to the right. For an added interest, I sometimes use oriental chopstick rests as knife rests.

## GLASSWARE

My philosophy is that even if you are serving only water at the dinner, serve it in a proper glass. Even water seems to taste much better.

It is boring to match everything on the table, so I like to mix and match to make the setting interesting. However, I do like to coordinate colored water glasses with the flowers on the table and/ or with the napkins.

A glass is considered the most important part of the drink. The proper etiquette for the party is to serve cocktails in appropriate glasses. Red wine is usually served in a large bowl stemware and white wine is served in a small, narrower one. For a change, you can also serve wine in small glasses similar to juice glasses, like the French and Italians do.

Tall high ball glasses are good for water, lemonade or iced tea. Based on the type of drinks you are planning to serve, you can collect specialty stemware such as martini glasses. If you are on a budget, settle for all-purpose glasses, such as ten to twelve ounce stemware, which can be used for wine, water or soft drinks.

The water glass should always be positioned at the tip of the dinner knife. Wine glasses for red wine go immediately to the right and above the smaller one for white wine. You need at least two glasses per person during the cocktail hour, in addition to the glasses at the table.

## COCKTAILS

Drinking alcohol is a very personal and cultural activity. Alcohol plays a major role in the Western style of entertaining, whereas in Indian culture, food takes the center stage. While growing up in a village, alcohol was never part of our lifestyle. I see many immigrant families still carrying on the tradition of not including alcohol in their lifestyle. When you are entertaining, it is important to respect the religious and cultural boundaries of your guests. I have adopted the custom of including alcohol in my entertaining. I enjoy making different mixed drinks with tropical flavors and serving them in elegant glasses.

I know I am not a wine connoisseur (which is why I requested help from an expert to pair the wine with the food, page 314). Food should complement the wine and vice-versa. It's all about balancing flavors. When I entertain, there is always a group of people who drink and those who don't. I always include non-

alcoholic beverages in the menu for kids and for adults who avoid alcohol.

## FLOWERS, CENTERPIECES AND CANDLES

Flowers can bring life to any party. Some people relax with music, others with flowers. I belong to the second category. I prefer to have fresh flowers all around the house including the bathroom. I planned my garden in such a way that I would have a supply of fresh flowers all year round.

The general rule of thumb in creating a centerpiece for the dining table is that it should be either above or below the eye level. The centerpiece should not obstruct the people's conversation and need not contain flowers. You can use a bowl of seasonal fruits with greenery from the backyard. For an added interest, open one or two fruits in the centerpieces. My Thanksgiving table is always set with seasonal backyard fruits and gourds.

If the container you are using for your arrangement is very ornate, keep the arrangement simple with single-colored flowers or use just greenery to bring out the beauty of the container.

I don't like using flowers or candles that have a lot of fragrance at the dinner table. Indian food is already very aromatic with its various spices. It is the aroma from the food that should entice people.

I prefer to keep the highly scented flowers at the entrance. This way the guests are welcomed by the fragrance from the fresh flowers.

Candles can brighten any room. Votive candles along the table are an elegant touch to any table. Everything looks better in candlelight. Limit the tall, bulky candles to the buffet table.

## LINENS

Whether it is a trip to the LA fabric district or the textile emporium in India, I'm always on the lookout for that special fabric to use on my table for my next party. It has been my hobby to collect fabrics. I use different styles of fabrics depending on the theme of the party. It is nice to have a collection of tablecloths in various colors. Bright Indian fabrics add an extra touch to a party with an Indian menu.

Taking proper care of your linens is very important. Most Indian curries have turmeric which can stain fabrics. It is important to spot-

*Detail: Using banana leaves in place of plates is an ethnic style very commonly seen in India.*

treat them and wash them according to the instructions. I soak some of heavy fabrics with 1% bleach solution for a short while before washing. Make sure you read the instructions before washing any fabric.

Napkins are essential to any table setting. It is fun to collect an array of napkins. Keep all your fabric possessions together. When I use a simple tablecloth, I use contrasting napkins to bring color to the table. You can set the table a different way each time, just by changing the napkins and a few accessories. You can mix and match colors of the same palate for a special touch.

## ACCESSORIES

Accessories are like jewelry; they bring that extra character and a whimsical touch to the table. Since most of my entertaining is with Indian-themed parties, I like to incorporate some ethnic accessories in my design. Look for these accessories in import stores like Cost Plus and Pier 1.

## MUSIC

Music is an important element of entertaining. Almost everybody relaxes with music. The music you choose to play at the party should go with the overall theme. My choice of music is usually Ravi Sankar's sitar pieces. I stay away from loud vocal music. The music should not interfere with your guests' conversation. Rather, it should make people relax and have good time.

## DETAILS

Place cards are useful when you are entertaining formally. This way, people don't have to guess where they will be sitting. Also, your guests feel special to be sitting at the table setting with their name on it.

Menu cards are important as well. A few years ago, I had a garden party for my neighbors. Not all of them were familiar with Indian food. So at every table I had menu cards that explained every dish with the ingredients used and how it was prepared. The guests had fun reading, learning and tasting an entirely different cuisine.

Buffet cards make it easier for people to choose what they want to eat, especially when they are specifically marked vegetarian or non-vegetarian.

## BUFFET

Setting the buffet table is like setting the stage for an orchestra and creating the music. Think outside the box when you are choosing the

tablecloth. I like to use an Indian sari or Indian-themed fabric to cover the buffet table and set the mood. I often create a focal point with a big centerpiece using a garden urn filled with seasonal backyard fruit combined with flowers. Unlike the dining table centerpieces, which should be above or below the eye level, buffet table flowers can be tall and dramatic.

I like to use a variety of platters with different textures. Depending on the dish I serve, I like to use bamboo trays lined with banana leaves to invoke the feeling of the tropics. It is also important to set the platters at varying heights to give a sense of interest and drama to the table.

I prefer to set the appetizers at one corner, so you can guide the guests to find their way to the appetizers and help themselves. You can also serve beverages in a buffet style with menu cards. A dessert buffet can be set at a different table or in a separate room. The placement of dishes is important as well. It is recommended to set the plates at the beginning of the buffet table and place silverware at the end, wrapped in the napkin so that guests don't have to juggle with the food and cutlery. Glasses should be set at the very end of the table or at a different table along with the drinks. It is important to set the table in a way that guests can navigate with ease. Buffet-style

entertaining gives the host some time away from the kitchen and an opportunity to mingle with the guests.

## PARTY FAVORS

Party favors are to thank people for coming and sharing the meal. It is not absolutely essential to have party favors, but they add a personal touch to any party. It is something that your guests take home to remember the good times. Party favors need not be expensive or out of the ordinary. Think of something that will flow with your theme and match your personal style. My favorite favors to give are homemade jams. I build up the inventory in the pantry during the summer by using the fruits from my backyard. Another favorite of mine is homemade garam masala powder or masala spice blend, neatly packed in a 4 ounce glass jar tied with raffia along with a note attached for instructions for use. Or it can be a small loaf of homemade tea cake or a few pieces of chocolate. Even the simplest gift can be elegantly presented with beautiful wrapping. You don't always have to set the favors at the dinner table. Things like a jar of spice blend can be handed out when the guests are leaving, one per family.

## Journal

It is nice to maintain a journal for all your possessions and the locations you store them in. This way you can find things when you need them. It is very important to maintain the journal, especially if you are like me. A small part of every room in my house is filled with entertaining gear. There is no point in having something if you can't find it when you need it.

## Garnishing

Presentation of food is very important. First you feast with your eyes and take in the aroma with your nose, and only then savor it. Garnish the dish with the ingredients you used in that dish. Good garnishes for Indian cuisine are chopped cilantro/coriander and mint, fried curry leaves, garam masala powder, a sprinkling of paprika or masala spice blend. Proper garnishing is not only pleasing to the eye, but it also enhances the flavor of the dish and gives it that finishing touch.

## Coffee and Tea

If I am serving a typical South Indian meal, I end the meal with coffee. More often my entertaining ends with chai. Chai is an Indian style milky tea, often flavored with cardamom or ginger, which is a perfect ending to any Indian meal. I also include Western-style tea because I like the elegance of serving tea from a tea pot with a cup and saucer. Many people cannot handle caffeine late at night, so I do include decaffeinated herbal teas as an option.

## Supari

Supari is a mouth freshener as well as a digestive aid taken after a heavy meal. It is offered in the same context as after dinner mints in the West. Supari is a delightful mixture of spices such as fennel seeds, dried fruits, nuts, tiny silver coated sugar balls and slivers of areca nuts. There are different combinations and concoctions available at Indian stores. Usually it is offered in a small, beautiful silver bowl with a small spoon for guests to help themselves. Put about one teaspoon of supari in the mouth and chew on it. Offering supari is the finale to any meal. Usually people don't eat or drink after chewing supari.

Most of all, entertaining is about being a gracious host. Being a good host does not mean having a spotless house and serving gourmet meals. It is about creating an atmosphere in which your guests will feel welcome and comfortable. Entertaining is about having a great time with the people you care about and creating memories with them.

# Indian Cuisine

*I*ndian cuisine wears its heritage with pride and dignity. The colorful and vibrant history, culture, and diversity of the nation is expressed through the incredible variety of food items from the various regions. Whether it is the cool cachumbar or the hot samosa, food touches all taste buds. It can be very addictive.

Indian food has evolved over the centuries. It is a complex cuisine that has been influenced by the waves of immigrants that came to this land from far and wide. The Persians and the Jews came to escape religious persecution, while the Moghuls and the Greeks came to conquer. The Portuguese came to colonize while the British came for trade, and warmed their way into becoming the rulers. Whatever their intentions, they brought with them their own culture and traditions.

Persian culinary technology, such as the gilding of food with silver and gold leaves, was introduced in India by the Moghuls. Rich sauces and elaborate rice dishes with nuts and dry fruits are also a Persian influence. With the combinations of Indian spices it eventually became the foundation of Moghul cuisine. The Portuguese introduced hot chilies, and after the colonization of Goa, chilies became an important ingredient of Indian cuisine.

India's many religions have also influenced its cuisine in a profound way. Hinduism, in one form or the other, is professed by about 80% of the population. Other prominent religions are Islam, Buddhism and Christianity. Jainism and Sikhism are prominent in some regions and Zoroastrianism is the faith of the Parsees. There are also many followers of Judaism. Each of these religions has its own particular restrictions and eating habits. Muslims, who make up about 13% of India's population do not eat pork. Hindus, Jains and Sikhs do not eat beef. Jains and many Hindus, particularly from the Brahmin caste, are strict vegetarians. Traditionally, the Jains refrain from eating anything that grows under the ground so as not to harm any insects. Their faith prohibits injuring life in any of its forms.

Vegetarianism is common in India, partly because of religious restrictions and partly out of necessity. Dal, a legume puree often laced with flavorful spice seasoning, is quintessential to Indian cuisine. Each region has its own specialty of seasonings. Dals play a vital role in the Indian diet. They are the primary source of protein for many vegetarians. The Indian vegetarian cuisine is a perfect combination of grains, beans and spices. It is nutritious, balanced and yet absolutely flavorful and delicious. Mahatma Gandhi used

vegetarianism to reinforce the concept of Ahimsa - the philosophy of nonviolence against any living creature. Some states like Gujarat follow this principle of nonviolence with great pride.

Rice has a place of honor in South Indian homes. The traditional way of inviting people for a meal is to ask them to come and eat rice. Yellow rice (tinted with turmeric) is used extensively in various ceremonies. For example, in the Hindu wedding ceremony, when the bride and groom pour yellow rice over each other's head, it signifies prosperity and fertility. Rice is the staple food in South India. Every dish is prepared to be eaten with rice. Basmati rice is usually consumed in the North. There are numerous varieties of rice consumed in the South and they are usually steam cooked without any fat or salt. In my house basmati rice is reserved for pulaos, biryanis and to serve with North Indian curries. For South Indian curries, chutneys, pickles, sambar and rasam, I prefer long grain or Thai jasmine rice.

In the North, however, with the exception of Kashmir, meals generally revolve around the flat breads called roti. Most of the flat breads are cooked on stove-top over the griddle. Some are deep fried such as pooris and bhaturas and some are stuffed with an array of fillings, such as parathas filled with vegetables or paneer. All these breads are a perfect accompaniment to any North Indian meal.

Native ingredients play an important role in regional cuisine. In the coastal state of Kerala, for example, coconut is used abundantly in most of the dishes whereas the state of Andhra Pradesh is famous for its flaming red hot pickle, Avakaya, made of raw mango, loaded with cayenne pepper. Indians like contrasting flavors and textures in their palate. All accompaniments such as pickles, chutneys, papadams, salads, yogurt raitas, bread and rice contribute to the great kaleidoscope of flavors and textures to the meal.

Pickles and chutneys contribute to the authenticity of the cuisine. Chutneys can be cooked or uncooked, sweet, hot or pungent. In the South, pickles are spicy and pungent with a generous use of cayenne, mustard, and fenugreek powder. North Indian pickles are salty and sour but not as hot. When I was growing up, pickle making was considered a talent that every village woman possessed. It became an art form in their expert hands. This was also the way to preserve vegetables for hot summers, when they would be in limited supply. Making chutneys and pickles from every possible vegetable was an important part of my mother's repertoire. However, none of her recipes existed on paper, all having been passed down from one generation to another. Village women take pride in stocking their cupboards with pickling jars and serving them as an accompaniment to the main meal. In Andhra Pradesh, people start their meal with lip-smacking pickles or chutneys and rice so that it activates the enzymes to crave for hot and spicy meals.

Along with pickles and chutneys, another important accompaniment with Indian food are papadams and vadiams (wafers). In my village, making these papadams and vadiams was a ritual during the summer. Flat rooftops are lined with bright sarees to air dry papadams and vadiams, taking advantage of the scorching summer heat. Papadams are usually made with stiff, pliable dough using urad dal or mung dal powder. They are rolled into 6 - 8 inch thin discs. Vadiams, on the other hand, can be made with rice flour, tapioca, and different beans. Vadiams can be cooked or uncooked batter dropped by spoonfuls onto the fabric lined surface and dried in the sun. Popular flavorings for these wafers include black pepper, garlic, green chilies, red chilies, cumin and ajwain. Once they are completely dried, they should be stored in an air-tight container to be used for the rest of the year. Not many people make these at home anymore (I still make vadiams during summer taking advantage of the California sunshine, just to keep my mother's tradition alive). You can buy arrays of papadams and vadiams (wafers) at Indian stores. These wafers can be quickly fried in hot oil before serving. Keep in mind that they will expand considerably in hot oil. These flavorful wafers are munched upon during the meal time. They not only give an extra crunch to the meal but also provide a different texture while eating rice with chutney, sambar or rasam. These wafers are like bread for South Indians. These can also be served as a snack with tea or cocktails.

Another important component of the Indian diet is yogurt. Meals often end with some form of yogurt. Raita, a combination of yogurt and vegetables or fruit is more popular in the North. In the South, yogurt is often eaten with plain rice to cool the stomach at the end of a hot, spicy meal. Making yogurt is an important culinary tradition in every Indian house. Even today, I continue to follow this tradition religiously by boiling milk for yogurt every morning.

Adding seasoning to the food is very important. The process of seasoning the food is called baghar or tadka in the North. Every Indian language has a different name for this process. Oil is heated to a high temperature, and the red chilies, different spices, dals, and curry leaves are added. When the spices start spluttering and popping, pour this hot sizzling mixture over the curries. Sometimes dishes are seasoned at the beginning while others are seasoned in the final stage.

Spices are synonymous with Indian cooking. In the West, the word "curry" is commonly used to describe Indian food. The British came up with this word based on the Tamil word "kari", which means black pepper. But it is strictly a Western invention. To the best of my knowledge, a universal curry powder does not exist in India. Instead, there are hundreds of spice combinations differing from region to region. Such combinations require dry and wet grinders. The big granite mortar and pestle are as common there as toasters are in American kitchens. Most of the spice blends are made after dry roasting spices to bring out their essential oils and aromas. A wet grinder is important for grinding ingredients such as garlic and ginger.

Another indispensable item in the kitchen is a pressure cooker. It saves a lot of time when cooking dals. On the other hand, ovens have never been a part of the Indian kitchens, except in Punjab, where the tandoor ovens have been used to make roti and to cook meat.

Marinating vegetables is not a common practice; however, several meat dishes are marinated with spices in order to tenderize the meat and infuse it with flavor prior to cooking.

In traditional Indian cooking, desserts are always cooked on the stove-top. Many North Indian sweets are made with milk and nuts. South Indian desserts, on the other hand, are typically made with rice flour, besan (chickpea flour), legumes and coconut. Fruit is also commonly served as dessert. Cardamom is the most commonly used flavoring in almost all Indian desserts. Some desserts are flavored with rose water and orange flavored water, which is a Persian influence.

Eating with your fingers is the common practice in Indian culture. It is customary to wash your hands and feet before you sit for the meal. You need practice and skill to eat with fingers like Indians do. We are allowed to eat with our right hand only, while the left hand is typically reserved for hygienic purposes. During meal time the left hand is used to drink water, pass the food around or to serve more food for oneself. North Indians use only the tips of their fingers to tear up the piece of chappati or naan and wrap it around the meat or vegetable to pick up and eat. They use their bread to mop the gravy from their plates, whereas South Indians use their fingers to mix rice with chutney or curry and to pick up the food and put it in the mouth. In both practices, they keep the palm of their hands clean.

Offering symbolic thambulam is an integral part of the Indian cultural heritage and a simple gesture of respect for the guests. In India, none of the religious and auspicious occasions end without offering thambulam. Simple thambulam consists of betel leaves, areka nuts and fruits. Offering thambulam was a ritual in my mother's life to wish a blessing for the newly married couple, a safe delivery to a pregnant woman, or to wish a safe journey to departing guests. People chew on betel leaves and areka nuts after meal as mouth fresheners and digestive aids.

Pan, on the other hand, along with betel leaves and areka nuts includes aromatic and sweet spices as cardamom, fennel seeds, tiny silver coated sugar balls and kawra. Chewing pan was a Northern tradition, passed on to the rest of the country. Pan became fashionable during the Moghul period. Beautifully crafted jeweled containers were used to hold the pan for the Moghul emperors.

*A well stocked pantry is essential to entertain with ease at any last-minute get-togethers.*

# Menus for Entertaining

*I* came to America as a young bride with very little experience in cooking or entertaining. I can still remember my first dinner party for six. I spent all day cooking nervously and had barely put together four dishes before the doorbell rang and the guests arrived. As time went by, I gained experience and developed a great passion for the finer points of cooking and entertaining.

After 25 years of experience as a home entertainer, I am ready to share what I have learned. Whether it is an intimate dinner party for six or a grand gala for twenty-five people, my goal is to provide recipes and guidelines for entertaining. These are some of my favorite menus which I use to entertain my friends and family. All these parties have different themes with an Indian flair. I hope you will have as much fun as I do at your parties.

## 1. Snack & Chaat Party

## 2. Tea Party

## 3. Dosa Party

## 7. Outdoor Candle Light Dinner

## 8. Elegant Dinner

## 9. Garden Party

4. BARBEQUE PARTY

5. MOGHUL BANQUET

6. DINNER BY THE FIRE

10. NELLORE DINNER

11. THALI

12. KERALA FEAST

*Detail: Using unexpected Indian musical instruments to display the food gives interest and drama to the buffet table.*

# Snack & Chaat Party

A Snack and Chaat party is similar to an appetizer party. Since an appetizer party does not involve formal seating, it gives the option to invite a handful to a houseful of guests. It has been my hobby to collect a diverse styles of platters and serving dishes. I enjoy mixing and matching my collection to serve appetizers. Use your imagination to display the food. I like to serve appetizers in interesting trays and baskets, using banana leaves as liners, garnishing food trays with one or two orchids or hibiscus flowers, or using ethnic Indian fabrics as tablecloths; this invokes the feeling of tropical India.

It is important to choose different textures in your menu. Go for a diverse tapestry of taste. For example, carrot salad complements a deep fried muruku, baked curry puffs contrasts with broiled lamb satays. Few well-chosen tropical drinks complement the Indian theme. Red wines such as Gewurztraminer and beer can be included in the menu.

The way the food is placed is also important. It is nice to set the appetizers up at multiple stations for easy access. This allows your guests to help themselves to the food as well as mingle with each other.

# The Menu

# PAPRI CHAAT

*Papri chaat is a typical North Indian snack/salad. It can be enjoyed at lunch, as an afternoon snack, or as an appetizer for a meal. I prefer to serve papri chaat buffet style so that it will provide an opportunity for guests to customize their serving according to individual taste. Papri chaat is nothing but an assortment of ingredients with different textures and flavors piled onto a plate. With each bite, you can taste a medley of flavors that tingle every sense in the mouth. It is important to assemble the papri chaat just before serving so that the moisture from chutneys and yogurt will not make the crunchy chips soggy.*

*Serves 6 - 8*
- tamarind/sweet chutney (page 300)
- cilantro chutney (page 298)
- 4 cups papri chips, homemade (page 309) or store-bought
- 1 pound russet potatoes
- 2 teaspoons salt
- two 15-ounce cans chickpeas, drained and rinsed
- 2 cups plain yogurt, whisked to smooth
- 1 - 3 teaspoons chaat masala powder, homemade (page 301) or store bought
- 1 - 3 minced fresh green chilies, such as serrano
- ¼ cup chopped cilantro
- 1 - 2 cups store-bought, thin, crispy sev

Prepare both chutneys. Prepare papri chips. Place potatoes with 2 teaspoons of salt in a large stock-pot. Add enough water so that the potatoes are completely immersed. Boil them over medium high heat until tender enough to be easily pierced with a fork or skewer. When the potatoes are ready, drain them into a colander. When they are cool enough to handle, peel and cut into 1-inch pieces. To assemble, layer the serving plate with papri chips, potatoes, and chickpeas. Drizzle with yogurt, and chutneys. Sprinkle chaat masala, minced chilies, cilantro and sev according to your taste.

# Carrot Salad

*This refreshing salad is popularly known as cachumbar in the state of Maharastra. This eye-catching carrot salad is a feast to the eyes as well as to the palate.*

*Serves 4 - 6*

- ⅓ cup mung dal
- 2 cups grated carrots
- ⅓ cup coarsely grated fresh coconut
- ⅓ cup grated raw mango (optional)
- 2 tablespoons oil
- 2 dry whole red chilies such as chile de arbol
- 1 teaspoon black mustard seeds
- 1 - 2 tablespoons lime juice
- 1 teaspoon salt or to taste
- ½ cup cilantro leaves

Soak dal in 2 cups of boiling water for 3 hours, and then drain. Combine dal, carrots, coconut and grated mango (if you are using) in a salad bowl. Heat oil in a small saucepan over medium heat. When the oil is hot add chilies. When the chilies start turning dark, add mustard seeds and cover until the spluttering subsides. Remove from the heat and pour it over the carrot mixture along with lime juice and salt. Gently toss to combine. Season to taste. Garnish with cilantro leaves.

*Cook's Note: If you are using a raw mango, you can adjust the amount of lime juice depending on the sourness of the mango.*

# CHICKEN 65

*There are many theories about how this name originated. Some people say it was the 65th item on one of the restaurant menus. Whatever the origin, this is the perfect dish to serve as an appetizer. There are many versions of this dish and I think this is the best one. This is a spicy dish. You can adjust the amount of cayenne according to your taste.*

*Serves 6 - 8*

2 pounds boneless, skinless chicken breast, cut into 1-inch pieces.

*Marinade:*

- ½ cup corn flour
- ½ cup all-purpose flour
- 2 eggs, slightly beaten
- 1½ teaspoons salt
- 1 - 3 teaspoons cayenne
- 1 teaspoon garam masala powder
- 4 tablespoons ginger garlic paste

- oil for deep frying

*Seasoning*

- ¼ cup vegetable oil
- 3 cloves garlic, sliced
- 1 green chili such as serrano, cut length wise into four
- 20 curry leaves
- 1 cup yogurt
- ½ - 1 teaspoon cayenne (optional)
- 1 teaspoon red food color

Mix all the ingredients for the marinade. Add chicken pieces to the marinade. Mix until all the pieces are evenly coated and refrigerate for a couple of hours. Pour oil into a wok or heavy-bottomed saucepan until it is ⅓ full (it should be 2 - 3 inches deep). Heat oil over medium high heat to 350° F. Fry chicken pieces in batches until golden brown. To season, add **¼** cup of oil to the separate skillet and heat over medium high temperature. When oil is hot add garlic, green chili and curry leaves. Fry for two minutes until garlic is soft and cooked. Add the fried chicken pieces to the skillet and stir to combine with the seasoning. Mix yogurt with cayenne and red food color. Add the yogurt mixture to chicken, 2 tablespoons at a time, while stirring constantly. Let the first 2 tablespoons of yogurt adsorb before adding next.

# SPICY FRIED PEANUTS

*This is the most popular snack sold on the beaches in India. The famous ad line 'no one can eat just one' is perfect for the dish. You can replace peanuts with cashews for variation.*

*Serves 4 - 6*

- 2 cups raw peanuts, with or without skin
- 1 cup chickpea flour/besan
- 2 tablespoons rice flour
- 1 teaspoon dry ginger powder
- 1 teaspoon cayenne
- ½ teaspoon cumin powder

- 1 teaspoon salt
- ⅛ teaspoon asafoetida
- pinch of baking soda
- 3 tablespoons lime juice
- 3 tablespoons water

- oil for deep frying

Mix peanuts with all the dry ingredients. Mix lime juice and water in bowl and add to peanuts. Mix all the ingredients together, making sure all the peanuts are covered with stiff batter. Add ½ to 1 tablespoon of water if necessary. Pour oil into a wok or heavy-bottomed saucepan until it is ⅓ full (it should be 2 - 3 inches deep). Heat oil over medium heat to 325º F. Add the peanuts in batches to the hot oil. Try to separate while adding. Fry until golden brown, about 3 - 5 minutes. Using a slotted spoon, remove from the oil on to a tray lined with paper towel. Repeat with the rest of the peanuts. Cool and store the peanuts in an airtight container.

# MURUKU

*To make muruku, you need a muruku press, which is available in most Indian stores. Muruku press comes with an assortment of design discs to make different shaped muruku.*

*Serves 6 - 8*

- 4 cups rice flour
- 1 cup chickpea flour/besan
- 2 teaspoons cumin or ajwain seeds
- ¼ teaspoon asafoetida
- 2 teaspoons salt
- 1 – 2 teaspoons cayenne
- ½ cup butter, melted
- 2 – 2 ¼ cups hot water

- oil for deep frying
- wax paper

Mix all the dry ingredients together in a bowl. Add melted butter and mix in to the dry ingredients. Add hot water, two tablespoons at a time, and mix in to make a pliable dough. Let the dough rest for an hour. Pour oil into a wok or heavy-bottomed saucepan until it is ⅓ full (it should be 2 - 3 inches deep). Heat oil over medium high heat to 350º F. Load muruku press, with the star disc, with the prepared dough. Keep a 10 x 10 inch wax paper. Hold muruku press 2 – 3 inches directly above the wax paper and press gently outwards from the center into 4 – 5 inch rounds. Lift the wax paper hold it 2 - 3 inches above the hot oil, invert gently and slip the dough in. Fry until golden brown. Using a slotted spoon remove from the oil onto paper lined bowl. Proceed with the rest.

Alternately you can hold the muruku press 2 - 3 inches above the hot oil press the dough directly into the oil, while gently moving the hand around. Fry as directed above and break them into pieces.
*Cook's Note: If muruku press is not available, use a pastry bag with star tip.*

# CURRY PUFFS

*Curry puffs are popular snacks sold in exhibitions and fairs in India.  This recipe is a variation of the traditional recipe.*

*Yield 24*

- one package frozen puff pastry (2 sheets), thawed overnight in the refrigerator
- 2 tablespoons vegetable oil
- 1 medium onion, finely chopped
- ½ red bell pepper, finely chopped
- ½ yellow bell pepper, finely chopped
- 2 cups finely chopped mushrooms
- 1 tablespoon coriander powder

- 1 teaspoon roasted cumin powder
- 1 teaspoon salt
- ½ teaspoon turmeric
- ½ - 1 teaspoon cayenne
- 3 tablespoons all-purpose flour
- 1 cup crumbled paneer (page 304)

- 1 egg beaten with 1 tablespoon water for egg wash
- 2 tablespoons black sesame seeds for garnish (optional)

Heat oil in a medium skillet.  Add onion and bell peppers.  Cook until the onions are soft and translucent.  Add mushrooms.  Fry until wilted.  Add coriander powder, cumin powder, salt, turmeric and cayenne.  Fry for a minute.  Add 3 tablespoons of flour to absorb extra moisture.  Cool the cooked mixture to room temperature.  Add the crumbled paneer and mix in gently.  Divide the filling into two portions, one for each sheet of puff pastry. Divide each portion of filling into 12 portions.

Meanwhile preheat oven to 375° F. Unfold each sheet of puff pastry and roll into 16 x 12-inches rectangle and cut into twelve 4 x 4 pieces.  Lightly moisten each piece at the edges with egg wash.  Place a portion of filling in the middle of each square.  Fold one corner over the filling to the opposite corner, making it a triangle.  Seal the edges with your fingers first and then with a fork.  Brush each puff with the egg wash. Sprinkle each puff with sesame seeds. Poke a few holes on top with a tip of a paring knife, for steam to escape from the filling.  Transfer them to the  ungreased sheet pans in a single layer, 2 inches apart to allow the puffs to expand. Bake for 20 - 25 minutes.

# VEGETABLE CUTLETS

*Corn flake crumbs make the cutlets light and crisp.*

*Yield 24*

- 1 ½ pounds potatoes
- 1 tablespoon + 2 teaspoons salt, divided
- ¼ cup vegetable oil
- 1 medium onion, finely chopped
- 1 tablespoon minced fresh ginger
- 2 minced fresh green chilies, such as serrano
- 3 cups sprouted mung beans*
- 1 teaspoon garam masala powder
- 1 tablespoon lemon juice
- 1 tablespoon finely chopped cilantro

Coating for cutlets:
- ¼ cup all-purpose flour
- ½ teaspoon cayenne
- ½ teaspoon salt
- ½ cup water

- 1 cup corn flake crumbs

- oil to fry

Place potatoes with 1 tablespoon salt in a large stock pot. Add enough water to cover the potatoes completely. Boil them over medium high heat until potatoes are tender enough to be pierced easily with a fork or skewer. When potatoes are ready, drain them into a colander. When they are cool enough to handle, peel them. Mash the potatoes, using a potato ricer or masher.

Heat oil in a skillet, over medium high heat. When the oil is hot add the chopped onion. Sauté until onion is translucent and edges begin to brown. Add ginger, green chilies and fry for a minute. Stir in sprouted mung beans. Cook until tender with 2 teaspoons salt, while stirring occasionally.  Add garam masala powder, lemon juice and cilantro and mix well. Add mashed potatoes and mix to combine. Let it cool.

Whisk all the coating ingredients together with the exception of cornflakes crumbs. Coating batter must be runny.
Divide the mixture into 20 - 24 portions. Make each portion into a round or oval patty. Dip each patty in the coating batter and then dredge in corn flake crumbs. Make sure the patties are evenly coated with the crumbs. Add 3 - 4 tablespoons of oil to a large heavy bottom non-stick skillet.  Heat over medium high heat.  When oil is hot, place patties in a single layer and cook until golden brown at the bottom. Gently flip it to the other side and drizzle more oil around the patties as needed.  Cook for another 3 - 4 minutes until cutlets have a crunchy golden crust.  Proceed with the rest. Serve with  onion tomato chutney (page 298).

***Cook's Note:*** *Sprouted mung beans are different from long bean sprouts. Sprouted mung beans are germinated seedlings available in Indian and health food stores.*

# LAMB SATAYS

*Serves 4 - 6*

- 2 pounds boneless leg of lamb, cut into wide strips against the grain.
- 2 tablespoons ginger garlic paste
- 2 tablespoons lime juice
- 1-2 teaspoons cayenne
- 2 tablespoons coriander powder
- 2 teaspoons salt
- Six inch wooden skewers soaked in water for at least 30 minutes.

Combine all the ingredients together and let it marinate in the refrigerator for an hour. Preheat oven to broiler. Keep two skewers flat, thread the meat while keeping the meat flat. Arrange satays on flat baking tray. Broil the meat for 2 - 3 minutes on each side. Serve with cilantro chutney.

# Spicy Pistachio Brittle

*Serves 6 - 8*

- 2 tablespoons white poppy seeds
- 2 tablespoons finely chopped roasted pecans
- 1 cup roasted pistachio nuts (unsalted)
- ½ teaspoon cayenne
- ½ teaspoon cinnamon
- ½ teaspoon salt
- 1 cup sugar
- 1 tablespoon corn syrup
- 2 tablespoons water

Spray the baking sheet and a spatula with non stick cooking spray. Dry roast poppy seeds in a small shallow pan over medium heat, until they turn a shade darker. Turn off the heat and add pecans, pistachio nuts, cayenne, cinnamon, and salt to the pan. Keep the nuts in the warm pan, while making the caramel.

Heat sugar, corn syrup and water in a small sauce pan over medium low temperature until sugar dissolves, while stirring occasionally. Increase temperature to medium high and cover for 3 minutes. Remove the lid and continue to cook until it turns into caramel. It takes approximately 5 minutes once the sugar melts. As soon as sugar syrup begins to caramelize, lift the sauce pan with both the hands using the hot pads and gently swirl to mix. Continue to cook until the mixture turns to caramel. As soon as it turns caramel color add nut mixture and mix in as fast as possible and turn off the heat. Immediately pour onto greased baking sheet and spread it with spatula. Let it cool, release it from the baking sheet and break into irregular pieces. Store in an air tight container in a cool place.

*Cook's Note: 1. Instead of spraying the baking sheet, I use silicone liner such as silpat.*
*2. Once the sugar is dissolved, it is important not to stir with the spoon.*

# SURYA CHANDRA

*Surya, which means "sun", signifies the spicy hot part of this drink. On the other hand, "chandra" which means "moon", stands for its sweeter and cooler side. This drink combines two of my most favorite fruits, pomegranates and meyer lemons. During fall, I get an abundant supply of pomegranates from my own orchard. With the intention to preserve the wholesome goodness of pomegranates for the rest of the year, I juice them and freeze the juice in the ice cube trays. Once they are frozen hard I save them in the Ziploc bags in the freezer. You can do the same thing with meyer lemon juice. Over the years, this drink has become a favorite at my weekend family lunches. It is best to use fresh pomegranate juice and meyer lemon juice. Most of the commercial brands add sugar, which I am not fond of. Look for the pomegranate juice and meyer lemons during late summer and fall at the farmers markets and health food stores. Unsweetened pomegranate juice is available in some supermarkets like Trader Joes. In this recipe the tartness of the pomegranate juice is balanced with the sweet meyer lemon juice. If unavailable, replace pomegranate juice with cranberry juice and meyer lemon with orange juice. Either way it is delicious.*

*Serves 4*
- 2 cups fresh pomegranate juice
- 1 cup meyer lemon juice
- ⅛ cup ginger juice (page 304)
- ½ teaspoon chaat masala powder, home made (page 301) or store brought
- ½ cup simple syrup (page 308)
- 10 fresh mint leaves, crushed

Mix all the ingredients together in the pitcher. Serve over ice cubes.

# AMRUTH

*Amruth means "nectar from the God". Once you taste this drink you will realize why I came up with this name. Aromatic cardamom and fragrant saffron complement this drink.*

*Serves 4*
- 4 cups mango nectar
- 1 cup canned coconut milk
- ¼ cup saffron-cardamom syrup (page 308)

Place all the ingredients in the blender. Blend for few seconds to combine. Serve over ice cubes.

# PASSION

*Cardomom's aromatic bouquet complements the citrus flavor and adds an exotic touch to the drink.*

*Serves 6*
- 2 cups pineapple juice
- 1 cup orange juice
- 1 cup passion fruit juice
- ½ cup Grand Marnier liquor
- ½ teaspoon green cardamom seed powder

Stir all the ingredients together in a pitcher. Serve over ice cubes

*It is fun to mix and match glassware for cocktails.*

# Tea Party

This is my favorite way to entertain on a leisurely afternoon. A traditional tea party has timeless charm and elegance. Whether it is a baby shower or bridal shower or just mid-afternoon tea with your close friends, it is an ideal style for entertaining.

This menu combines an international charm with an ethnic touch such as open faced chutney sandwiches to satisfy your sense of taste and style.

The Menu

# ALMOND APRICOTS

*Yield approximately 36*
*Coating*
- 1 cup almonds
- ½ - ⅔ cup water
- 2 cups sugar
- ½ cup ghee
- ½ teaspoon green cardamom seed powder
- few drops of yellow food color
- 1 teaspoon rose water
- 1 tablespoon milk, if necessary

*Filling*
- ½ cup roasted pistachio nuts, ground into course powder
- 2 tablespoons powdered sugar
- 2 tablespoons cream

- ⅛ cup raw pistachios, cut lengthwise to use as a stem

*Additional Equipment Needed*
- paintbrush
- pink petal dust (available at gourmet food shops)

To make the coating, place the almonds in a bowl and add two cups of boiling water. When almonds are cool enough to handle, peel the skin off and let the peeled almonds soak in water for 4 – 5 hours. Drain the almonds from the soaking liquid and transfer them to a grinder. Grind into a fine paste using ½ - ⅔ cup water. Transfer almond paste in a nonstick skillet and cook over medium heat while stirring occasionally until some of the moisture evaporates. When the mixture starts forming a lump, add sugar. Cook for another 15 - 20 minutes while stirring often. Add ghee, 2 tablespoons at a time. Make sure the first 2 tablespoons are mixed well before adding the next. Continue stirring until mixture starts forming white bubbles underneath, for about 6 - 8 minutes. Stir in cardamom seed powder and couple of drops of yellow food color. Mix well and turn off the heat. Let it cool.

Meanwhile, prepare the filling. In a small bowl, stir in the ground pistachios and powdered sugar. Add cream to moisten and make a paste.

Transfer almond mixture and rose water to the food processor fitted with metal blade. Process until it becomes a smooth dough like consistency. If necessary, add a tablespoon of milk.

Divide almond paste into 36 portions. Take one portion and spread it in the palm of your hand into a 2-inch round circle. Place ¼ teaspoon of pistachio filling in the middle. Gather the ends together and make it into a ball with pistachio filling inside. Using the blunt side of the dinner knife, make an indentation on one side to resemble an apricot. Use a paintbrush and brush some petal dust on the side of the apricot to emulate blush. Insert a stem on top. Serve it with tea. Your guests will be impressed with this dessert.

# FRUIT TARTS

*Yield 24-2 ½ inch tarts*

*Rum Syrup*
- ¼ cup sugar
- ¼ cup water
- 2 tablespoons rum

*Coconut Pastry Crust*
- 1 ½ cups all-purpose flour
- pinch of salt
- ½ cup (1 stick) cold butter, diced
- ½ cup sugar
- ⅓ cup finely grated unsweetened dry coconut
- 1 egg, slightly beaten
- 1 teaspoon coconut flavored rum or vanilla

- ½ cup warm apricot preserve

*Filling*
- ½ cup (1 stick) butter at room temperature
- ¾ cup powdered sugar
- 2 eggs
- 2 teaspoons all-purpose flour
- 1 cup ground almonds
- 1 teaspoon coconut flavored rum or vanilla

- assorted fresh fruits such as strawberries, raspberries, kiwis, mandarin oranges, blueberries
- 2-inch tart pans

- apricot glaze (recipe follows)

To make the rum syrup, boil sugar and water over medium heat until sugar dissolves.  Stir in rum and let it cool to room temperature.

To make the pastry crust, add flour and salt to the food processor fitted with metal blade.  Pulse few times to mix it well.  Add butter and process until mixture resembles bread crumbs.  Add sugar and coconut.  Pulse few times till it is combined.  Add egg and rum.  Process until dough comes together.  Transfer dough to a work surface.  Cover the dough with plastic wrap.  Let it rest in the refrigerator for 30 minutes.

Preheat oven to 350º F.

Flatten the dough with the palm of your hand and roll it into ⅛-inch thickness.  Using a 3-inch round cookie cutter, cut into 3-inch circles.  Fit each circle into a 2-inch tart pan.  Press the dough into tart pans and trim off extra pastry.  Transfer tart pans to the sheet pan.

Spoon ½ a teaspoon of warm preserve into the pastry lined tart pans.

To make the filling, cream butter and sugar in an electric mixer with a paddle attachment until light and creamy.  Add eggs one at a time and mix until creamy.  Add all-purpose flour and ground almonds.  Mix until combined.  Stir in rum or vanilla.  Transfer filling into a pastry bag.  Pipe about 2 tablespoons of filling into each tart pan.  Bake for 25 - 30 minutes.  As soon as you remove them from the oven, glaze the tarts with rum syrup.  Cool the tarts to room temperature and release the tarts from the tart pans.

Arrange fresh fruit on each tart.  Glaze the fruit with apricot glaze and serve

## APRICOT GLAZE

- 1 cup apricot preserve
- ¼ cup sugar
- 2 tablespoons water
- 1 tablespoon lemon juice or rum

To make the glaze, place the preserves into a fine mesh sieve set over a bowl. Use a rubber spatula to push the preserve through the sieve. Discard any leftover solids from the sieve. Combine sugar and water, in a small saucepan.  Bring it to a boil over medium high heat. Boil for 2 minutes.  Stir in strained preserve into the sugar syrup.  Bring it to boil for 1 minute.  Stir in lemon juice or rum.  Let it cool. This glaze can stay fresh in the refrigerator for several months.

# Swan Éclairs

*The shells of these éclairs are made of choux (pronounced "shoo") pastry. This is a unique pastry because the batter is cooked before it is baked. Once you have mastered the technique of making choux pastry, the possibilities are unlimited. You can fill them with a savory or sweet filling.*
*Yield approximately 24*

- 1 cup milk
- ½ cup (1 stick) butter
- 1 tablespoon sugar
- ¼ teaspoon salt
- 1 cup all-purpose flour
- 4 eggs

- saffron custard cream filling (recipe follows)

Combine milk, butter, sugar and salt in a saucepan. Heat over medium high heat. Bring the mixture to a boil. Remove from the heat. Add flour all at once. Stir vigorously with a wooden spoon until the flour is completely blended into the milk mixture. Reduce heat to medium. Bring the saucepan back to the stove. Cook until mixture leaves the sides of the pan and becomes a ball. Remove from the heat and let it cool for 2 - 3 minutes.

Meanwhile whisk one egg in a small bowl. Make a well in the center of the dough; add whisked egg and beat with the wooden spoon until thoroughly incorporated. Add remaining eggs one at a time, whisking each egg and beating into the batter. After adding the last egg, beat for another minute until the dough is smooth and shiny. Let the dough cool before shaping and baking. The finished dough should be a smooth paste.

Preheat oven to 400º F. Line the sheet pan with parchment or silicone liner such as silpat. To shape the swan's neck, fit the pastry bag with ⅝ inch rose tip (number 124). Fill the bag until it is ¼ full. Fold the piping bag to close and hold the bag in such a way that the pointed end of the tip faces upward. Pipe the dough in an "S" shape for the swan's neck on to a prepared pan. Make extra necks in case a few break. Bake the necks for 10 minutes.

To pipe the body of the swan, fit the pastry bag with ¾-inch plain tip. Pipe out 4-inch long and ¾-inch wide logs of pastry. Space the logs at least 2 inches apart to allow the dough to expand. Bake for 25 – 35 minutes or until golden brown. Turn off the oven and remove the pastries from the oven. Using a thin skewer or a toothpick, prick the sides of each pastry a few times. Return pastries to the oven. Leave the door ajar. Allow pastries to dry out in a warm oven for ½ an hour. Let the pastries cool completely on a wire rack.

To make the swans, cut off the top ⅓ off from the body. Cut the top piece lengthwise into 2 for wings. Fill the bottom of the puff with custard cream filling. Insert the neck to one end. Insert both wings to the sides. Refrigerate until ready to serve.

**Cook's Note:** *Preheat oven to proper temperature. Do not open the oven door during the first ½ of the baking period. If the pastry is not completely dry inside, it will collapse.*

## Saffron Custard Cream Filling

- ¾ cup sugar
- 6 tablespoons flour
- ¼ teaspoon salt
- 2 cups milk

- ½ teaspoon loosely packed saffron
- 6 egg yolks, slightly beaten
- 2 teaspoons vanilla extract

Stir in sugar, flour and salt in a heavy bottomed saucepan. Add milk and saffron. Using a wire whisk, stir until blended without any lumps. Place the saucepan over medium high heat. Cook until mixture comes to a boil while stirring often. Meanwhile whisk egg yolks in a bowl. Remove ½ a cup of hot milk mixture and slowly add to egg yolks, while whisking constantly (this is called tempering the egg yolks. By tempering, you are raising the egg yolks temperature to that of the milk mixture. In doing so, the addition of egg yolks to the milk mixture will not cause curdling). Return egg yolk mixture to the saucepan. Cook over low heat while stirring constantly until mixture thickens and covers the back of the spoon. Remove from the heat. Stir in vanilla. Pour through a fine-mesh sieve into a bowl. Cover the surface of the custard with plastic wrap to prevent a layer being formed. Cool to room temperature and refrigerate until ready to use. Use to fill the swan éclairs or serve with fresh fruit.

# PETITS FOURS

*Yield about 32*

*Cake*

- 1 cup butter at room temperature
- 1 ½ cups sugar
- 4 eggs
- 1 teaspoon mixed fruit essence or vanilla
- 2 ¾ cups cake flour
- ¼ teaspoon salt
- 2 teaspoons baking powder
- 1 cup milk

*Icing*

- 8 cups powdered sugar
- ½ cup hot water
- ½ cup corn syrup
- 1 tablespoon lemon juice
- 1 tablespoon rose water

- candied flowers (page 306)

Preheat oven to 350º F. Grease and flour 13 x 9 inch cake pan.

In an electric mixer fitted with paddle attachment, cream butter and sugar together until light and fluffy for about 3 – 4 minutes. With the mixture on medium speed add eggs one at a time, incorporating the first one before adding the next. Make sure you stop and scrape the sides of the bowl with a spatula in between. Stir in mixed fruit essence or vanilla. In a separate bowl, whisk the flour, salt and baking powder together. When the mixer is on low, add flour mixture in 3 installments, alternating with 2 installments of milk, beginning and ending with the flour mixture until just combined. Finish folding with the spatula to make sure that the batter is completely mixed. Pour batter into the prepared pan. Bake for 35 – 40 minutes, until a cake tester comes out clean.

Let the cake cool in the pan for 10 - 15 minutes. Unmold on to the wire rack and let the cake cool completely. Cut the cake into small bite-sized squares or rectangles. Place these mini cakes on a wire rack over a pan to catch drippings from the icing.

To make the icing, combine powdered sugar, hot water, corn syrup, lemon juice and rose water. Whisk until everything is mixed together without lumps. You can either dip the little cakes in the icing or ladle icing on top of the cakes, making sure that the entire surface is covered. Once the icing is set, decorate with candied flowers.

# OPEN FACED CHUTNEY SANDWICHES

## CUCUMBER

*Yield about 20*
- one loaf of any rich egg bread, sliced lengthwise into ¾-inch thickness, crust trimmed
- ½ cup butter at room temperature
- 1 tablespoon cilantro chutney (page 298)
- 1 large English cucumber

In a small bowl, mix butter and chutney until well combined. Spread a thin layer of the mixture on 1 side of the sliced bread. Repeat with the rest of the slices.

Using a mandoline, slice cucumbers lengthwise into paper-thin slices. On the buttered side of the bread, shingle sliced cucumbers. Trim the edges and cut into a triangle. Serve with tea.

## TOMATO

*Yield about 20*
- one loaf of any rich egg bread, sliced lengthwise into ¾-inch thickness, crust trimmed
- ½ cup butter at room temperature
- 1½ teaspoons tomato pickle (page 299)
- 6 tomatoes, preferably red and gold, sliced into thin rounds

In a small bowl, mix butter and pickle until well combined. Spread a layer of the mixture on 1 side of the sliced bread. Repeat with the rest of the slices.

On the buttered side of the bread, arrange sliced tomatoes so that they are slightly overlapping. Trim the edges and cut into triangles. Serve with tea.

# Coconut Ginger Scones

*Yield 18 mini scones*
- 2 cups all-purpose flour
- ½ cup sweetened coconut flakes
- 2 tablespoons sugar
- 1 tablespoon baking powder
- ½ teaspoon salt
- 2 teaspoons lemon zest
- ⅓ cup minced crystallized ginger
- ½ cup cold butter, diced
- ¾ cup heavy cream

*Topping*
- 1 tablespoon turbinado sugar
- ½ teaspoon cinnamon
- ½ teaspoon green cardamom seed powder

- 2 tablespoons cream or milk

Preheat oven to 425º F. In a bowl, stir to combine flour, coconut, sugar, baking powder, salt, lemon zest and ginger. Add butter to dry ingredients. Using a pastry blender or 2 dinner knives, cut the butter into the flour mixture until it resembles very coarse crumbs. Pour the cream over the dry ingredients. Gently mix until dry ingredients are moistened. Do not over mix.

Transfer the dough onto the work surface. Quickly gather the dough until it clings together. Pat the dough into 9 x 9 square. Cut the dough into nine 3-inch squares. Cut each square into 2 triangles.

To make the topping, mix sugar, cinnamon and cardamom. Brush the scones with cream or milk. Sprinkle flavored sugar on top. Transfer scones to a parchment or silicone lined baking tray. Bake for 20 minutes. Transfer to a wire rack to cool. Serve with jam or lemon curd.

# MADELEINES

*Madeleines are delicate cakes/cookies baked in a special shell shaped pan. They are a popular snack to serve with tea.*

Yield 10 - 12

- ½ cup all-purpose flour
- ½ teaspoon green cardamom seed powder
- 2 eggs
- ⅓ cup sugar
- ¼ teaspoon salt
- ¼ cup unsalted butter, melted and cooled
- 1 teaspoon lemon zest

Preheat oven to 375º F. Butter and flour madeleine mold pans thoroughly. Whisk flour, and cardamom powder in a bowl and set aside.

In an electric mixer fitted with paddle attachment, cream eggs, sugar and salt together until light and fluffy for about 5 minutes. Remove the bowl from the mixer. Sprinkle flour mixture on top of the egg mixture. Using a rubber spatula, quickly fold the flour mixture into the egg mixture. Do not over mix. Add melted butter and lemon zest. Gently fold until butter and lemon zest are incorporated into the batter. Divide the batter among the molds, filling each mold ⅔ full. Bake madeleines for 10 minutes or until they are spongy to touch. Transfer them to a metal rack to cool for 10 minutes. Invert the pan to unmold. Dust with powder sugar and serve with tea.

*Cook's Note: The traditional shell shaped madeleine molds are available at gourmet kitchen supply stores.*

# MEYER LEMON CURD

- 1 teaspoon meyer lemon zest
- ¾ cup butter
- ¾ cup sugar
- 2 eggs
- ½ cup meyer lemon juice
- ⅛ teaspoon salt

Cream zest, butter and sugar in the bowl of an electric mixer fitted with paddle attachment. Add eggs 1 at a time. Then add lemon juice and salt. Mix until combined.

Remove the bowl from the mixer and set over a saucepan of simmering water. Cook while stirring constantly with a wooden spoon. The lemon curd is ready when it is thick and coats the back of the spoon, for about 20 minutes or until candy thermometer register's at 175ºF . Try not to overcook to avoid curdling. Remove from the heat. Chill in the refrigerator. Serve with scones or fresh fruit.

**Cook's Note:** *You can substitute regular lemon juice for meyer lemon juice.*

*Detail: I like to coordinate colored water glasses with the flowers on the table and/or with the napkins.*

Dosas are an all-time favorite breakfast item for southerners. Dosas are crispy, tangy crepes, that can be stuffed with an array of filling. The most favorite filling is masala potato which is usually accompanied by sambar and coconut chutney. This is a very popular item with Indians as well as non-Indians at Indian restaurants. People are always excited by the crispy look and the length of the typical dosa that is about 18 - 20 inches. I never get tired of eating dosas. Even though dosas were meant to be eaten for breakfast, in my household in America, most of my brunch entertaining features dosas. Crispy brown plain dosas without any filling can be served with a variety of chutneys. Advanced preparation is needed to make the dosa batter. The rice and urad dal need to be soaked, blended and fermented a day earlier.

# MASALA DOSA

*Masala dosas are stuffed with potato curry, and are usually eaten with coconut chutney and sambar for breakfast in South India. In this country, we are accustomed to eating dosas during lunchtime. Making dosas is not a difficult process, it just needs a little practice. When you are planning to make dosas, plan 30 hours in advance for soaking and fermentation.*

*Yield 14 - 18 dosas*

- 2 ½ cups long grain rice
- ½ cup plain Uncle Ben's converted rice
- 1 cup white urad dal
- 2 teaspoons fenugreek seeds
- 2 ½ - 2 ¾ cups water

- 1 tablespoon salt
- 2 tablespoons plain yogurt

- vegetable oil to drizzle on top of the dosas
- masala potato stuffing (page 62)

In a bowl, combine rice, converted rice, white urad dal and fenugreek seeds. Wash with several changes of water. Soak them for 4 - 6 hours with enough water to cover 2 - 3 inches above the surface of the rice.

Drain the rice mixture. Transfer mixture to a blender and grind it into a fine batter, using 2 ½ - 2 ¾ cups of total water. You can grind the mixture in 2 - 3 batches. Empty the batter into a bowl. Stir in salt and yogurt. Cover and leave it in a warm place to ferment overnight. The batter will rise with tiny bubbles during the fermentation process. Have masala patoto ready. Heat flat nonstick griddle or skillet over medium high heat. When you sprinkle a tiny bit of water, it should sizzle immediately. Add 1 teaspoon of oil to the griddle. Wipe with paper towel. This step will ensure that the dosa doesn't stick to the pan. Using a metal soup ladle, pour about ½ cup of batter onto the middle of the hot griddle. Using the bottom of the soup ladle, spread the batter outwards from the center in a continuous spiral motion into a 10 - 12 inch circle, smoothing out any ridges along the way. Drizzle a teaspoon of oil on top of the dosa and another teaspoon of oil along the edges. As the dosa sets, it turns golden brown at the bottom. Gently lift dosa with a spatula and flip onto the other side. After 5 - 10 seconds, flip it back to the other side again. The underside of the dosa should be rich golden color, whereas the other side should be cooked but not browned. Add half a cup of masala potato in the middle. Fold both sides so that they overlap on top of the filling. Serve with coconut chutney and sambar.

*Cook's Note:*
*1) Don't use food processor to grind the batter. If you do, the batter won't be as smooth.*
*2) Leftover batter can be stored in the refrigerator for up to a week.*

# Masala Potato Stuffing

- 2 pounds, potatoes, preferably red
- 1 tablespoon + 1 teaspoon salt, divided
- ¼ cup vegetable oil
- 2 dry whole red chilies, such as chile de arbol
- 1 teaspoon black mustard seeds
- 1 teaspoon cumin seeds
- 1 teaspoon chena dal

- 1 teaspoon white urad dal
- 20 curry leaves
- 1 onion, cut lengthwise, sliced and cut in the middle
- 1-inch piece fresh ginger, minced
- 1 - 2 minced fresh green chilies, such as serrano
- 1 large tomato, chopped
- ½ teaspoon turmeric
- 1 teaspoon lime juice or to taste

Place potatoes with 1 tablespoon of salt in a large stock-pot.  Add enough water to cover 2 - 3 inches above the surface of the potatoes.  Boil them over medium high heat until tender enough to be easily pierced with a fork or skewer.  When potatoes are done, drain them into a colander.  When they are cool enough to handle, peel them and cut into 1-inch pieces and set aside.

Heat oil in a large skillet over medium high heat.  When oil is hot, add red chilies.  As the chilies turn darker, add mustard seeds and cover with a lid until spluttering subsides.  Uncover, stir in cumin seeds.  As soon as cumin seeds sizzle, add chena dal and white urad dal.  As soon as the white urad dal turns golden, add curry leaves and fry until they are crisp.  Add onions.  Sauté until onions are translucent and edges begin to brown.  Stir in ginger and minced green chilies.  Stir fry for about 1 minute.  Add tomatoes.  Cook while stirring occasionally until tomatoes are soft and some of the moisture evaporates.  Add turmeric and 1 teaspoon of salt.  Add potatoes and stir fry for two minutes.  Stir in lime juice and use it as stuffing for dosas.

*Cook's Note: Whole red chilies are added to flavor the dish, but not meant to be eaten.*

# Sambar

*Sambar is a very popular lentil vegetable soup of South India, especially with vegetarians.  Each state has its own variation of sambar.  It can be eaten with rice or with dosas.*

*Serves 8*

- one recipe cooked toor dal (page 309)
- 2 tablespoons vegetable oil
- ¼ teaspoon asafoetida
- 2 dry whole red chilies such as chile de arbol
- 1 teaspoon black mustard seeds
- 1 teaspoon cumin seeds
- 20 curry leaves
- 1 onion, cut into 1 ½-inch chunks
- 1 - 3 fresh green chilies such as serrano, cut in the middle lengthwise

- 2 cups mixed vegetables, such as green bell peppers, green beans, cucumbers, carrots, okra, drumsticks* and eggplant, cut into 1 ½-inch pieces
- 2 medium tomatoes, cut into 1½-inch pieces
- 1 tablespoon salt
- 1 teaspoon turmeric
- 1 teaspoon cayenne
- 2 - 3 tablespoons tamarind paste, homemade (page 300) or store-bought
- sambar podi (page 63)
- 2 tablespoons chopped cilantro/coriander

Prepare cooked toor dal and set aside.

Heat oil in a large saucepan over medium high heat.  Add asafoetida and red chilies.  When chilies start turning dark, add mustard seeds and close with the lid until the spluttering subsides.  Uncover and add cumin seeds.  When cumin seeds start to sizzle, add curry leaves.  As soon as curry leaves are crisp, add onion.  Sauté onion until translucent.  Add all the vegetables.  Cook vegetables until tender but not soft, while stirring occasionally for about 5 minutes.  Add tomatoes and cook for about 2 minutes.  Add salt, turmeric, cayenne and tamarind paste.  Stir for another minute.  Add cooked toor dal and stir in 4 cups of water.  Bring it to boil, reduce heat and simmer for 20 - 25 minutes.  Just before serving, stir in sambar podi and cilantro/coriander.  Taste and adjust the seasoning for salt.  Serve hot either with plain rice or dosa.

*Cook's Note:*
*1. Whole red chilies and green chilies are added to flavor the dish, but not meant to be eaten.*
*2. *The most popular vegetable to add to sambar are drumsticks, available at Indian stores, fresh or frozen.  To eat drumsticks, scrape the flesh with the teeth and discard the fibrous shell.*

# COCONUT CHUTNEY

*This is the most commonly used chutney for breakfast in South Indian states.*

*Serves 4 - 6*
- 1 - 3 fresh green chilies, such as serrano
- 1 tablespoon vegetable oil
- ½ cup chena dal
- 1 cup freshly grated coconut or grated dry coconut
- 1 teaspoon salt
- 1 cup water
- 1 teaspoon lime juice

*Seasoning*
- 1 tablespoon vegetable oil
- ⅛ teaspoon asafoetida
- ½ teaspoon black mustard seeds
- ½ teaspoon cumin seeds
- 10 curry leaves

Pierce green chilies twice with the tip of a paring knife twice to prevent from exploding in hot oil. Heat oil in a skillet over medium high heat. Add chena dal and green chilies. Stir fry until chena dal is one shade darker. Remove from the heat and stir in the coconut. Let it cool. Transfer dal mixture to grinder. Add salt and grind into a grainy paste using 1 cup of water. Empty chutney into a serving bowl. Stir in lime juice.

To season the chutney, heat oil in a small sauce pan over medium high heat. When oil is hot, add asafoetida and mustard seeds and cover until spluttering subsides. Uncover and add cumin seeds. When cumin seeds sizzle, add curry leaves. As soon as curry leaves are crisp, add the seasoning to chutney and stir in. Serve with dosas.

## SAMBAR PODI

*Podi is a course spice powder, in this case especially made to be used in sambar.*

- 1 teaspoon vegetable oil
- ⅛ teaspoon asafoetida
- 1 - 2 dry whole red chilies such as chile de arbol
- 1 tablespoon coriander seeds
- ½ teaspoon fenugreek seeds
- 1 teaspoon chena dal
- 1 teaspoon toor dal
- 1 teaspoon white urad dal
- 1 tablespoon grated dry or fresh coconut
- 10 fresh or dry curry leaves

Heat oil in a small skillet. When oil is hot, add asafoetida, red chilies, coriander seeds, fenugreek seeds, chena dal and white urad dal. Fry until white urad dal turns golden brown, while stirring often. Add grated coconut, and curry leaves. Remove from the heat and let it cool. Transfer contents to a spice grinder. Grind to make a powder.

# Barbeque Party

While barbequing is a time honored tradition in America, Punjab is the only region in India where tandoor ovens are used to cook meat and bread outdoors. Here in America, the sun-drenched Californian weather provides the best opportunity to barbeque and spend leisurely afternoons with friends and family, sipping mango and pomegranate margaritas. The seductive floral aroma of meyer lemon lemonade with lemon verbena adds a refreshing touch to the backyard barbeque garden party.

*Detail: Getting ready for the BBQ party.*

# The Menu

# BARBEQUED WHOLE FISH
# WRAPPED IN BANANA LEAVES

*This dish is highly flavorful with a dramatic presentation.*

*Serves 4 - 6*

- 1 whole fish, such as salmon or bluefish (4 - 5 pounds), gutted and scaled, with bones removed but head, skin and fillet left intact.

*1st Marinade*
- ½ teaspoon salt
- ½ teaspoon turmeric
- ½ teaspoon cayenne

*2nd Marinade*
- 4 tablespoons vegetable oil
- 4 cups roughly chopped red onions
- ¼ cup ginger garlic paste
- 2 tablespoons tomato paste
- 2 tablespoons coriander powder
- 2 teaspoons cumin powder
- 2 teaspoons salt
- ½ - 1 teaspoon cayenne
- 1 teaspoon sugar
- 1 teaspoon garam masala powder
- 3 tablespoons lime juice
- ½ cup fresh mint and coriander leaves

- banana leaves and kitchen twine

Mix 1st marinade ingredients and rub all over the fish. Let it marinate in the refrigerator while the 2nd marinade is being prepared.

Preheat barbeque grill to medium temperature.

In a medium sized skillet, heat oil over medium high heat. Add onions and sauté until translucent. Add ginger garlic paste and tomato paste and stir fry for 2 - 3 minutes. Stir in coriander powder, cumin powder, salt, cayenne and sugar. Stir fry for another minute. Remove from the heat and stir in garam masala powder, lemon juice, mint and coriander leaves. Once the mixture comes to room temperature, transfer to the food processor and process to a coarse paste.

Remove the fish from the refrigerator. Generously spread the paste on to both sides of the flesh part of the fish. Fold it over to close. Spread banana leaves in 2 - 3 layers on to a work surface. Transfer fish onto the banana leaves. Fold the leaves over the fish to cover, securing with toothpicks if necessary. Use kitchen twine to tie the fish and completely encase it with the leaves. Grill for an hour, while flipping it in between for even cooking. When it is ready, transfer the whole fish onto a serving platter. Cut strings open and serve.

# LAMB KABOBS

*Lamb kabobs are best served as an appetizer but they can also be served as part of the main meal.*

*Serves 4 - 6*

- 2 pounds boneless leg of lamb, all visible fat removed and cut into 1½ inch cubes

*Marinade*
- 2 tablespoons vegetable oil
- 2 tablespoons ginger garlic paste
- 2 tablespoons tamarind paste (page 300)
- 1 tablespoon coriander powder
- 1 teaspoon cumin powder
- 1 tablespoon paprika
- 1 teaspoon – 1 tablespoon cayenne
- 1 ½ teaspoons salt

- metal or bamboo skewers
- 2 tablespoons ghee for basting

Mix all the marinade ingredients in a bowl. Add lamb cubes to the bowl and mix to coat evenly with marinade. Refrigerate for 4 - 24 hours.

If you are using bamboo skewers, soak them in water for at least ½ an hour in advance. Preheat grill to medium heat. When the meat is ready, thread the meat pieces on to the skewers. Place the threaded skewers on to the rack and grill them while turning from time to time to ensure even charring. Grill for about 20 minutes until meat pieces are tender. During the last minute of cooking, baste the meat pieces with melted ghee. When they are ready, transfer them to the serving platter.

# GRILLED SPICY NAAN

*By replacing all-purpose flour with bread flour, this dough has extra gluten to withstand direct heat from the grill. By incorporating spices into the dough, this naan is a perfect companion to all barbequed meats.*

*Yield 8 - 10*

- 1 teaspoon yeast
- 1 teaspoon sugar
- ⅓ cup milk, heated to 110º F
- 2 cups bread flour
- ¾ teaspoon salt
- ½ tablespoon kasuri methi (dry fenugreek leaves)
- 1 teaspoon cumin powder

- 1 teaspoon paprika
- ½ teaspoon cayenne
- ¼ teaspoon garlic powder
- ½ cup yogurt
- 2 tablespoons ghee or vegetable oil

- extra flour for rolling
- extra ghee or oil for basting

In a bowl, add yeast, sugar and milk. Stir and set aside for 5 to 10 minutes to activate the yeast. Add flour, salt, kasuri methi, cumin powder, paprika, cayenne, garlic powder, yogurt, and ghee or oil to the yeast mixture and knead to form a dough. Transfer dough to work surface and knead for 5 minutes until dough is smooth and silky. Alternately, this step can be done in a food processor or Kitchen Aid mixer using dough hook.

Brush a large bowl lightly with oil. Transfer dough to the bowl. Cover with plastic wrap or a kitchen towel. Let it rest for 2 - 3 hours. This allows the yeast to ferment and makes the dough rise to double its size. You can also refrigerate the dough for a day.

Divide the dough into 8 - 10 balls. Let them rise again for ½ an hour. Preheat the barbeque grill to medium high. Roll each ball into 6 - 7 inch circles. Transfer 2 - 3 pieces of rolled dough at a time to the grill rack. Cook until bread puffs up. It takes about ½ - 1 minute. Carefully using the spatula, turn the bread and cook for another 1 - 1 ½ minutes. Just before removing from the fire, baste the naan with ghee, or oil. Transfer the naans to a platter. Cover them with foil or clean kitchen towel. Proceed with remaining dough. Serve with barbequed meats.

# TAMARIND GLAZED PORK RIBS

*Traditionally, pork ribs are not a part of Indian cuisine. We acquired the taste for pork ribs after coming to this country . My children cannot imagine a barbeque without these succulent ribs.*

*Tamarind is widely used as a souring agent in India. It has a tangy, sweet and sour taste. Tamarind, along with aromatic spices, can perk up the flavor of any meat. To avoid burning, glaze the ribs with the tamarind chutney a few minutes before removing the meat from the grill.*

*Serves 4*
- 1 rack baby back pork ribs, about 3 - 3 ½ pounds
- 2 tablespoons vegetable oil
- 1 teaspoon salt
- ¼ cup masala spice blend (page 301)
- 1 cup tamarind/sweet chutney (page 300)
- extra tamarind/sweet chutney to serve with ribs

Mix oil, salt and masala spice blend into paste.  Rub the spicy paste all over the ribs and marinate in the refrigerator for 4 - 24 hours.

Meanwhile prepare the tamarind/sweet chutney.

Preheat grill to medium low heat.  Place the ribs onto the grill rack.  Grill ribs for 2 - 3 hours until tender, while turning every 15 minutes.  During the last 15 minutes of grilling, baste with tamarind chutney.  Remove from the grill and serve with more chutney.

Alternately, you can bake these ribs in a conventional oven.  Preheat the oven to 325º F.  Place ribs on a shallow baking sheet lined with a metal rack.  Bake for 2 - 2 ½ hours until tender.  During the last 15 minutes of baking, baste with tamarind chutney.  Remove from the oven and serve with more chutney.

# TANDOORI CHICKEN

*Tandoor oven*

*Traditionally, tandoori chicken is baked in a tandoor clay oven. This is where the dish gets its name from. You can achieve similar results by grilling or baking. This is the most popular dish in all Indian restaurants. Children and adults alike get attracted to this vibrantly colored chicken. Color is added for a visual appeal while the real flavor comes from the spicy yogurt marinade.*

*Serves 6 - 8*
- 3 - 4 pounds chicken thighs and legs or whole chicken, skin removed and cut into big pieces

*1st marinade*
- ½ teaspoon salt
- 1 tablespoon lime juice

*2nd marinade*
- 2 tablespoons vegetable oil
- 1 medium onion, roughly chopped
- 1 tablespoon coriander powder
- 1 teaspoon roasted cumin powder
- 1 teaspoon - 1 tablespoon cayenne
- 2 teaspoons salt
- 3 tablespoons ginger garlic paste
- 3 tablespoons lime juice
- 2 tablespoons malt vinegar or white vinegar
- 1 cup whole milk yogurt, whisked to smooth
- 2 teaspoons red food color
- 1 teaspoon yellow food color
- ¼ cup of ghee for basting

Mix salt and lime juice for the first marinade. Using a sharp knife, cut 2 - 3 long slashes on each piece of chicken. Add chicken to first marinade. Set aside for ½ an hour.

Meanwhile, prepare the 2nd marinade. Heat oil in a small skillet over medium heat. Add onions and fry until translucent. Add coriander, cumin and cayenne. Turn off the heat and let onions come to room temperature. Transfer onion mixture to the blender. Add salt, ginger garlic paste, lime juice and malt vinegar. Blend into a smooth paste. Transfer marinade to the bowl. Stir in yogurt and the food colors and add this marinade to the chicken. Mix well to make sure that the marinade gets into the slits and coats all the chicken pieces. Cover and refrigerate for 6 - 24 hours.

Preheat grill to medium high temperature. Transfer chicken pieces onto the grill rack. Grill the chicken for about 20 - 25 minutes or until done. During the last 5 minutes of grilling, baste with melted ghee. Transfer chicken to the serving platter. Garnish with lime wedges and sliced onions.

***Cook's Note:*** *You can bake this chicken in a preheated oven at 400º to 450º F for 30 - 35 minutes.*

# CORN SEEKH KABOBS

*In India, during the peak season, you can see fresh corn being roasted on coal stoves on street corner. Passersby cannot resist the aroma of fresh-roasted corn.*

*Serves 4*

- 1 pound red potatoes
- ½ tablespoon + 1 teaspoon salt, divided
- 1½ cups frozen or fresh corn, divided
- 1 - 2 minced green chilies, such as serrano
- 1-inch piece ginger, minced
- ¼ cup corn starch
- 1 teaspoon amchoor powder
- ½ teaspoon garam masala powder
- 2 tablespoons finely chopped green onion

- bamboo or metal skewers
- 2 tablespoons ghee for basting

If you are using bamboo skewers, soak them in water for at least ½ an hour.

Place potatoes along with ½ tablespoon of salt in a medium saucepan. Add enough water to cover 2 - 3 inches above the surface of the potatoes. Boil them over medium high heat until tender enough to be easily pierced with a fork or a skewer. Drain potatoes in a colander. When potatoes are cool enough to handle, peel and mash potatoes. You can use a potato ricer for this. Transfer ½ cup of corn to the food processor bowl, pulse few times to mince the corn. Add minced corn to potatoes along with green chilies, ginger, corn starch, amchoor powder, garam masala powder, green onions and 1 teaspoon salt. Mix thoroughly.

Preheat grill to medium high heat. Divide the dough into 8 portions. Take each portion and press them onto the skewer in the shape of a sausage. Stud the kabobs all over with left over corn. Spray the grill rack with nonstick cooking spray. Grill the kabobs until evenly charred for about 10 - 15 minutes, while turning once after 5 - 7 minutes. During the last minute of grilling, baste with ghee.

Alternately, you can bake them in the oven. Preheat oven to 375° F. Line the baking tray with a wire rack. Spray the wire rack with nonstick cooking spray. Place kabobs on to the wire rack. Bake until evenly browned for 10 - 12 minutes. Turn over in between once or twice for even browning. After removing from the oven, baste them with ghee.

Serve with onion tomato chutney.

# PANEER AND VEGETABLE KABOBS

*Whenever we have a barbeque party, we usually have a few strict vegetarians. These kabobs are perfect for a vegetarian's palate. The vegetables and paneer cubes are marinated with strained yogurt, spices and chickpea flour. The marinade becomes the coating for the vegetables and paneer, which helps to lock in the moisture.*

*Serves 4 - 6*

- 16 - ounces paneer, cut into 1½ - 2 inch cubes
- 2 green bell peppers, cut into 2-inch chunks
- 1 medium red onion, cut into 2-inch chunks
- ½ cup strained yogurt (page 307)
- 2 tablespoons ginger garlic paste
- 1 tablespoon lime juice
- 2 tablespoons chickpea flour/besan
- ½ - 1 teaspoon cayenne
- ½ teaspoon turmeric
- ¼ teaspoon ajwain powder
- ½ teaspoon salt or to taste
- 1¼ teaspoons chaat masala powder, homemade (page 301) or store bought, divided

- metal or bamboo skewers

If you are using bamboo skewers, soak them in water for at least ½ an hour.

In a medium sized non-reactive bowl, add yogurt, ginger garlic paste, lime juice, chickpea flour, cayenne, turmeric, ajwain powder, salt and 1 teaspoon chaat masala. Stir to combine. Add paneer and rest of the vegetables. Mix thoroughly until all the pieces are evenly coated with the marinade. Cover and marinate for ½ - 1 hour in the refrigerator.

Preheat grill to medium high. Thread the paneer and vegetables onto the skewers. Grill them until evenly charred.

Alternately, you can broil these kabobs in the oven. Place skewers on a baking sheet lined with metal rack. Place baking sheet with skewers 5 - 6 inches below the heating element. Broil while turning in between once or twice for 5 - 7 minutes or until golden brown. Remove from the oven. Sprinkle with ¼ teaspoon of chaat masala and serve.

# GRILLED VEGETABLE CHAAT

*You can use any vegetable of your choice for this recipe.*

Serves 4 - 6
- 5 - 6 assorted colored bell peppers
- 1 pound Indian or Japanese eggplant
- 2 pounds mushrooms
- 3 zucchini squash
- 2 red onions
- ¼ cup vegetable oil
- 1 - 2 tablespoons chaat masala powder, homemade (page 301) or store bought
- salt and pepper to taste

Cut the colored bell peppers into big chunks.  Cut mushrooms in the middle.  Cut zucchini and red onions into thick rounds. In a bowl, mix vegetables and oil, making sure that all the vegetables are evenly coated with a thin film of oil. Preheat grill to medium heat.  Grill all the vegetables until lightly charred.  Remove them onto a platter.  Sprinkle with chaat masala.  Gently toss the vegetables to mix. Season with salt and pepper. Serve with barbeque meats.

# SPICED FRUIT SALAD

*Fresh fruit salad is jazzed up with spicy syrup.*

Serves 6 - 8

Syrup
- 1 cup sugar
- 1 ½ cups water
- 1-inch piece ginger, sliced
- 1 teaspoon pepper corn
- 1 teaspoon fennel seeds
- 1 star anise
- one 2-inch stick cinnamon
- mint springs

- 1 papaya, peeled, seeded and cut into chunks
- 2 mangos, peeled, seeded and cut into chunks
- 1 pineapple, peeled, cored and cut into chunks
- 2-inch piece ginger, julienned
- mint springs to garnish

To make the syrup, heat sugar, water, ginger, pepper corn, fennel seeds, star anise, cinnamon stick and mint springs in a medium saucepan over medium high heat.  Bring it to boil.  Reduce heat to medium.  Simmer for 5 minutes.  Turn off the heat and let it steep for ½ an hour. Strain the syrup and cool in the refrigerator

Meanwhile, prepare the fruit. Pour the syrup on top of the prepared fruit. Gently toss to make sure all the fruits are covered with the syrup.   Garnish with julienned ginger and mint sprigs.

# MANGO SALSA AND CHIPS

*Serves 4 - 6*
- ¼ cup finely chopped onion
- 1½ teaspoons salt, divided
- 1 large ripened mango, peeled and cut around the pit and finely diced
- 4 large yellow or golden tomatoes, finely chopped
- 1 - 4 minced fresh green chilies, such as serrano
- 3 tablespoons lime juice or to taste
- ¼ cup chopped cilantro leaves

- blue corn chips

Sprinkle ½ a teaspoon of salt over chopped onions and mix. Let it steep. After 15 minutes, squeeze as much water as possible from the onions and discard the water.

In a medium bowl, stir in onions, mango, tomatoes, green chilies, 1 teaspoon salt, lime juice and cilantro. Season to taste with salt. Serve with blue corn chips.

# MEYER LEMON LEMONADE WITH LEMON VERBENA

*Meyer lemon is a cross between lemon and mandarin orange. It is not only sweeter than regular lemon, but also has very distinct floral aroma which I have fallen in love with. This is my most favorite lemonade and I hope it becomes yours too.*

*Serves 4 - 6*
- 2 cups sugar
- 6 cups water
- 2 cups meyer lemon juice
- ½ cup lemon verbena leaves
- ½ teaspoon salt

In a small saucepan, place 2 cups sugar and 2 cups of water and bring it to boil. Stir until sugar dissolves. Turn off the heat and cool the syrup to room temperature. To a large pitcher, add meyer lemon juice, the remaining 4 cups of water, lemon verbena leaves, salt and 2 cups of sugar syrup (or to taste). Mix everything together. Refrigerate 2 - 3 hours to chill. Serve over ice.

**Cook's Note:** *Look for meyer lemons at farmers market and specialty supermarkets.*

# Iced Tea with Saffron and Cardamom

*Serves 4 - 6*
- 6 cups hot water
- 4 tea bags
- 1 cup saffron-cardamom syrup or to taste (page 308)
- mint sprigs for garnishing

Place tea bags in a large pitcher. Add 6 cups of hot water to the tea bags. Let it steep for about 5 - 6 minutes. Remove tea bags from the water. Add sugar syrup and stir together. Chill in the refrigerator until ready to serve. Serve over ice cubes with mint sprigs as garnish.

# Pomegranate Margaritas

*This margarita has a beautiful vibrant color. For added interest, toss in some fresh pomegranate seeds to the glass before pouring the drink.*

*Serves 1*
- salt and lime wedge for the rim of the glass
- ⅛ cup Tequila
- ⅛ cup orange liquor such as Cointreau
- 1 tablespoon fresh lime juice
- ½ cup unsweetened pomegranate juice
- 1 tablespoon ginger syrup (page 308)
- 1 cup ice cubes

Run a lime wedge around the rim of margarita glass to moisten, then dip the rim in salt.
Combine tequila, orange liquor, lime juice, pomegranate juice and ginger syrup in a shaker along with ice cubes.
Shake for few minutes. Strain into salt-rimmed glass and serve.

If you prefer frothy margarita, place all the ingredients in the blender and blend until frothy. Serve in a salt-rimmed glass.

# MANGO MARGARITAS

*Margaritas are a classic Mexican drink. They are popular at parties in America, especially at barbeques.*
*Serves: 1*

- sugar and lime wedge for the rim of the glass

- 3 tablespoons tequila
- 2 tablespoons Grand Marnier or Triple sac
- 4 tablespoons lime juice
- ½ cup mango nectar or juice
- 2 tablespoons ginger syrup (page 308)
- 1 cup crushed ice

- mango slice for garnishing

Run a lime wedge around the rim of margarita glass to moisten, then dip the rim in sugar.

Place all the ingredients in the cocktail shaker and shake for few minutes. Strain it into the sugar-rimmed margarita glass. Garnish with mango slice and serve.

If you prefer frothy margarita, place all the ingredients in a blender and blend until frothy. Serve in a sugar-rimmed glass.

# KULFI

*Kulfi, or Indian ice cream, is a favorite dessert for many Indians. Kulfi is made of a combination of flavors such as saffron, cardamom and rose water. Nuts are added to give it another layer of flavoring and crunchiness. It is traditionally made with thickened whole milk, but this recipe is an instant foolproof method. Even though traditional kulfi has a denser texture, I use an ice cream maker to make this dessert. The end result is a creamy and smooth dessert which melts in your mouth. Kulfi molds are available at Indian stores. If you can't find them, freeze them in 6 - 8 ounce ramekins or paper cups. To serve, dip ramekin in hot water before unmolding. If you are using paper cups, you can simply tear the cup away from the kulfi and serve.*

- ice cream maker

- 1 teaspoon loosely packed saffron
- ¼ cup hot milk
- one 14 ounce can sweetened condensed milk
- one 12 ounce can evaporated milk
- 2 cups heavy cream
- ½ teaspoon green cardamom seed powder
- ¼ cup chopped pistachio nuts

Follow the directions for the ice cream maker. You may need to freeze the ice cream bowl before you proceed to make kulfi.

In a small skillet over low heat, fry saffron for a few seconds until it turns one shade darker. It takes less than a minute. Crumble saffron over hot milk and let it steep for 30 minutes. In a bowl, mix saffron milk, condensed milk, evaporated milk, heavy cream and cardamom powder.

Transfer the milk mixture to the ice cream bowl and freeze according to the manufacturer's directions. During the last 15 minutes of freezing, add chopped nuts and continue with the process. When mixture is frozen and creamy, transfer to the kulfi molds and freeze. When you are ready to serve, dip the molds in the hot water and unmold into the serving bowl.

**Cook's Note:** *If you don't have an ice cream maker, freeze the mixture in a shallow tray. When it is semi-solid, transfer to a food processor bowl fitted with metal blade. Process for a few seconds until it becomes creamy. Transfer to kulfi molds and freeze.*

# VEGETABLE KABOBS

*Serves 4 - 6*

- 1 ½ pounds potatoes
- 1 tablespoon salt, divided
- 3 tablespoons vegetable oil
- ½ cup finely chopped carrots
- ½ cup finely chopped green beans
- 1 cup finely chopped cabbage
- 1 cup grated paneer
- 1 teaspoon chaat masala powder, homemade (page 301) or store bought

- 1 tablespoon minced fresh green chilies, such as serrano
- 1 tablespoon minced fresh ginger

- metal or bamboo skewers
- 2 tablespoons ghee for basting

If you are using bamboo skewers, soak them in water for at least ½ an hour.

Place potatoes along with 2 teaspoons of salt in a medium saucepan. Add enough water to cover 2 - 3 inches above the surface of the potatoes. Boil them over medium high heat until tender enough to be easily pierced with a fork or a skewer. Drain potatoes in a colander. When potatoes are cool enough to handle, peel and mash the potatoes. You can also use a potato ricer for this. Stir-fry each vegetable separately for 2 to 3 minutes, using about a tablespoon of oil for each vegetable. Add cooked vegetables, grated paneer, chaat masala, green chilies, ginger, and 1 teaspoon salt to the mashed potatoes and mix in.

Preheat oven to 375° F.

Divide the dough into 12 portions. Take each portion of dough and make a sausage shape around the skewer. Line the baking tray with a wire rack. Spray wire rack with nonstick cooking spray. Arrange skewers on top of the rack and place it into the preheated oven. Bake for 10 to 12 minutes. In between you can turn skewers once or twice for even browning. During the last minute of baking, baste with ghee. Serve with cilantro chutney.

# CHICKEN KABOBS

*Kabobs and tikkas were introduced to North India by the Moghul emperors. This is a spectacular recipe from the Moghul restaurant Sahib Sindh Sultan in Bangalore.*

*Serves 4 - 6*

- 2 pounds boneless chicken thigh meat, cut into two pieces.
- 2 tablespoons vegetable oil
- 2 tablespoons chickpea flour/besan
- 2 tablespoons ginger garlic paste
- ¼ cup malt vinegar or white vinegar
- 1 ½ teaspoons salt

- 1 - 2 teaspoons cayenne
- ⅛ cup caramelized onion powder (page 309)
- ½ teaspoon cinnamon
- 1 tablespoon coriander powder
- 1 teaspoon Moghul garam masala powder (page 86)

- metal or bamboo skewers
- 2 tablespoons ghee for basting

Heat 2 tablespoons oil in a small skillet. When oil is hot, add chickpea flour and mix until well-combined. Remove from heat and cool the flour mixture. In a bowl, combine fried chickpea flour, ginger garlic paste, vinegar, salt, cayenne, onion powder, cinnamon, coriander powder and Moghul garam masala. Add chicken pieces. Mix thoroughly to make sure all chicken pieces are coated with the marinade. Marinate the chicken in the refrigerator for 4 to 24 hours.

If you are using bamboo skewers, soak them in water for at least half an hour.

Preheat grill to medium high heat. Thread marinated pieces onto metal or bamboo skewers. Grill the kabobs, while turning occasionally until cooked and evenly charred for about 20 to 25 minutes. During the last few minutes of grilling, baste them with ghee.

Alternately, you can cook these in a preheated oven at 375° F for 20 to 25 minutes. For the last 2 to 3 minutes, you can put them under the broiler while turning once in the middle to char the meat pieces.

# MOGHUL DUM BIRYANI

*This is another authentic dish from the Moghul era. Dum is a classic Moghul technique of slow-cooking food in a sealed pot. Traditionally, it is done by placing the marinated meat layered with parboiled rice in a pot and using the dough to seal the pot with the lid. While cooking this dish over the coal stove, hot coals are placed on top of the dish. While the meat is being cooked, the rice is simultaneously cooked by absorbing flavors from the meat with the heat from the coals. Similar results can be achieved by cooking in the convenience of a modern oven. This is another sumptuous one-dish party meal. It needs just a simple raita as an accompaniment.*

*Serves 6 – 8*

- 2 pounds leg of lamb or goat meat, cut into 2-inch pieces
- ½ cup vegetable oil
- ¼ cup golden raisins
- ¼ cup sliced almonds
- 2 medium onions, halved lengthwise and sliced thinly
- ⅛ cup red chili paste (page 304) or ⅛ cup paprika
- 2 tablespoons ginger garlic paste
- ¼ cup lime juice
- ½ teaspoon shea jeera powder (black cumin powder)
- 1 teaspoon roasted cumin powder
- 1 teaspoon Moghul garam masala powder (recipe follows)

- 2 - 5 minced fresh green chilies, such as serrano
- ¾ cup strained yogurt
- ½ cup chopped cilantro
- ½ cup chopped mint leaves
- 3 tablespoons + ½ teaspoon salt, divided
- 3 cups basmati rice
- 1 teaspoon loosely packed saffron
- ½ cup hot milk
- ¼ cup hot water
- ¼ cup ghee
- extra Moghul garam masala powder to garnish

Heat oil in a shallow pan over medium heat. Add almonds and fry until golden brown. Remove from the pan using a slotted spoon onto a tray lined with paper towel. To the same pan add raisins and fry until they plump up, remove them to the same tray as almonds. Increase the heat to medium high and add the onions. Fry onions while stirring occasionally at the beginning and often at the end, until they turn golden brown evenly. Remove onions with the slotted spatula and with another spatula gently press the onions between the two spatulas to release excess oil. Spread them on to the sheet pan to crisp up and cool. Reserve leftover oil from the pan for the marinade. Remove half of the fried onions; grind them into a powder using the spice grinder. Reserve rest of the onions for the garnish along with almonds and raisins.

To the medium bowl, add onion powder, reserved oil, red chili paste, ginger garlic paste, lime juice, shea jeera powder, cumin powder, Moghul garam masala powder, minced chilies, yogurt, cilantro and mint, and 2½ teaspoons of salt. Mix everything together. Add to lamb cubes. Mix to make sure all the meat pieces are coated with marinade. Marinate for 8 to 24 hours in the refrigerator.

Place rice in a large bowl. Wash rice with several changes of cold water. Add 1 teaspoon salt and enough water to cover 2 inches above the rice. Let it soak for at least 3 hours.

In a small skillet over low flame, fry saffron threads for a few seconds until they become a shade darker. Crumble saffron over the hot milk. Let it steep for ½ an hour to 1 hour. Meanwhile, bring 10 cups of water to boil in a large saucepan. Add 2 tablespoons of salt to it. Drain the rice and slowly add to the boiling water. Boil for 3 minutes. Drain the rice immediately into a colander.

To assemble biryani, preheat oven to 375° F. Transfer marinated meat to a large oven-proof casserole dish. Add ¼ cup of hot water to the meat mixture and mix well. Spread the rice on top of the meat evenly. Drizzle saffron milk and ghee over the rice. Cover the dish with aluminum foil first and then with the lid. Bake for 45 minutes. Let it rest for 10 minutes. Mix gently just before serving. To keep the rice grains with triple color do not over mix the rice. Transfer to a platter. Garnish with reserved nuts, raisins, caramelized onions and a sprinkling of Moghul garam masala powder.

## MOGHUL GARAM MASALA POWDER

*What sets the Moghul garam masala powder apart from the regular garam masala is that it is more fragrant than others because of the addition of mace and nutmeg.*

- 2 tablespoons cumin seeds
- 1 tablespoon shea jeera seeds (black cumin seeds)
- 2 inch stick cinnamon, broken into small pieces
- 1 tablespoon cloves
- 2 tablespoon black pepper corns

- 1 tablespoon green cardamom seeds
- 1 teaspoon saffron
- ½ teaspoon ground mace
- ½ teaspoon ground nutmeg

Transfer cumin seeds, shea jeera, cinnamon, cloves, black pepper and cardamom to the small skillet. Heat over medium heat, roast spices while stirring, and shaking the skillet, until aromatic for about 2 minutes. Let it cool. Using a spice grinder, grind the roasted spices into powder along with saffron, mace and nutmeg. Store in an air tight container in a cool dark place.

# MOGHUL EGG KORMA

*Kormas are a part of the culinary heritage of the Moghul dynasty. They are often enriched with onion, ginger, garlic, cream, and nuts.*

*Serves 4 -6*

- ⅓ cup vegetable oil
- 2 cloves
- ½-inch cinnamon stick
- 2 cardamom pods, split open
- 1 medium-sized onion, finely chopped
- 1 tablespoon ginger garlic paste
- 2 tablespoons tomato paste
- 2 tablespoons coriander powder
- 1 teaspoon cayenne

- 1 tablespoon kashmiri chili powder or paprika
- 1 teaspoon salt
- ¼ cup almond paste (page 303)
- ½ cup heavy cream
- 4 cups water
- 2 teaspoons lime juice
- 8 hard-boiled eggs, peeled and cut lengthwise in half
- chopped cilantro/coriander leaves to garnish

Heat oil in a wide-bottom skillet over medium high heat. When oil is hot, add cloves, cinnamon, and cardamom pods. Stir-fry for a few seconds. Add onion. Sauté onion until edges begin to brown. Add ginger garlic paste and stir for a minute. Add tomato paste and stir-fry for 2 minutes. Add coriander powder, cayenne, and kashmiri chili powder or paprika. Stir fry for a minute. Add salt and 4 cups of water and bring it to a boil. Reduce heat and simmer the sauce until thickened for about half an hour. Stir in almond paste and cream. Cook for 2 minutes. Add lime juice and stir to mix. Spread the eggs, cut side up in a single layer over the sauce. Simmer gently for 2 to 3 minutes. Garnish with coriander leaves. Serve with rice or chappati.

***Cook's Note:*** *Whole spices are added for flavor only and are not meant to be eaten.*

# Roti Pae Boti

*Roti means bread and boti means a piece of meat with bone. Traditionally, meat with bone is used to make this dish, but this recipe is made with boneless meat. Roti pae boti translates to "piece of meat on the bread".*

Serves 6 - 8

- 1 sheet puff pastry, thawed in the refrigerator over night

- 2 tablespoons vegetable oil
- 1 pound lamb or goat meat, minced
- 1 tablespoon ginger garlic paste
- ½ teaspoon cumin powder
- 1 tablespoon red chili paste (page 304) or 1 tablespoon paprika

- ¼ teaspoon turmeric
- 1 teaspoon salt
- ½ teaspoon Moghul garam masala powder (page 86)
- ¼ cup whole milk yogurt
- 1 tablespoon caramelized onion powder (page 309)
- 2 tablespoons shredded mint leaves
- ¼ cup sour cream for garnish (optional)
- mint leaves to garnish

Heat oil in a medium shallow pan over medium high heat. Add minced meat and cook until all the water evaporates and the meat is cooked. Add ginger garlic paste, cumin powder, red chili paste, turmeric and salt. Stir fry for 2 to 3 minutes. Add garam masala powder and fry for 1 minute. Add the yogurt, one tablespoon at a time. Wait until the first tablespoon is absorbed before you add the next. Cook, stirring occasionally, until yogurt begins to fry for 1 to 2 minutes. Stir in onion powder and mint leaves and set aside.

Preheat oven to 425° F. Roll pastry into 16 x 16 inch square. Prick all over the surface with fork to prevent the dough from rising while baking. Using 3 ½ -inch round cookie cutter, cut the dough into 16 round pieces. Place them on a cookie sheet and cover with parchment paper. Place another cookie sheet on top of the parchment paper to weigh it down and bake for 8 to 10 minutes or until golden brown.

To serve, place 1 tablespoon of meat mixture on top of each baked roti. Garnish with 1 teaspoon of sour cream and a mint leaf in the middle.

# MIXED BELL PEPPER AND PANEER IN MOGHUL SAUCE

*The sauce is enriched with cashew nut paste and cream. This is characteristically a Moghul sauce.*

*Serves 4 - 6*
- 12 ounces fried paneer pieces (page 304)
- 2 tablespoons vegetable oil
- 2 to 3 cardamom pods, split open
- ¼ cup onion paste (page 303)
- 1 tablespoon ginger garlic paste
- ½ - 1 teaspoon green chili paste or to taste
- 3 multi-colored bell peppers, cut into 2 x 1 pieces
- ¼ cup cashew paste (page 303)
- ¾ teaspoon salt or to taste
- ¼ teaspoon cinnamon
- ½ teaspoon black pepper
- ¼ cup yogurt
- ¼ cup heavy cream
- 1 cup water

Have paneer ready and set aside. Heat oil in a skillet over medium heat. Add cardamom pods and fry for few seconds. Add onion paste. Stir fry until some of the moisture evaporates for about 5 minutes. Add ginger garlic and chili paste, fry for 2 minutes while stirring often. Stir in peppers and fry about 5 minutes, while stirring often. Add cashew paste and stir fry for another two minutes. Add salt, cinnamon, and black pepper. Add yogurt one tablespoon at a time, incorporating the first tablespoon before adding another. Stir in cream and water and bring it to a simmer. Stir in paneer pieces, continue to simmer for 5 minutes. Serve with rice or chappati.

# THADKA DAL

*Thadka means seasoning. Every region has its own version of seasoning. This is very creamy, tasty and satisfying dal. Mung dal is a favorite of North Indians.*

*Serves 6*
- 1 ½ cups mung dal
- 6 cups water
- 1 teaspoon turmeric
- ¾ cup heavy cream
- 1 teaspoon salt or to taste

*Seasoning*
- ¼ cup ghee
- 1 teaspoon cumin seeds
- ½ cup chopped onion
- 2 teaspoons minced garlic
- 2 - 5 minced fresh green chilies, such as serrano
- 1 teaspoon kashmiri chili powder or paprika

Wash dal with several changes of water. Boil dal with 6 cups of water in a large heavy bottom stock pot over medium high heat. Bring it to boil and reduce heat to medium. Cook dal uncovered, while stirring occasionally for 10 - 15 minutes. Reduce heat to medium low, stir in salt and simmer for another 30 minutes or until dal is cooked and soft. Mix in cream and cook for another 10 - 15 minutes.

To season, in a small skillet heat ghee over medium heat. When it is hot, add cumin seeds. When the cumin seeds start sizzling, add onion and garlic. Sauté until edges of the onions begin to brown. Add green chilies and stir fry for 1 minute. Add chili powder. Fry for a few seconds. Add seasoning to cooked dal. Heat through and serve.

# NAAN

*"Naan" means "bread" in Persian. This bread was introduced in India by Moghuls who came from Persia to rule India. Traditionally, the bread is cooked in tandoor clay ovens. The bread is slapped against the inside walls of a very hot tandoor oven. It cooks almost instantly, locks in moisture, and has a crispy outside. Even though it is impossible to replicate the taste and the texture without a tandoor oven, you will get similar results by cooking the bread under the broiler. Use a heavy baking tray and turn the bread once in the middle of baking.*

*Yields 8 - 10*

- 1 teaspoon yeast
- 1 teaspoon sugar
- ¼ cup milk, warmed to 110°F
- 2 cups all-purpose flour
- ½ teaspoon salt

- ½ cup yogurt
- 2 tablespoons ghee or vegetable oil
- extra flour for rolling
- 2 tablespoons ghee for basting
- 1 teaspoon black poppy seeds

To a bowl, add yeast, sugar and milk. Stir and set aside for 5 - 10 minutes to activate yeast. Add flour, salt, yogurt and ghee or oil to the yeast mixture. Knead for 5 minutes until dough is smooth and silky. Alternately, this step can be done in a food processor or Kitchen Aid mixer using dough hook.

Brush a large bowl lightly with oil. Transfer dough to the bowl. Cover with plastic wrap or a kitchen towel. Let it rest for 2 - 3 hours. This allows the yeast to ferment and makes the dough rise to double its size. You can also refrigerate the dough for a day.

Divide the dough into 8 - 10 balls. Let them rise again for ½ an hour. Set the metal rack in the oven, 5 - 6 inches below the heating element. Preheat oven to broiler at high temperature.

Roll out each ball into 6 - 7 inch circles. Transfer 2 - 3 circles at a time onto the baking sheet and place them under the broiler. Broil until the bread puffs up and acquires a few golden spots. It takes about ½ - 1 minute. Carefully, using the spatula, turn the bread and cook for another 1 - 1 ½ minutes. Remove bread from the oven and baste with ghee. Sprinkle with poppy seeds and transfer naans to the platter. Cover them with a foil or a clean kitchen towel. Proceed with the rest. Serve warm with any curry with gravy.

# PINEAPPLE KA PANNA

*This is a variation of the traditional mango ka panna, with a contrast of flavors that are sweet, spicy and aromatic.*

*Serves 8*

- 1 pineapple, peeled, cored and cut into 1 ½-inch pieces
- 6 cups water
- 1 cup simple syrup (page 308)
- 1 teaspoon black salt
- 1 teaspoon chaat masala powder, homemade (page 301) or store bought
- ½ teaspoon salt
- 1 teaspoon roasted cumin powder
- ¼ cup chopped mint
- ¼ cup chopped cilantro/coriander

Preheat oven to 375º F. Spread pineapple pieces on a sheet pan. Roast them in the oven for 40 - 45 minutes or until the bottom of the pieces are caramelized. Let them cool to room temperature. Transfer roasted pineapple, water, simple syrup, black salt, chaat masala, salt, cumin powder, mint and cilantro to the grinder. Grind them until smooth. You can do this in 2 - 3 batches. Strain through a fine metal sieve. Discard any leftover solids from the sieve. Taste and adjust the seasoning. Garnish with a sprig of mint before serving.

# RABDI WITH LYCHEES

*Rabdi, a creamy north Indian dessert, is traditionally made by simmering milk, while stirring often until almost all the moisture evaporates. Sweeteners and flavorings are added at the end to enhance the flavor. By using pre-made khoya in the recipe, cooking time can be reduced by half without sacrificing the taste and quality.*

*Serves 4 - 6*

- ¼ teaspoon loosely packed saffron threads
- ¼ cup hot milk
- 2 cups whole milk
- 2 cups half and half
- 1 cup grated khoya*
- ¼ cup sugar
- ¼ teaspoon green cardamom seed powder
- one 14-ounce can lychees, drained
- silver leaves to garnish

In a small skillet, over low flame, fry saffron threads until they become a shade darker for a few seconds. Crumble saffron over hot milk. Let it steep for ½ an hour.

In a large heavy bottom skillet, boil 2 cups of milk and 2 cups of half and half over medium high heat while stirring often. Once it reaches its boiling point, reduce heat to medium and continue to simmer for 40 to 45 minutes or until the volume is reduced by half, while stirring occasionally. While it is simmering, you will notice skin forming on top of the liquid. Simply stir it back in. Add grated khoya and stir in for 10 minutes until khoya dissolves into the milk mixture. Add sugar and stir for 5 minutes until the sugar melts and is incorporated with the other ingredients. Stir in the saffron milk and cardamom powder into the milk mixture. Remove the skillet from the stove, cover and cool to room temperature. Transfer to serving bowl. Cover with plastic wrap and chill in the refrigerator. To serve, add 3 to 5 lychees to individual bowls. Pour ½ cup of rabdi over lychees and garnish it with silver leaf.

*Cooks Note: *Khoya is available at Indian stores in the refrigerator section.*

*Detail: During the Moghul period, delicacies were garnished with very thin leaves of 24 carat gold and silver.
This symbolized the opulence and power of the Moghuls.*

*Detail: Comfortable cushions around a low table in front of a fireplace provide a warm setting for relaxed and intimate conversations.*

# Dinner by the Fire

A dinner by the fire with a few close friends is the best way to spend cozy winter evenings. I like to set a low table in front of the fireplace and use oversized cushions for people to sit on the floor around the table. Sitting on the cushions at a low table invites intimate conversation. Little touches like these make cozy gatherings extra-special.

## The Menu

# PEANUT CHAAT

*Peanuts are called ground nuts in India. When I visited Delhi, I ate this chaat in a canteen at an army golf club. It instantly became my favorite snack.*

*Serves 6*

- 1 ½ cups roasted, shelled peanuts
- ½ cup chopped red onion
- 2 tablespoons lime juice
- salt to taste
- 1 - 3 minced fresh green chilies, such as serrano
- 4 tablespoons chopped cilantro
- 1 teaspoon chaat masala powder, homemade (page 301) or store bought

Gently toss all the ingredients together. Serve in individual bowls as an appetizer.

# Tomato Soup

*This flavorful spicy soup can be an ultimate comfort food during the cold winter months as you sip it by the fire. This can also be a great summer soup using garden fresh tomatoes.*

*Serves 6*

- 2 tablespoons vegetable oil
- 2 cloves garlic, sliced
- 1 teaspoon cumin seeds
- 1 cup grated carrots
- 4 cups wine ripened chopped tomatoes
- 2 tablespoons all-purpose flour
- 6 cups water
- ½ teaspoon cayenne
- ½ cup chopped cilantro, including stems
- ½ teaspoon green cardamom seed powder
- ½ - 1 teaspoon freshly ground black pepper
- 2 teaspoons salt
- 1 tablespoon sugar or honey
- extra cilantro leaves for garnishing

Heat oil in a large saucepan over medium high heat. When oil is hot, add garlic and cumin seeds. As soon as cumin seeds sizzle, add the carrots. Stir fry for 5 minutes or until carrots are soft. Add tomatoes and cook until soft and some of the moisture evaporates. Stir in flour and fry for about a minute. Add water, cayenne, cilantro, cardamom powder, black pepper, salt and sugar or honey. Bring it to a boil and reduce the heat to medium. Simmer for 30 minutes. Let it cool. Let the soup pass through a food mill or a fine mesh strainer into a bowl. If you prefer a smoother consistency, once the contents are cool, transfer to a blender. Blend until you have a smooth puree, then pass it through a strainer. Return strained soup to the saucepan. Heat over medium heat until soup is hot. Season to taste. Serve in soup bowls and garnish with cilantro.

# Okra Fry

*To select tender okra, snap the tip off with your fingers. If the tip snaps and breaks off, the okra is tender. If it doesn't, it is fibrous. Okra is called "bhindi" in Hindi.*

*Serves 4*

- 1 ½ pounds okra
- 2 tablespoons vegetable oil
- 1 - 2 dry whole red chilies such as chile de arbol
- 1 teaspoon black mustard seeds
- 1 teaspoon cumin seeds
- 10 curry leaves

- ½ cup chopped onion
- 1 teaspoon salt or to taste
- ½ teaspoon turmeric
- ½ teaspoon cayenne

Rinse and dry okra with paper towels. Trim the ends and cut into ¾-inch pieces. Heat oil in a wok or skillet over medium high heat. When oil is hot, add the red chilies. When the chilies turn dark, add mustard seeds and cover with a lid until the spluttering subsides. Uncover and stir in cumin seeds. When cumin seeds sizzle, add curry leaves. As soon as curry leaves are crisp, add the chopped onion. Sauté onion until translucent. Stir in okra, salt, turmeric and cayenne. Reduce heat to medium and fry until okra is cooked for about 20 - 25 minutes while stirring occasionally. Serve as a side dish to any Indian meal.

*Cook's Note:*
*1. After the addition of okra to the pan, you can transfer the whole mixture to a microwave safe dish and cook in the microwave for 15 - 20 minutes, uncovered at full power, stopping and stirring once or twice in the middle of cooking.*
*2. Whole red chilies are added for flavor. They are not meant to be eaten.*

# Coconut Chicken with Peppers

*Serves 4 - 6*

- ¼ cup vegetable oil
- 1-inch cinnamon stick
- 8 cloves
- 1 bay leaf
- 1 onion, finely minced
- 2 tablespoons ginger garlic paste
- 1 tablespoon coriander powder
- 2 teaspoons salt
- ½ teaspoon turmeric

- ½ - 1 teaspoon cayenne
- 1 tablespoon paprika
- 2 pounds boneless, skinless chicken breasts, cut into 2-inch pieces
- 2 tomatoes, blanched, peeled and pureed in blender (page 298)
- 3 multi-colored bell peppers, cut into 2-inch pieces
- ½ cup coconut milk, homemade ( page 302) or canned
- 1 teaspoon garam masala powder
- cilantro for garnishing

Heat oil in a large saucepan over medium high heat. When oil is hot, add cinnamon stick, cloves and bay leaf. When cloves plump up, add the onions. Sauté onions until light golden. Stir in ginger garlic paste, coriander powder, salt, turmeric, cayenne and paprika. Stir fry for about 2 minutes. Add chicken. Stir fry for about 5 - 10 minutes or until chicken turns white. Add pureed tomato. Cook for another 15 - 20 minutes or until chicken is almost cooked. Add the bell peppers and cook for another 5 - 7 minutes while stirring occasionally. Reduce heat to medium and stir in coconut milk. Gently heat through and stir in garam masala powder. Transfer to a serving dish and garnish with cilantro. Serve with any flat bread or rice.

***Cook's Note:*** *Whole spices are added for flavor, not meant to be eaten.*

# KHATTE CHOLE
## (SOUR CHICKPEA CURRY)

*Chole served with bhatura, puri or chappati can be a wholesome meal. Chole – Bhatura is one of the popular items on Indian restaurant menus. This dish gets its tangy taste with the addition of tamarind paste. I prefer serving chole as a vegetarian chili.*

**Serves 6**

- ¼ cup vegetable oil
- 2 cups chopped red onion
- 1 tablespoon minced fresh ginger
- 1 - 3 sliced or minced fresh green chilies, such as serrano
- 1 tablespoon coriander powder
- 1 teaspoon roasted cumin powder
- 2 teaspoons salt
- ½ teaspoon turmeric
- 1 teaspoon cayenne
- 1 teaspoon sugar
- 2 large tomatoes, chopped
- 2 tablespoons tamarind paste (page 300)
- four 15-ounce cans chickpeas, drained and rinsed well
- ½ teaspoon garam masala powder

### Raw Seasoning
- 1 - 2 tablespoons lime juice
- 1 - 3 sliced or minced fresh green chilies
- ¼ cup chopped fresh cilantro leaves
- ½ cup chopped red onions

Heat oil in a large saucepan over medium high heat. When the oil is hot, add the onions. Sauté until onions are translucent and edges begin to brown. Stir in ginger, green chilies, coriander powder, cumin powder, salt, turmeric and cayenne. Stir fry for 2 minutes. Add sugar and tomatoes. Cook until tomatoes are soft and some of the moisture evaporates. Add the tamarind paste and cook through. Stir in chickpeas. Cook while stirring occasionally for 5 minutes. Stir in 2 cups of water. Bring it to boil and reduce heat to medium. Cook until sauce is thick. Stir in garam masala powder.

For raw seasoning, mix everything together in a bowl. Stir in just before serving.

### Cook's Note:
*Don't mix in raw seasoning until just before serving to keep the onions crunchy.*

# METHI ROTI

*Methi is the tender fenugreek leaves available at Indian stores. The addition of methi leaves give an interesting flavor to the basic roti.*

*Yields 8*

- 2 cups chappati flour (atta)
- 1 teaspoon salt
- ½ teaspoon coarsely ground ajwain seeds
- ½ teaspoon cayenne
- 2 tablespoons vegetable oil
- 1 cup methi leaves

- extra flour for rolling
- 3 - 4 tablespoons ghee or oil for basting

Stir in flour, salt, ajwain and cayenne in a bowl. Add oil. Using your fingers, rub oil into the flour mixture. Stir in methi leaves. Add ¾ cup of water to the flour mixture and mix in to form a soft, pliable dough. Transfer dough to the work surface. Knead for 5 minutes. Place dough in an oiled bowl. Cover and let it rest for 30 minutes allowing the gluten to develop. Divide the dough into 8 portions and form each portion into a ball. Work with one piece of dough at a time, keeping the rest covered to prevent drying. Roll out each piece of dough into 7-inch circles on a floured surface. Heat griddle over medium high heat. When griddle is hot, cook one roti at a time. Cook on one side until it is cooked and acquires a few rich golden brown spots. Flip it over and cook until other side is also covered with rich golden brown spots. Brush lightly with ghee or oil. Flip it again and apply ghee or oil to the other side. Remove from the griddle. Cover with a kitchen towel while you are preparing the rest of the rotis. Serve with any gravy curry.

*Cook's Note: Equal parts of whole wheat flour and all-purpose flour can be used in place of chappati flour.*

# PEAS PULAO

*This is a simple pulao that can be served as a part of any Indian menu.*

*Serves 6*

- ¼ cup vegetable oil
- ½ tablespoon cumin seeds
- 1 bay leaf
- 6 cloves
- 1-inch cinnamon stick

- ½ cup sliced onion
- 1 - 3 fresh green chilies, such as serrano cut lengthwise into two
- 2 teaspoons salt
- 1 cup frozen peas, thawed
- 2 cups basmati rice

Heat oil in a medium saucepan over medium high heat. When oil is hot, add cumin seeds, bay leaf, cloves and cinnamon stick. Stir fry until the cinnamon stick sizzles and the cloves plump up. Add onions and green chilies. Fry until onions are translucent and edges begin to brown. Stir in salt and peas and stir fry for 2 - 3 minutes. Add basmati rice. Mix thoroughly until all the rice grains are coated with a thin film of oil and spices. Stir in 3 ½ cups of water. At this point, you can transfer rice mixture to an automatic rice cooker and finish cooking. Alternately, bring rice mixture to boil and reduce heat to the lowest setting. Cover with the lid and cook until rice is done for about 20 - 25 minutes. Let the rice rest for 5 - 10 minutes before serving.

*Cook's Note: Whole spices and green chilies are added for flavor, but not meant be eaten.*

# APPLE RAITA

*Serves 4-6*

- 4 cups plain yogurt
- 2 granny smith apples, peeled, cored and grated
- 1 teaspoon roasted cumin powder
- ½ teaspoon cayenne
- 1 teaspoon salt or to taste

Place yogurt in a bowl. Stir in apples, cumin powder, cayenne, and salt. Serve with any Indian meal.

# PHIRNI
## (CREAMY RICE PUDDING)

*Serves 6*

- ½ cup long grain rice
- ¼ cup water
- 6 cups whole milk
- 1 cup sugar
- 1 teaspoon green cardamom seed powder
- 1 teaspoon rose essence
- ½ cup coarsely chopped roasted nuts such as slivered almonds and pistachio nuts
- pistachio nuts and rose petals for garnishing

Soak rice in two cups of water for 3 - 4 hours. Drain the rice and transfer to the blender along with ¼ cup of water and grind into fine paste. Mix rice paste with milk in a medium saucepan. Boil over medium to medium high heat for about 15 minutes while stirring often, until it becomes creamy. Add sugar and cook for another 7 - 8 minutes while stirring often. Mix in cardamom powder and essence. Stir in the chopped nuts. Transfer them to individual serving dishes. Cover with plastic wrap. Cool in the refrigerator. Just before serving, garnish with pistachio nuts and rose petals.

# Outdoor Candlelight Dinner

*Detail: Adding individual salt and pepper shakers with a matching knife rest adds flair to the setting.*

A beautiful luscious garden under a moonlit sky, the fragrance of flowers in the air and the dazzling stars above along with a tantalizing cuisine, candlelights and good friends – this is as good as it gets. It is a magical setting to relax all your senses. Offer guests drinks as they arrive and reserve time for a garden tour before relaxing under the stars.

## The Menu

# CHICKEN TIKKA MASALA

*This is not a traditional Indian recipe, but was developed in England in one of the restaurants as a solution for using leftover grilled chicken. Recently chicken tikka masala is said to have replaced England's national dish, fish and chips.*

*This recipe is included upon request from my son, Naveen. According to him, this is the most popular dish among his peers at Berkeley whenever they go out to eat at Indian restaurants*

- 1 recipe chicken tikka (page 210)
- 4 tablespoons ghee
- 1 bay leaf
- 2 - 3 cardamom pods, lightly crushed to open the shell
- 1 cup finely chopped onion
- 1-inch piece fresh ginger, minced
- 1 minced fresh green chili, such as serrano
- ½ teaspoon cinnamon
- 1 teaspoon roasted cumin powder
- ½ - 1 teaspoon cayenne
- ¼ teaspoon turmeric
- 1 teaspoon kasuri methi (dried fenugreek leaves)
- 1 teaspoon salt or to taste
- one 8-ounce can tomato sauce
- ½ cup heavy cream
- ¼ cup cashew paste (page 303)
- 1 teaspoon garam masala powder
- 2 tablespoons chopped cilantro/coriander

Have chicken tikka ready. Heat the ghee in a large sauce pan over medium high heat. When the ghee is hot, add bay leaf and cardamom pods. Stir for a minute. Add the chopped onion and sauté until edges begin to brown. Add minced ginger and chili and fry for a minute. Stir in cinnamon, cumin powder, cayenne, turmeric, kasuri methi and salt and fry for couple of minutes. Add tomato sauce and one cup of water and bring it to boil. Reduce heat to medium and simmer for 5 minutes. Stir in chicken pieces. Continue to simmer for about 5 minutes until the chicken is heated through. Stir in cream and cashew paste and cook for 5 more minutes. Sprinkle garam masala powder and mix it in. Transfer to a serving dish and garnish with cilantro leaves. Serve with any paratha or rice.

***Cook's Note:*** *Whole spices are added for flavor only, they are not meant to be eaten.*

# FISH IN BANANA LEAF POCKET

*Persians of Zoroastrain faith migrated to India due to religious persecution over 1000 years ago, mainly settling in Gujarat and Mumbai (formerly known as Bombay). Even though they are well integrated into the Indian society, they still maintain their customs and traditions. Their food is one of the traditions that has been preserved over the years. This dish is served at at Persian wedding banquets.*

*Serves 4 - 6*
- 1 ¼ pound any firm white fish fillet, such as cat fish or sea bass.
- 3 cups grated fresh coconut
- 3 cloves garlic, minced
- 1-inch piece ginger, minced
- 1 - 3 minced fresh green chilies, such as serrano
- 2 tablespoons chopped cilantro/coriander

- 5 tablespoons peanut or vegetable oil, divided
- 1 teaspoon black mustard seeds
- 1 teaspoon cumin seeds
- 1 teaspoon salt or to taste
- ½ teaspoon sugar
- 1 tablespoon lime juice

- banana leaves
- kitchen twine

Rinse the fish fillet under cold water and cut into 3-inch steaks. Pat dry with paper towels and set in the refrigerator until ready to use. To the food processor set with a metal blade, add coconut, garlic, ginger, green chilies, and cilantro. Process into a course paste.

Heat 2 tablespoons of oil in a medium skillet over medium heat. When the oil is hot, add mustard seeds and cover until the spluttering subsides. Uncover and add cumin seeds. Once they sizzle, reduce heat to medium low, add coconut paste and stir fry for 5 minutes. Stir in salt, sugar and lime juice. Let it cool to room temperature.

Meanwhile, prepare banana leaves. Cut the banana leaves into 10 x 10 inch squares. Cut as many pieces as that of the fish. Heat 6 - 8 cups of water in the sauce pan until hot. Dip banana leaves in hot water for few seconds, to make them pliable. Remove them from the water and dry with paper towels.

Place banana leaf squares onto the work surface. Brush lightly with oil. Place a piece of fish in the middle of each square. Divide coconut paste equally among the fish pieces. Cover the fish with coconut paste. Fold one side of the leaf over the fish and fold the other side to overlap. Fold opposite ends like a package and tie it with a kitchen twine.

Heat 2 tablespoons of oil in a wide skillet over medium high heat. Place fish pockets in a single layer and fry for 5 minutes. Flip it over and fry for another five minutes. Cover with the lid and cook for 5 more minutes. Cut and remove the twine before serving.
*Cook's Note: If you don't have banana leaves, use aluminum foil.*

# MANGO DAL

*This is called "mamidi kaya pappu" in Telugu. This dal is a childhood favorite of mine and still is.*

*Serves 4 - 6*

- 1 cup toor dal
- 4 - 6 cups water
- 1 green raw mango, peeled, and cut around the pit into 1-inch pieces
- 1 cup chopped onion
- 2 - 5 fresh green chilies, such as serrano, cut lengthwise into two
- ½ teaspoon turmeric
- 1 teaspoon salt or to taste

*Seasoning*

- 2 tablespoons vegetable oil
- 2 dry whole red chilies such as chile de arbol
- 1 teaspoon black mustard seeds
- 10 - 20 curry leaves
- 2 tablespoons chopped onion

Place dal with 3 cups of water in a large sauce pan. Bring it to a boil over medium high heat. Boil for 5 minutes. Reduce heat to medium and simmer for 15 minutes while stirring occasionally. As the dal is being cooked, you will notice some of the scum rises to the top, simply stir it back in. Add mango, onion, green chilies, turmeric and salt and continue to cook. Add more water as needed. Cook for about 25 – 30 minutes until dal is creamy and the mango pieces are soft but still intact.

To season, heat oil in a small skillet over medium high heat. Add red chilies. When red chilies turn one shade darker, add mustard seeds and cover with the lid until spluttering subsides. Uncover and add cumin seeds. Once they sizzle, add curry leaves. As soon as the curry leaves are crisp, add onions. Fry until onion turns golden brown. Add the seasoning to the cooked dal and stir in. Season to taste and serve with rice or chappati.

*Cook's Note: Whole green chilies and dry chilies are added for flavoring. They are not meant to be eaten.*

# BEETS FRY

*Serves 4 - 6*

- 3 beets, tops trimmed
- 2 tablespoons vegetable oil
- 1 dry whole red chili, such as chile de arbol
- 1 teaspoon black mustard seeds
- 1 teaspoon cumin seeds
- 1 teaspoon white urad dal
- 10 - 20 curry leaves
- ½ - 1 teaspoon salt or to taste
- ½ teaspoon turmeric
- ½ teaspoon cayenne
- ¾ cup coarsely grated fresh coconut

Peel and grate beets (use kitchen gloves to avoid stains on your hands). Heat oil in a medium skillet over medium high heat. When oil is hot, add red chili. When the red chili turns dark, add mustard seeds, and cover with the lid until spluttering subsides. Uncover, add cumin seeds. When cumin seeds sizzle, add white urad dal. When the white urad dal turns golden, add the curry leaves. As soon as the curry leaves are crisp add grated beets. Add salt, turmeric, and cayenne. Stir fry until beets are cooked about 5 - 7 minutes. Stir in coconut and fry for 2 minutes more. Transfer to a serving dish and serve with rice.

*Cook's Note: Whole dry chilies are added for flavoring, not meant to be eaten.*

# SPINACH RAITA

*Frozen spinach is convenient to use and is available at almost all supermarkets.*

- one 10 ounce package chopped frozen spinach
- 1 tablespoon vegetable oil
- 2 dry whole red chilies such as chile de arbol
- 1 teaspoon black mustard seeds
- 1 teaspoon salt or to taste
- ½ teaspoon cayenne
- 1 teaspoon roasted cumin powder
- 2 cups plain yogurt
- 1 teaspoon paprika

Defrost spinach. Heat oil in a medium sauce pan over medium high heat. Add dried chilies. Fry until red chilies turn a shade darker. Then add mustard seeds and cover until the spluttering subsides. Uncover and add spinach. Cook for five minutes and stir in salt, cayenne, and cumin powder. Let it cool to room temperature. Stir yogurt into the spinach mixture, transfer to a serving dish and garnish with paprika.

# TOMATO PULAO

*Serves 4 - 6*

*Masala paste:*
- 1-inch piece ginger, chopped
- 5 cloves garlic, chopped
- ½ cup grated fresh coconut
- 1 tablespoon coriander powder

- ⅓ cup vegetable oil
- 2 bay leaves
- 10 cloves
- 2-inch stick cinnamon
- 5 green cardamom pods, slightly crushed to open the shell
- 1 star anise

- ¼ cup raw cashew nuts
- 2 cups sliced onion
- 1 - 3 fresh green chilies such as serrano, cut lengthwise into two
- 4 cups chopped tomato
- 2 teaspoons salt
- ½ teaspoon turmeric
- 1 teaspoon garam masala powder
- 2 cups basmati rice
- 1 cup milk
- 2 ½ cups water
- 2 tablespoons each chopped mint and cilantro/coriander

To make masala paste, transfer ginger, garlic, coconut, coriander powder along with ¼ cup of water to the grinder and grind into a smooth paste.

Heat oil in a medium sauce pan over medium high heat. When oil is hot, add bay leaves, cloves, cinnamon stick, cardamom pods and anise star. Fry until cloves plump up. Add cashew nuts and fry until golden. Add onion and sauté until edges begin to brown. Add reserved masala paste and fry for 2 minutes. Add tomatoes and cook until they are soft and some of the moisture evaporates. Add salt, turmeric and garam masala, stir to combine. Stir in basmati rice and mix well to coat all rice grains with the tomato mixture. Stir in milk and water. Sprinkle with mint and cilantro. At this point you can transfer this rice mixture to an automatic rice cooker and finish cooking.

Alternately, you can bring rice mixture to boil. Reduce heat to the lowest setting, cover with lid and cook until rice is cooked about 20 - 25 minutes. Remove from the heat. Let it rest for 10 minutes. Fluff up the rice and serve.

*Cook's Note: Whole spices and whole chilies are added for flavoring only, they are not meant to be eaten.*

# Mango–Cucumber Chaat Salad

*This salad gets its distinct flavor with the addition of chaat masala. This sweet, sour and crunchy salad can be munched along with the meal or can be served as an appetizer.*

*Serves 4 - 6*

- 1 English hot house cucumber, peeled and cut into ¾-inch pieces.
- 1 large ripened mango peeled and cut around the pith into ¾-inch pieces.
- ½ cup chopped red onion
- ½ cup chopped cilantro
- 2 tablespoons lemon juice
- 1 teaspoon to 1 tablespoon minced fresh green chilies, such as serrano
- 1 teaspoon chaat masala powder, homemade (page 301) or store bought
- ½ teaspoon salt or to taste

Stir all the ingredients together in a bowl and serve.

# Paneer Stuffed Parathas

*In North India, parathas are stuffed with an array of fillings. Paneer is a rich filling used at special occasions.*

*Yields 8*

- basic paratha dough (page 124 )

*Filling*

- 1 cup paneer (page 304), crumbled
- ¼ cup finely chopped red onion
- 1 tablespoon minced fresh ginger
- 1 minced fresh green chili, such as serrano
- ¼ teaspoon Anardhana (dried pomegranate seed powder)
- ½ teaspoon coriander powder
- ¼ teaspoon garam masala powder
- ¼ teaspoon black pepper
- ⅛ teaspoon cayenne
- ¼ - ½ teaspoon salt or to taste

- extra flour for dusting and rolling
- extra ghee or oil for basting

Prepare the paratha dough. Transfer the dough to an oiled bowl and cover with plastic wrap. Let it rest for at least ½ an hour allowing the gluten to develop.

To make the filling, stir everything together.

To roll, divide dough into 8 balls. Work with one ball of dough at a time, make sure to cover the rest with plastic wrap to prevent it from drying. Take one ball of dough and roll out into a 5 - 6 inch circle. Place 2 tablespoons of stuffing in the middle. Pinch edges together and make a ball again. Flatten the ball into 2 - 3 inch disc. Using extra flour to dust, roll each disc into 7 - 8 inch circles. Sometimes, due to extra moisture in the stuffing, the parantha develops a hole while rolling. If this happens, dust with extra flour over the hole and roll.

Heat a griddle on top of the stove over medium high heat. When griddle is hot, place stuffed parathas and cook until bottom is covered with few brown spots. It takes about a minute or so. Flip to the other side. Cook until other side is also covered with brown spots and baste with ghee or oil on each side. Cook on each side for few seconds more. Remove from the griddle. Cover with a kitchen towel or a foil and proceed with the rest.

# COCONUT CARDAMOM FLAN

*The addition of coconut and cardamom gives this Spanish flan an Indian touch.*
*Serves 6 - 8*

- 1 ½ cups sugar, divided
- 3 whole eggs
- 5 large egg yolks
- one 13.5 ounce can coconut milk
- one 12 ounce can evaporated milk
- ½ teaspoon green cardamom seed powder
- 3 tablespoons coconut flavored rum
- Assorted fruit for garnishing

Preheat oven to 325º F.

Have ready a 9-inch cake pan.

To make the caramel, heat ¾ cup sugar in a heavy bottomed skillet over medium heat. Cook until sugar begins to melt. Swirl the pan and continue to cook for about 5 - 7 minutes until color changes to amber. Remove from the heat and pour into reserved pan. Quickly swirl the pan to coat the bottom evenly. Set aside to cool.

In a large mixing bowl, whisk together eggs, egg yolks, and salt. Avoid forming too many air bubbles. Whisk in remaining sugar, coconut milk, condensed milk, cardamom powder and rum. Slowly strain the mixture through a fine-mesh sieve into the caramel coated pan. Set the pan in a large roasting pan and place it in the oven. Pour boiling water into the roasting pan, until water is halfway up the sides of the pan and bake for an hour. Remove the flan from the oven and water-bath and let it cool completely. Chill the flan in the refrigerator.

When ready to serve, run a knife around the flan. Place serving dish onto the pan and invert quickly and gently shake to release the flan. Garnish with fruit and serve.

*Cook's Note:*
*1. While making the caramel do not stir with the spoon.*
*2. You can make this dessert in eight 6 ounce individual baking cups. If you are using the individual cups, bake for only 25 minutes.*

# Guava Daiquiri

The first frozen Daiquiri with rum, lime/lemon juice and a touch of sugar is said to have been created in Cuba during early 20th century. Since then, this recipe has gone through many modifications with the addition of different fruit purees This is my version of Guava daiquiri. Guava nectar is readily available at all well-stocked super markets.

Serves: 2
- 1 cup guava nectar
- ⅛ cup Captain Morgan spiced rum
- 1 tablespoon lime juice
- 1 tablespoon rose syrup (page 308)
- 1 cup crushed ice

Place all the ingredients in the blender and blend until it becomes frothy. Pour into glasses and serve.

# Elegant Dinner

A formal dinner party does not have to be intimidating. An elegant dinner party needs just a few extra touches, such as using a formal table, using the best china, and having an elegant centerpiece and candles. One option is for the food to be plated in the kitchen and brought to the guests. Food can also be brought to the table on big platters so that the guests can help themselves and pass the food around.

More often, I like to set the table before cooking the food. This gives me the inspiration to cook a terrific menu to compliment the table. Here, an oriental monochromatic theme is the inspiration for the table setting.

*Detail: In place of salt and pepper, a masala spice blend is served in a sake cup with a tiny spoon at each place setting to spice up meals according to individual preferences. Notice: an oriental chopstick rest is used as a knife rest. Instead of a traditional flower arrangement, a single bloom in a sake pot is used to add a touch of elegance, welcoming every guest at the table.*

*The Menu*

# SHRIMP COCONUT SOUP

*Serves 4 - 6*

- 1 pound medium shrimp, shell on and rinsed
- 2 tablespoons vegetable oil
- 1 teaspoon cumin seeds
- 10 curry leaves
- ½ cup  onion paste (page 303)
- 1 - 3 fresh green chilies, such as serrano, cut lengthwise into two
- 1 tablespoon minced fresh ginger
- 1 tablespoon coriander powder
- ½ teaspoon turmeric
- ½ teaspoon salt or to taste
- 2 tomatoes, blanched, peeled and pureed (page 298)
- 2 cups shrimp stock (recipe follows)
- 1 cup coconut milk, homemade (page 302) or canned
- 1 tablespoon lime juice
- sliced green onions and chopped cilantro for garnishing

Peel and de-vein the shrimp.  Save the shells for the stock.  While the stock is being made, refrigerate the shrimp.  Once the stock is done, proceed with making the soup.

Heat oil in a medium saucepan over medium high heat.  When the oil is hot, add cumin seeds.  Once the cumin seeds sizzle, add curry leaves.  When the curry leaves are crisp, add onion paste and green chilies.  Fry the onion paste until light golden, while stirring constantly.  Add ginger, coriander powder, turmeric and salt and fry for 2 minutes.  Add pureed tomatoes and cook for another 5 minutes or until sauce is thick.  Add shrimp and cook until the shrimp turns pink.  Stir in the shrimp stock, coconut milk and bring it to a boil.  Reduce heat to medium and simmer for 5 - 10 minutes and stir in lime juice.  Season to taste.  Garnish soup with green onions and cilantro.

*Cook's Note: Fresh whole green chilies are added for flavoring the dish.  They are not meant to be eaten.*

## SHRIMP STOCK

- shells from 1 pound shrimp
- 1 cup roughly chopped onions
- 1 cup roughly chopped carrots
- 1 - 3 fresh green chilies, such as serrano, cut lengthwise into two
- 1-inch piece ginger, sliced
- 10 curry leaves
- 6 cups water
- 1 teaspoon salt

Place all the ingredients in a medium stock-pot.  Bring it to a boil over medium high heat.  Reduce heat and simmer for 25 - 30 minutes.  Strain the stock into a bowl using a mesh strainer.

# GOBI MASALA (CAULIFLOWER CURRY)

*Serves 4-6*

- 3 tablespoons vegetable oil
- 1 onion, finely chopped
- 1-inch piece ginger, minced
- 1 minced fresh green chili, such as serrano
- 1 tablespoon coriander powder
- 1 tomato, chopped

- 1 teaspoon salt or to taste
- ½ teaspoon turmeric
- 1 ½ - 2 pounds cauliflower, washed and cut into florets
- 1 teaspoon garam masala powder
- cilantro to garnish

Heat oil in a heavy bottom skillet over medium high heat. When the oil is hot, add the onion. Fry until soft and edges begin to brown. Add minced ginger and chili and stir fry for 1 minute. Add the coriander powder and stir for another minute. Add the tomato and cook until it is soft and some of the moisture evaporates. Stir in salt, turmeric and cauliflower. Cover the pan and cook for 10 minutes while stirring occasionally. If there is a lot of liquid in the pan, remove the lid and cook until almost all the liquid evaporates. At the end, stir in garam masala powder. Mix thoroughly. Garnish with cilantro.

# VEGETABLE BIRYANI

*Serves 8*

- 3 cups basmati rice
- 2 tablespoons + 2 teaspoons salt, divided
- 1 teaspoon loosely packed saffron
- ½ cup hot milk
- ⅓ cup vegetable oil
- ¼ cup raw cashew nuts
- 1 tablespoon cumin seeds
- 4 - 5 cloves
- 1-inch piece cinnamon stick
- 4 - 5 cardamom pods, slightly crushed to break the shell
- 2 bay leaves
- 1 large onion, cut lengthwise, thinly sliced, and cut in the middle
- 1 - 3 fresh green chilies, such as serrano, cut lengthwise into two
- 2 tablespoons ginger garlic paste
- 6 cups washed and cut vegetables, such as potatoes, mixed colored bell peppers, carrots, green beans and peas
- 1 ¼ cups yogurt, whisked smoothly
- 1 teaspoon garam masala powder
- ¼ cup roughly chopped fresh cilantro/coriander
- ¼ cup roughly chopped fresh mint
- 2 tablespoons lime juice
- ½ teaspoon green cardamom seed powder

Wash the rice with several changes of water. Soak the rice with 1 teaspoon of salt and with enough water to cover 2 - 3 inches above the rice, for 3 hours. In a small skillet, over a low flame, fry saffron threads until they become a shade darker for a few seconds. Crumble saffron over hot milk. Let it steep for at least ½ an hour. Meanwhile, prepare the vegetables. Heat oil in a large saucepan over medium heat. When the oil is hot, add cashews. Fry the cashews until light golden and remove cashews from hot oil using a slotted spoon. Drain them onto a paper towel and reserve for garnishing.

Add cumin seeds to the same pan. When the cumin seeds sizzle add cloves, cinnamon stick, cardamom pods and bay leaves. When the cloves plump up, add onions and green chilies. Sauté until edges begin to brown. Add ginger garlic paste and stir fry for 1 minute. Add potatoes and cook for 5 minutes. Stir in rest of the vegetables with 1 teaspoon salt and cook for 5 - 7 minutes, while stirring occasionally. Add yogurt 2 tablespoons at a time. Let the first 2 tablespoons of yogurt absorb before adding the next 2 tablespoons. Stir in garam masala powder and cook for about 2 – 3 minutes until yogurt is fried and coats the vegetables. Remove from the heat.

Preheat the oven to 350º F. Bring 10 cups of water to boil in a large stock-pot over medium high heat. Add 2 tablespoons of salt to the water. Drain the rice and slowly add to boiling water. Cook for 5 minutes. Drain the rice immediately to the colander.

To assemble biryani, spread ½ the rice in a casserole dish. Spread the vegetables evenly on top of the rice. Sprinkle with ½ of mint and cilantro. Spread the rest of the rice on top. Lace the rice with lime juice and saffron milk. Sprinkle cardamom powder on top. Cover with aluminum foil first and then with the lid. Bake for 30 - 35 minutes. Just before serving, fluff the rice with spoon and garnish with cashew nuts and the rest of the cilantro and mint.

*Cook's Note:* *Whole spices are added for flavoring, are not meant to be eaten.*

# MATAR PANEER

*This is a hearty vegetarian dish that can make a meal when served with chappati or paratha.*

*Serves 4 - 6*

- 12 ounces fried paneer pieces (page 304)

*Gravy*
- 2 tablespoons vegetable oil
- 1 cup finely chopped onions
- 1 tablespoon ginger garlic paste
- 1 tablespoon coriander powder
- 1 teaspoon cumin powder
- 1 teaspoon cayenne
- ½ teaspoon turmeric

- ½ cup tomato sauce
- 1 teaspoon salt or to taste
- 1 ½ cups hot water
- 1 cup frozen peas
- 1 teaspoon garam masala powder
- ¼ cup heavy cream
- 2 tablespoons chopped fresh cilantro/coriander

Have paneer ready and set aside.

Heat oil in a medium saucepan over medium high heat. When the oil is hot, add the onions. Sauté until onions are translucent and the edges begin to brown. Add ginger garlic paste and stir fry for 1 minute. Stir in coriander powder, cumin powder, cayenne and turmeric and fry for about 2 minutes until all the spices are fried with the onion mixture. Add tomato sauce and salt. Cook for another 2 - 3 minutes while stirring occasionally. Add hot water and peas. Reduce heat to medium, cover and cook for about 10 minutes until peas are tender. Stir in garam masala and cream and cook for 2 – 3 minutes. Stir the paneer into the gravy and heat through. Garnish with cilantro and serve.

# LAMB VINDALOO

*Vindaloo, meaning "with vinegar", is a signature dish from Goa. It can be made with pork, goat, or lamb. The Portuguese, who ruled Goa from 1510 to 1961, introduced chilies and vinegar to India. Can you even imagine Indian food without chilies? It would be like Italian food without tomatoes (tomatoes were introduced to Italy during the 16th century by Spanish explorers). This is a tongue-scorching spicy and sour dish.*

*Serves 4 - 6*

- 2 pounds leg of lamb, all visible fat trimmed and cut into 1 ½-inch pieces.
- ⅓ cup vegetable oil
- 1 cup sliced onion
- 6 - 8 dry whole red chilies, such as chile de arbol
- 1 tablespoon coriander seeds
- 1 teaspoon cloves
- 1 teaspoon black pepper corns
- 2 teaspoons cumin seeds
- 1 teaspoon green cardamom seeds
- 1-inch piece cinnamon stick

- 2 teaspoons black mustard seeds
- ¼ teaspoon fenugreek seeds
- 2 teaspoons salt
- ¼ teaspoon turmeric
- 1 teaspoon jaggery or light brown sugar
- 5 tablespoons malt or white vinegar
- 20 curry leaves, preferably fresh
- 2 tablespoons ginger garlic paste
- 1 - 3 minced fresh green chilies, such as serrano
- 2 medium tomatoes, chopped

Heat ⅓ cup of oil in a skillet over medium high heat and add the onions. Fry while stirring occasionally at the beginning and often at the end until the onions turn golden brown evenly. Remove onions with a slotted spatula and with an another spatula gently press the onions to release excess oil. Spread the onions on a sheet pan lined with a paper towel to crisp up and cool. Reserve the leftover oil. Grind the fried onions into a powder using a spice grinder and reserve for part of the marinade.

In a small skillet, dry roast red chilies, coriander seeds, cloves, pepper corn, cumin seeds, cardamom seeds, cinnamon stick, mustard seeds, and fenugreek seeds over medium heat while stirring and shaking for about 2 minutes or until it turns one shade darker. Let it cool to room temperature. Using a spice grinder, grind them into a fine powder. Transfer this powder to a medium bowl. Add salt, turmeric, jaggery, malt or white vinegar, and onion powder and stir to combine. This is the vindaloo paste.

Add the vindaloo paste to lamb. Mix to ensure all the pieces are coated with the marinade evenly. Refrigerate for 4 - 12 hours.

Heat reserved oil from onions in a large nonstick saucepan over medium high heat. Add curry leaves. Fry until crisp. Add ginger garlic paste and chilies and stir fry for 2 minutes. Add tomatoes and cook until tomatoes are soft and some of the moisture evaporates. Add the marinated lamb to the saucepan. Cook for 8 - 10 minutes, while stirring often. Reduce heat to medium and cook for about 40 - 45 minutes the meat until tender while stirring occasionally. Add more water if necessary. When it is ready, transfer to a serving dish and serve with rice.

# TOMATO PACHADI

*Serves 6 - 8*

- 2 tablespoons vegetable oil
- 1 teaspoon black mustard seeds
- ¼ teaspoon fenugreek seeds
- 10 - 20 fresh or dry curry leaves
- ½ cup sliced onions
- 1 tablespoon minced fresh ginger
- 1 minced fresh green chili, such as serrano
- 2 medium tomatoes, chopped
- ¾ teaspoon salt or to taste
- ¼ teaspoon turmeric
- 2 cups yogurt

Heat oil in a small saucepan. When the oil is hot, add mustard seeds. Cover with a lid until the spluttering subsides. Uncover and add fenugreek seeds. When the fenugreek seeds turn one shade darker, add curry leaves. As soon as curry leaves are crisp, add the onions. Sauté until onions are translucent and edges begin to brown. Add ginger and green chili and stir fry for 2 more minutes. Add tomatoes, salt and turmeric and cook until tomatoes become soft and some of the moisture evaporates. Remove from the heat, cool for 10 minutes and stir in the yogurt.

# PARATHAS

*Yield 8*

*Basic paratha dough*
- 2 cups chappati flour (atta)
- ½ teaspoon salt
- ¾ cup water
- 2 tablespoons ghee or oil

- extra flour for rolling
- ghee or oil for basting

Stir flour and salt in a bowl. Add water to the flour mixture and mix into a soft, pliable dough. If the dough feels too dry, add water 1 tablespoon at a time and mix. If the dough feels sticky, add flour 1 tablespoon at a time. Transfer dough onto a work surface. Knead for 3 - 5 minutes. Cover the dough with plastic wrap and let it rest for ½ an hour allowing the gluten to develop.

Divide the dough into 8 equal portions. Work with 1 portion at a time and keep the rest covered to prevent from drying. Roll out the dough into 5-inch circles. Brush the surface with a little ghee or oil. Sprinkle 1 teaspoon of dry flour on top. Make a cut from the center to the edge. Roll the dough from 1 cut side to the other. Press down the pointed end in the middle to make a disc. Roll the disc into 7 - 8 inch circles.

Heat the griddle over medium high heat. When the griddle is hot, place rolled parathas onto the hot griddle. When the bottom is cooked and dotted with brown spots, flip it to the other side. When the other side is also covered with a few brown spots, baste the top with ghee or oil. Flip it back and baste the other side with ghee or oil. Remove from the griddle. Cover parathas with a kitchen towel or foil while preparing the rest.

# MANGO MOUSSE

*Serves 6 - 8*

- 1 ½ cups canned mango puree
- ½ cup + 2 tablespoons sugar, divided
- 1 envelop unflavored gelatin (¼ ounce)
- ¼ cup water
- 1 cup sour cream
- 1 cup heavy whipping cream

In a bowl, stir together mango puree and ½ cup of sugar until sugar dissolves. Sprinkle gelatin over water in a heat-proof bowl. Let it stand for 5 - 10 minutes for gelatin to soften. Place gelatin bowl over a pan of simmering water and stir until the gelatin is completely dissolved. Remove gelatin from the heat, stir into the mango puree mixture and let it cool for 5 minutes. Add sour cream. Stir with a whisk until sour cream is completely incorporated into the pure.

Using an electric mixer with a balloon whisk, beat cream with 2 tablespoons of sugar until soft peaks form. Stir 2 tablespoons of whipped cream into mango puree mixture to lighten. Fold in remaining whipped cream. Transfer mousse into a serving dish and refrigerate until set. Alternately, you can spoon mousse into individual desert bowls. Let it chill in the refrigerator, before serving.

# STUFFED DATES

*Yield 36*

- 36 medjool dates

*Filling*
- 1 recipe for coating in almond apricots (page 49)

Prepare the coating for almond apricots, according to the directions.

Using a paring knife, make a slit lengthwise in the middle of the dates. Make sure you don't cut through the date. Remove the seed. Divide the filling into 36 portions. Roll each portion into a 1-inch long roll. Stuff the date cavity with this almond roll.

# ROLLED BAKLAVA

*As opposed to traditional Greek baklava, which is made with almonds and/or walnuts, this baklava is made with cashew nuts and perfumed with exotic Persian spices - rose water and saffron.*

*Yield 50*

- 1 cup cold syrup (recipe follows)
- ¾ cup clarified butter*
- 2 cups raw ground cashew nuts
- ½ teaspoon green cardamom seed powder
- ½ teaspoon cinnamon
- ¼ cup sugar
- 1 pound frozen phyllo dough, thawed overnight in the refrigerator

Place a rack in the middle of the oven. Preheat oven to 325º F. Brush a 13 x 18 sheet pan with clarified butter. Set aside.

In a medium bowl, combine ground nuts, cardamom powder, cinnamon powder and sugar. Set aside.

Work with 1 sheet of phyllo at a time. Make sure you cover the rest of the phyllo with a towel to prevent drying. Place one sheet of phyllo on a work surface. Brush with clarified butter. Place another sheet of phyllo over the first and brush with clarified butter again. Leaving a 1-inch border, spread 3 tablespoons of nut mixture in a 1-inch wide line along 15-inch side of phyllo. Fold 1-inch border of phyllo over the nuts to cover and roll like a cigar till the end. Transfer it to a sheet pan, placing it seam side down. Repeat with the remaining phyllo and filling, laying each roll parallel to the next. Cut rolls crosswise into 3-inch pieces. Brush with the remaining butter. Transfer them to the oven. Bake for about 30 - 35 minutes until light golden brown. Remove the pan from the oven. Drizzle cold syrup over the pastry. Let all the syrup absorb into the pastry, and let it cool to room temperature . You can store baklava in the refrigerator for up to a month.

*Cook's Note:* To make the clarified butter, melt 1 cup unsalted butter over medium heat until butter is melted and foamy. Pour melted butter into a glass bowl. You will see three layers, the foam layer on top, clear liquid in the middle and milk solids at the bottom. Using a spoon, discard the foam from the surface. Carefully pour clear liquid into another bowl. This is the clarified butter. Discard the milk solids.*

## BAKLAVA SYRUP

- ½ cup sugar
- ½ cup water
- ¼ cup honey
- 1½ tablespoons lemon juice
- 1 teaspoon rose water
- ½ teaspoon loosely packed saffron
- ½ teaspoon green cardamom seed powder

To make the syrup, combine sugar, water and honey in a small saucepan. Place over medium heat and stir until sugar dissolves. Increase heat to medium high and boil the syrup for 2 minutes. Turn off the heat. Stir in lemon juice, rose water, saffron and cardamom powder. Let it steep for ½ an hour. Refrigerate the syrup until needed. (You can make this syrup up to 1 week in advance).

# PARADISE

*Like the name suggests, this drink has all the elements
of a tropical paradise.*

*Serves 4*
- 1 cup mango juice/nectar
- 1 cup pineapple juice
- 1 cup guava nectar
- 1 tablespoon lime juice
- ½ cup coconut flavored rum, such as Malibu
- 1 tablespoon rose syrup ( page 308)

Stir all the ingredients together in a pitcher. Serve it
over ice cubes in the glasses.

With a lush garden as the perfect backdrop, the warm summer weather and the soothing perfume from the gardenia and michelia champaka inspires me to have garden party.

Just because it is a garden party doesn't mean that you have to sacrifice the elegance and ambiance of a dinner party. Set the table with crisp table linens. Informal center pieces can be made from flowers gathered from the garden and candles can be lit as the sunlight fades. The menu showcases the season's bounty of garden fresh vegetables. Cocktails and appetizers can be served at a different location.

# The Menu

**Appetizer:**

Vegetable Bajjis (page 138)

**Drink:**

Tropical Punch (page 131)

**Main Course:**

Palak Gosht (page 132)

Loki Kofta (page 135)

Kadhai Paneer Vegetables (page 133)

Black Eyed Peas Dal (page 134)

Heirloom Tomato Salad (page 139)

Cucumber Dill Raita (page 139)

Zafrani Pulao (page 134)

Garlic Naan (page 140)

**Dessert:**

Mango Crisp with Ice Cream and

Saffron Cashew Gajjak (page 136)

*Detail: Japanese dipping bowls work wonderfully for serving chutneys and sauces for appetizers.*

# TROPICAL PUNCH

*Serves 20*

- 3 ½ - 4 cups canned mango pulp
- 12 ounces frozen concentrate pineapple juice
- 6 ounces frozen concentrate lemonade
- 12 ounces frozen concentrate orange juice
- 2 liters ginger ale
- 1 cup rum (optional)
- sliced strawberries and mint leaves for garnishing

To the punch bowl, add all the ingredients and stir to dissolve. Add 6 cups of ice. Garnish with sliced strawberries and mint leaves.

*Gosht is a Persian word for red meat, used widely in Moghul cuisine.*

# PALAK GOSHT (LAMB WITH SPINACH)

*This is a classic Moghul dish that is very popular in Punjabi households. You can replace lamb cubes with lamb chops for variation. Lamb and goat can be used interchangeably in this recipe or in any other recipe for that matter.*

Serves 4 – 6

- 4 tablespoons vegetable oil, divided
- 1 ½ pounds lamb, shoulder or leg meat, all visible fat trimmed and cut into 1 ½-inch cubes
- 2 bay leaves
- 4 cloves
- 3 cardamom pods, slightly crushed to break the skin
- 2 cups chopped red onion
- 2 tablespoons ginger garlic paste
- 1 teaspoon coriander powder
- 1 teaspoon roasted cumin powder
- 1 tablespoon paprika

- 1 - 2 teaspoons cayenne
- ¼ teaspoon turmeric
- 1 ½ teaspoons salt
- 2 tomatoes, finely chopped
- 1 - 3 minced fresh green chilies, such as serrano
- 1 teaspoon kasuri methi (dry fenugreek leaves)
- ½ cup yogurt, whisked
- 1 ½ cups water
- 1 teaspoon garam masala powder
- 10 ounces spinach, finely shredded
- 2 tablespoons chopped cilantro/coriander

Add 1 tablespoon of oil to the lamb. Mix to make sure each piece of meat is covered with a thin film of oil. Heat a heavy bottomed nonstick skillet over high heat. When the skillet is hot, add a few pieces of meat at a time. Sear the meat while tossing and turning until evenly browned. Remove and place them onto a platter. Repeat with the rest of the pieces, in batches.

Heat 3 tablespoons of oil in a large skillet over medium high heat. When the oil is hot, add bay leaves, cloves, and cardamom pods. When the cloves plump up (it takes only a few seconds), add the chopped onions. Sauté onion until edges begin to brown. Add ginger garlic paste and fry for 2 minutes. Add coriander powder, roasted cumin powder, paprika, cayenne, turmeric and salt. Stir fry for 2 minutes or until all the dry spices are fried. Add tomatoes and cook for about 4 - 5 minutes until tomatoes are soft and some of the moisture evaporates. Stir 2 tablespoons of yogurt at a time into the onion-tomato mixture, make sure the 1st 2 tablespoons are fully incorporated before adding the next 2 tablespoons, while stirring constantly. This will prevent the yogurt from curdling. Stir in green chilies and kasuri methi cook for 2 - 3 minutes more. Transfer the meat to the onion-tomato mixture and mix well. Add 1 ½ cups of water and bring it to a boil. Reduce heat to medium, and cover with the lid. Cook until the meat is tender and coated with thick gravy, while stirring occasionally. It will take about 1 - 1 ½ hours.

Alternately, you can cook the meat in a pressure cooker. Place prepared meat in the pressure cooker with 1 cup of water. Close the lid and heat over medium high. Cook on high pressure for 3 minutes and turn off the heat. Let the pressure drop on its own. It takes about 12 - 15 minutes. Open the lid. Check if the meat is tender. If not, continue to cook on the stove-top until the meat is cooked and the sauce is thick.

Stir in spinach and garam masala powder. Cook until spinach is wilted and cooked through. Adjust the seasoning. Transfer to a serving dish. Garnish with chopped cilantro leaves. Serve with naan.

*Cook's Note: Whole spices are added for flavoring, are not meant to be eaten.*

# Kadhai Paneer Vegetables

*Kadhai is an Indian wok-shaped cooking pan, which can be used for stir fry or to cook any curry. However, this dish gets its name from the spice blend used to flavor it, rather than the pan that is used for cooking.*

*Serves 8 - 10*

- ½ cup vegetable oil
- 1 large red onion, cut into chunks
- 2 tablespoons ginger garlic paste
- 3 - 4 multicolored bell peppers, cut into chunks
- ½ head cauliflower, cut into chunks
- 1 pound asparagus, peel the bottom ⅔ length and cut into 3-inch pieces
- ½ pound eggplant, cut into 1 ½-inch cubes
- ½ pound green beans, trim the ends and cut in the middle
- ½ pound paneer, cut into 1 ½-inch cubes
- ½ pound okra, trim the ends
- 3 - 6 tablespoons kadhai masala, homemade (page 302) or store-bought
- 2 teaspoons salt or to taste

Heat 1 tablespoon of oil in large nonstick wok or skillet over medium high heat. Add onion chunks and stir fry the onions for 2 - 3 minutes until cooked but still crisp. Add ginger garlic paste. Stir fry for a minute. Using a slotted spoon, remove onto a tray. Using 1 tablespoon oil for each vegetables, stir fry separately until they are crisp and tender. Stir fry paneer using 1 tablespoon of oil until light brown. Add all the stir-fried onions, vegetables, and paneer to the wok. Sprinkle kadhai masala and salt, mix and heat through. Serve with any roti or rice.

# BLACK EYED PEAS DAL

*In this recipe, seasoning is added to the cooked dal and the raw seasoning is added just before serving, to keep the onions crunchy.*

*Serves 4 - 6*
- 1 ½ cups black eyed peas

- ¼ cup vegetable oil
- ⅛ teaspoon asafoetida
- 2 dry whole red chilies, such as chile de arbol
- 1 teaspoon black mustard seeds
- 1 teaspoon cumin seeds
- 10 fresh or dried curry leaves
- 2 cups chopped onions
- 1 tablespoon minced garlic
- 1 teaspoon coriander powder
- 1 teaspoon roasted cumin powder

- ½ - 1 teaspoon cayenne
- ½ teaspoon turmeric
- 1 ½ teaspoons salt
- 2 large tomatoes, chopped
- 

*Raw Seasoning*
- 2 tablespoons chopped red onion
- 2 tablespoons lime juice
- 1 - 3 minced fresh green chilies, such as serrano
- 2 tablespoons fresh cilantro/coriander leaves

Wash the black eyed peas with several changes of water. Add enough water to cover 2 - 3 inches above the peas. Let them soak overnight. Discard the soaking liquid. Transfer soaked peas to a large heavy bottomed saucepan with 6 cups of water and heat over medium high heat. Bring it to a boil. Reduce heat to medium and cook until peas are soft and creamy. Mash the peas with the back of a spoon. The dal should be soft and creamy, but should have some texture.

Alternately, you can cook the peas in a pressure cooker. Place the soaked peas with 3 ½ cups of water in a pressure cooker. Close with the lid and heat over medium high heat. Cook on high pressure for 1 ½ minutes and reduce heat to medium. Cook for 10 - 12 minutes and turn off the heat. Let the pressure drop on its own. It takes about 12 - 15 minutes. Open the lid and check if the peas are soft. If they are, mash them with the back of a spoon. If not, add 1 more cup of water and cook over medium heat until the peas are soft and creamy.

Heat oil in a medium saucepan over medium high heat. Add asafoetida and red chilies. When red chilies turn darker, add mustard seeds, and cover until the spluttering subsides. Uncover, and add cumin seeds. As soon as the cumin seeds sizzle, quickly add the curry leaves and onion. Sauté onion until the edges begin to brown. Add garlic and stir fry for a minute. Stir in coriander powder, cumin powder, cayenne, turmeric and salt. Add tomatoes. Cook until tomatoes are soft and some of the moisture evaporates. Add cooked peas along with one cup water, and simmer over medium heat for 15 - 20 minutes. Add more water if necessary. Just before serving, mix all the raw seasoning ingredients together and stir into the dal. Serve with chappati or naan.

*Cook's Note:* *Whole red chilies are added for flavoring, are not meant to be eaten.*

# ZAFRANI PULAO

*Zafrani means saffron. This is a simple but elegant Persian rice dish prepared using the world's most expensive spice, saffron. This delicately flavored rice gets its yellow hue from the saffron.*

*Serves 6 - 8*
- 1 teaspoon lightly packed saffron
- 4 tablespoons ghee
- 2 bay leaves
- 4 cloves
- 4 green cardamom pods, slightly crushed to open the shell

- 2-inch piece cinnamon stick
- 1 ½ cups basmati rice
- 1 teaspoon salt
- 2 ¾ cups water

- rose petals for garnish

In a small skillet over a low flame, fry saffron threads for a few seconds until they become a shade darker and set aside. Heat ghee in a medium saucepan over medium high heat. When the ghee is hot, add bay leaves, cloves, cardamom pods and cinnamon stick. As soon as the cloves plump up add basmati rice. Stir to mix basmati rice with flavored ghee to coat all rice grains with a thin layer of ghee. Add the fried saffron, 2 ¾ cups of water and salt. At this point, you can transfer the rice mixture to a rice cooker and cook according to the manufacturer's directions. Alternately, bring rice mixture to a boil. Reduce heat to lowest setting and cover with the lid and cook until rice is done. It takes about 20 - 25 minutes. Let it rest for 10 minutes and transfer to a platter, garnish with rose petals and serve.

# LOKI KOFTA (OPO SQUASH KOFTAS)

*Loki is opo squash, a light green colored squash available at Indian stores and well-stocked supermarkets. The good thing about this recipe is that you can make koftas and the gravy ahead of time and freeze them separately until ready to use.*

Yield 16

### Koftas

- 3 - 3 ½ pounds opo squash
- 1 teaspoon salt
- ¾ cup chickpea flour/besan, divided
- 1 teaspoon garam masala powder
- ½ - 1 teaspoon cayenne
- 2 tablespoons finely chopped fresh cilantro/coriander

- oil for deep frying

### Gravy

- ⅓ cup vegetable oil
- 2 cups minced onion
- 2 tablespoons ginger garlic paste
- 3 tablespoons coriander powder
- 1 teaspoon cayenne
- ½ teaspoon turmeric
- 1 ½ teaspoons salt
- 1 cups tomato sauce
- ¼ cup sour cream
- 1 teaspoon garam masala powder
- 2 tablespoons fresh cilantro/coriander for garnishing

Using a sieve, sift chickpea flour/besan in to a bowl to remove any lumps. Transfer ½ cup of chickpea flour/besan to a small skillet, dry roast over medium heat until flour loses its raw smell and turns one shade darker, while stirring constantly.

To make koftas, peel and remove seeds from the opo squash. Using a food processor with grater attachment or box grater, grate opo squash and measure 5 cups. Heat a medium saucepan over medium high heat. Add grated opo squash with 1 teaspoon salt. Cover and cook for 10 - 12 minutes, while stirring occasionally. Transfer the cooked opo squash to a colander set over a bowl to catch any extra moisture and let it come to room temperature. Transfer the cooked opo squash to a bowl, add roasted chickpea flour/besan, garam masala powder, cayenne, and chopped cilantro and mix thoroughly. (You can finish the recipe up to this point and refrigerate for a couple of days.) Divide the dough into 16 parts. Using wet fingers, working with 1 portion at a time, make it into a ball. Roll each ball in the remaining chickpea flour. Shake off excess flour and finish the rest of the dough in the same manner.

Fill the wok or heavy bottomed saucepan until it is ⅓ full of oil (oil should be 2 - 3 inches deep). Heat oil to 325º F or when you add a piece of bread, it should rise to the top in 15 - 20 seconds. Add as many koftas as the pan can hold, without crowding them. Fry until evenly golden brown, while turning from time to time with a slotted spoon. Using a slotted spoon, remove koftas from the hot oil onto a tray lined with paper towel and proceed with the rest of the koftas.

To make the gravy, heat ⅓ cup of oil in a heavy bottomed skillet over medium high heat. When oil is hot, add minced onion. Sauté onion for about 10 - 12 minutes until light brown. Add ginger garlic paste and stir fry for 2 minutes. Add coriander powder, cayenne, turmeric and salt. Fry everything together for another 2 minutes. Add tomato sauce along with 2 ½ cups of water and bring it a boil. Reduce heat to medium and cook for about 15 minutes until oil rises to the top. Stir in sour cream into the gravy, one tablespoon at a time, making sure the 1st tablespoon is fully incorporated before adding the next, while stirring constantly. Stir in garam masala powder. Add koftas to the gravy in a single layer and heat through. Transfer to a serving dish and garnish with cilantro. Serve with chappati or naan.

# MANGO CRISP WITH ICE CREAM AND SAFFRON CASHEW GAJJAK

*Crisps are an American tradition. In this recipe the all-American crisp gets an Indian makeover. This dish smells heavenly while it is baking. I suggest baking this crisp just before your guests arrive. They will be greeted with an enticing aroma, as soon as they enter.*

*Serves 6 - 8*

- 6 mangos, preferably Kent variety, ripened but still firm
- 1 pint fresh red raspberries
- zest of 1 lemon
- 2 tablespoons lemon juice
- 2 tablespoons all-purpose flour
- 1 cup light brown sugar
- 1 teaspoon cinnamon
- ½ teaspoon grated nutmeg
- ½ teaspoon green cardamom seed powder

**Topping**

- ¾ cup all-purpose flour
- 1 cup quick cooking oats
- ½ cup sweetened coconut flakes
- ½ cup cold butter, cut into small cubes
- 1 teaspoon cinnamon
- ½ teaspoon green cardamom seed powder
- ½ teaspoon grated nutmeg
- ½ teaspoon salt

- vanilla ice cream
- saffron cashew gajjak (recipe follows)

Preheat oven to 350º F and butter a 9 x 13 x 2 inch baking dish. Peel the mangoes and cut around the pit into 1-inch pieces; toss with raspberries, lemon zest and lemon juice and set aside. Combine all-purpose flour, light brown sugar, cinnamon, nutmeg, and cardamom powder. Add to the mango mixture, gently toss to mix and transfer to the baking dish.

To make the topping, combine flour, oats, coconut, butter, cinnamon, cardamom, nutmeg, and salt in a bowl. Mix with a pastry blender or with your fingers until the mixture is crumbly. Spread the topping evenly over the mangos.

Place the baking dish on a sheet pan and bake for 1 hour in the middle rack of the oven until the top is brown and the filling is bubbly. Serve hot with a scoop of ice cream and saffron cashew gajjak.

## SAFFRON CASHEW GAJJAK

*Gajjak's are Indian nut brittle, a speciality of Gujarat. You can replace cashews with any kind of nuts. The rose water added for flavor gives it a Persian touch.*

*Serves 6 - 8*
- 1 cup sugar
- 1 tablespoon light corn syrup
- 2 tablespoons water
- 1 cup salted roasted cashews, roughly chopped
- 1 teaspoon rose water
- ¼ teaspoon loosely packed saffron
- ½ teaspoon green cardamom seed powder

Spray the baking sheet and spatula with a nonstick cooking spray and keep aside. Combine sugar, corn syrup, and water in a 4 quart saucepan. Heat sugar mixture over medium temperature until the sugar dissolves. Increase heat to medium high. Cover with a lid for 3 minutes. Remove the lid and continue to cook until the sugar syrup begins to caramelize. Lift the sauce pan with both hands using hot pads and gently swirl to mix. Continue to cook until the mixture turns to caramel. As soon as it turns to caramel, add cashew nuts, rose water, saffron and cardamom powder. Mix caramel and nut mixture very quickly, using a wooden spoon. Turn off the heat and pour onto a baking sheet immediately. Spread it as quickly as possible with a spatula and let it cool. After it cools, release from the baking sheet and break into irregular pieces. Store in an airtight container in a cool place. This can be made for up to 3 - 4 days in advance.

*Cook's Note:*
*1. Instead of spraying the baking sheet with nonstick cooking spray, I use silicone liner such as silpat.*
*2. Once the sugar is dissolved, it is important not to stir.*

# VEGETABLE BAJJIS

*Serves 6 - 8*

- cilantro chutney (page 298)
- tamarind /sweet chutney (page 300)
- orange bell pepper chutney (page 298)

- 2 cups chickpea flour/besan
- 2 tablespoons rice flour
- 1 teaspoon slightly crushed ajwain seeds
- 1 teaspoon salt
- 1 teaspoon cayenne
- ½ teaspoon baking soda
- 1 ¼ - 1 ½ cup water
- 2 pounds assorted vegetables such as sliced potatoes, sliced eggplants, sliced onions, cauliflower florets, and colored bell peppers cut into strips

- oil for deep-frying

Prepare the chutneys.

Sift chickpea flour into a medium bowl. Stir in rice flour, ajwain seeds, salt, cayenne, and baking soda. Add 1 ¼ cup of water and use a whisk to make smooth batter. The batter should coat the vegetables evenly. If the batter seems to be runny, mix in besan one tablespoon at a time. If the batter seems too thick, add water 1 tablespoon at a time and mix.

Pour oil in a wok or heavy-bottomed saucepan until it is ⅓ full (it should be 2 - 3 inches deep). Heat oil over medium high heat to 350° F or when you drop a tiny bit of batter into the hot oil, it should rise to the top. Dip sliced vegetables in the batter. Lightly tap it into inside of the bowl to release excess batter and gently drop into the hot oil. Add as many pieces as the wok can hold comfortably without crowding. Using a slotted spoon, turn a few times to ensure even frying. When bajjis are golden brown, remove them from the pan onto a tray lined with a paper towel. Repeat with the rest of the vegetables. Serve with cilantro chutney, tamarind/sweet chutney or orange bell pepper chutney.

*Bajjis are batter coated vegetables fried in the oil, similar to Japanese Tempura. You can serve Bajji's with one or more chutneys.*

# CUCUMBER DILL RAITA

*This cool and refreshing raita can be a terrific addition to any Indian meal.*

*Serves 6 - 8*

- 1 English cucumber
- 2 cups yogurt
- 2 tablespoons sour cream
- 1 tablespoon lemon juice
- 2 tablespoons olive oil
- 1 small bunch dill, finely chopped
- 1 garlic clove, finely minced

Peel and grate cucumber in a food processor and squeeze out some of the water. Mix yogurt, sour cream, lemon juice, olive oil, dill and garlic with grated cucumber. Season with salt to taste. Serve with any Indian meal.

# HEIRLOOM TOMATO SALAD

*Serves 6 - 8*

- 2 - 3 pounds heirloom tomatoes, sliced
- salt to taste
- pepper to taste
- 1 tablespoon lime juice
- cilantro leaves for garnishing

Arrange sliced tomatoes on a platter. Sprinkle salt and pepper. Drizzle with lime juice and garnish with cilantro leaves.

# GARLIC NAAN

*This is a richer bread than the original naan recipe. The addition of egg to the dough makes it silky smooth.*

*Yield 8 - 10 pieces*

**Dough**

- 1 teaspoon yeast
- 1 teaspoon sugar
- ¼ cup milk, warmed to 110º F
- 2 cups all-purpose flour
- ½ teaspoon salt
- 1 egg, slightly beaten
- ⅓ cup yogurt
- 2 tablespoons ghee or vegetable oil

**Topping**

- ¼ cup ghee
- 1 tablespoon minced garlic
- 2 tablespoons finely chopped fresh cilantro/coriander

Add yeast, sugar and milk to a bowl. Stir and set aside for 5 - 10 minutes to activate yeast. Add flour, salt, egg, yogurt and ghee or oil to yeast mixture. Knead for 5 minutes until dough is smooth and silky.

Brush a large bowl with oil and transfer dough to the bowl. Cover with plastic wrap or a kitchen towel. Let it rest for 2 - 3 hours. This allows the yeast to ferment and makes the dough rise to double its size. You can also refrigerate the dough for a day at this point.

Meanwhile, make the topping. Warm the ghee in a small saucepan over medium heat. Add minced garlic and cilantro. Remove from the heat and let it steep for 10 - 15 minutes.

Divide the dough into 8 - 10 balls. Let them rise again for ½ an hour. Set the metal rack in the oven 5 - 6 inches below the heating element. Preheat oven to broiler at high temperature.

Roll out each ball into 6 - 7 inch circles. Transfer 2 - 3 circles at a time onto a baking sheet. Place them under the broiler. Broil until bread puffs up and acquires a few golden spots. It takes about ½ - 1 minute. Carefully using the spatula, turn the bread and cook for another 1 - 1 ½ minutes. Remove bread from the oven and baste with topping. Transfer naans to a platter and cover them with foil or a clean kitchen towel. Proceed with the remaining dough. Serve warm with any curry with gravy.

# Nellore Dinner

My husband is from Nellore, a district in the state of Andhra
Pradesh. Chepala pulusu (fish stew) is the speciality of this
region. They have a unique way of cooking that distinguishes
their dishes from the rest of Andhra Pradesh. This menu is
from my in-laws' kitchen. My mother-in-law would have been
pleased with the inclusion of this menu.

Historically, Nellore is not only famous for its unique cuisine
but also for its jewelry merchants. That is the inspiration for
the theme of the buffet.

*The Menu*

# Masala Vada

*Traditionally, these vadas are made with chena dal but I prefer to use yellow split peas. When you use split peas, vadas not only taste better but they stay crisp at room temperature for a longer time, which makes them the perfect appetizer for a party.*

### Yield 12
- 1 cup yellow split peas
- 1 teaspoon salt
- ½ tablespoon minced fresh ginger
- 1 minced fresh green chili, such as serrano
- ¼ cup finely chopped onion
- ½ teaspoon garam masala powder
- 2 tablespoons chopped cilantro/coriander
- vegetable oil for deep frying

Wash peas with several changes of water, and soak them overnight. Drain into a colander. Place dal in the food processor, process with 1 teaspoon of salt until it becomes a grainy paste. Remove from the food processor. Mix in ginger, green chili, chopped onion, garam masala powder and cilantro.

Pour oil in a wok or heavy-bottomed saucepan until it is ⅓ full (it should be 2 - 3 inches deep). Heat oil over medium high heat to 350° F. Take ⅛ cup of batter. Make it into 2 - 3 inch patty, and gently drop into the hot oil  Add as many vadas as the wok can hold comfortably without crowding. Fry the vadas until golden brown while turning as needed with a slotted spoon. Remove from the hot oil and drain onto paper towels. Proceed with the rest of the batter.

*Cook's Note: If you are having trouble forming a patty, you can mix in a tablespoon of chickpea flour/besan into the batter.*

# Mango-Eggplant Curry

### Serves 4 - 6

- 2 tablespoons vegetable oil
- 1 dry whole red chili, such as chile de arbol
- 1 teaspoon black mustard seeds
- 1 teaspoon cumin seeds
- 1 teaspoon white urad dal
- 20 curry leaves
- 1 cup chopped onion
- 2 - 4 finely chopped fresh green chilies, such as serrano
- 1 medium firm raw green mango, peeled and cut around the pit into 1-inch pieces
- 1 ½ pounds Indian or Japanese eggplant, cut into 1-inch pieces
- 1 teaspoon salt or to taste
- ½ teaspoon turmeric

Heat oil in a wok or skillet over medium high heat. When oil is hot, add red chili. Fry until red chili turns a shade darker. Add mustard seeds and  cover until the spluttering subsides. Uncover and add cumin seeds and white urad dal. Fry until cumin seeds sizzle and white urad dal turns golden. Add curry leaves. Fry until curry leaves are crisp. Add the onions and green chilies and fry until the edges of the onion begin to brown. Stir in eggplant and mango pieces. Reduce heat to medium. Add salt and turmeric. Cook while stirring occasionally until vegetables are cooked and tender (about 20 - 25 minutes).

*Cook's Note: 1. Raw mangoes are available at Indian stores.*
*2. Whole red chili is added for flavor only and are not meant to be eaten.*

# NELLORE CHEPALA PULUSU
## (NELLORE-STYLE FISH STEW)

*Chepalu means fish and Pulusu means "sour gravy curry". It is usually made with tamarind and is a specialty of Nellore in the state of Andhra Pradesh. This dish is known for being notoriously hot and sour. People from Nellore always brag about their chepala pulusu being the best, incomparable to any other regions of Andhra Pradesh. You can replace part of the cayenne with paprika if you prefer a milder version. You can also drizzle 1 teaspoon of melted ghee with each serving to lessen the spiciness. If your stomach can handle the killer hot and spicy pulusu, replace paprika with cayenne. Chepala pulusu is usually served with a generous portion of plain rice.*

*Typically chepala pulusu is cooked in a wide, shallow pan so that the pieces can be cooked in a single layer without breaking.*

*After tasting all world-famous cuisines from my kitchen, this is my daughter Silpa's all-time favorite accompaniment to white rice. As a child, she would eat this curry while wiping tears from her cheeks because of the spiciness of the chili powder. Over a period of time, she developed a tolerance for the spiciness and learned to love and devour the hot and spicy pulusu. I experimented with a milder version of the recipe to include in this book but she flatly refused the modified version, saying that I should not change the tradition. Here is the original recipe of Nellore chepala pulusu, in honor of my daughter, Silpa.*

*Serves 6 - 8*

- ⅓ cup tamarind without seeds, packed
- 4 cups water
- 1 tablespoon paprika
- 3 tablespoons cayenne
- 1 tablespoon coriander powder
- 4 teaspoons salt or to taste
- 2 pounds any white firm fish fillet, such as catfish, bluefish, trout, or sea bass.
- ¼ cup vegetable oil
- 2 dry whole red chilies, such as chile de arbol
- 1 teaspoon black mustard seeds
- ¼ teaspoon fenugreek seeds
- 20 curry leaves, fresh or dried
- 2 cups finely chopped red onion or shallots

To make tamarind water, soak the tamarind in 1 cup of hot water for ½ an hour. Using your fingers, mash the tamarind to release as much pulp as possible. Pour the mixture into a mesh sieve set over a bowl to extract pulp, by pushing it through the sieve. Transfer fibrous remains to the bowl. Add another cup of hot water. When it is cool enough to handle, mash with your fingers again to extract any remaining pulp. Pour the mixture into the sieve set over a bowl again. Push it through. Discard the fibers left in the sieve. Add enough water to make 4 cups of tamarind water. To the tamarind water, add paprika, cayenne, coriander and salt. Mix it together until salt is dissolved. Set aside until ready to use.

Clean the fish under cold, running water and cut into 2 – 3 inch steaks.

Heat oil in a large, wide shallow skillet over medium high heat. When oil is hot, add red chilies. When the chilies turn darker, add mustard seeds, and cover until the spluttering subsides. Uncover, and add fenugreek seeds and curry leaves. When the curry leaves are crisp, add onions and fry until the edges begin to brown. Add the reserved tamarind water. Cook for about 20 - 25 minutes until the sauce is reduced to half. Gently add fish pieces in a single layer into the boiling sauce. Cook for about 10 - 15 minutes until fish is cooked and sauce is thick. Transfer to a serving dish. Serve with generous portions of white rice and ghee.

***Cook's Note:** 1. **Whole** red chilies are added for flavor only and are not meant to be eaten.*
*2. Sourness of the tamarind can vary.*

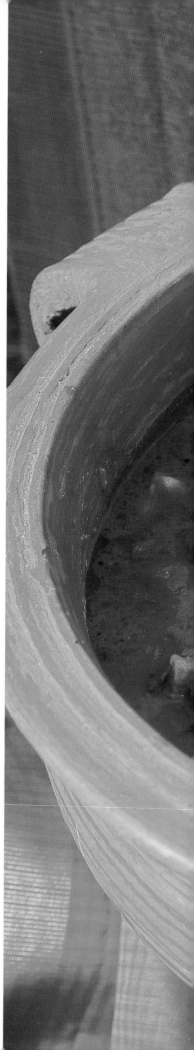

# Ridge Gourd–Chena Curry

## (Beerakaya – Senaga pappu kura)

*Ridge gourd is called Beera Kaya in Telugu and Tori in Hindi. It is a very popular vegetable in Southern states.*

*Serves 4 - 6*

- ¼ cup chena dal, soaked in water for 2 hours
- 2 ½ pounds ridge gourd
- 2 tablespoons vegetable oil
- 4 cloves
- 2-inch stick cinnamon
- 20 curry leaves, fresh or dry
- 1 cup chopped onion
- 1 teaspoon salt
- ½ teaspoon turmeric
- ½ - 1 teaspoon cayenne
- masala podi (recipe follows)

Using a vegetable peeler, peel the ridges and skin from the ridge gourd. Cut into ½-inch pieces.

Heat 2 tablespoons of oil in a wok or skillet over medium high heat. When the oil is hot, add the cloves and cinnamon stick. As soon as the cloves plump up, add curry leaves and fry until they are crisp. Add onion and fry until edges begin to brown. Add ridge gourd pieces, salt, turmeric, cayenne, and soaked chena dal and cook until almost all the water is evaporated and the dal is cooked, while stirring occasionally.

This vegetable leaves a lot of water. That water is enough to cook the chena dal. There is no need to add extra water to this dish while cooking. Stir in the masala podi, remove from the heat and serve with rice.

## Masala Podi

*Masala podi means spice powder. Cooks in India express their personal flair in cooking through the unique combination of spice blends they use. This particular spice blend is my mother-in- law's specialty.*

- 1 tablespoon coriander seeds
- 1 teaspoon white poppy seeds
- 1 tablespoon grated dry coconut
- 1 clove garlic, finely minced

In a small skillet, dry roast coriander seeds over medium high heat for 2 minutes, while shaking and stirring. Reduce the heat to medium, stir in poppy seeds and coconut and turn off the heat. Let it cool. Using a spice grinder, grind the spices into powder. Add minced garlic to the powder and mix well.

# Pappu Rasam

*Serves 6 - 8*

- 1 cup cooked toor dal (page 309)
- 1 tablespoon ghee
- 2 dry whole red chilies, such as chile de arbol
- ⅛ teaspoon asafoetida
- 1 teaspoon black mustard seeds
- ¼ teaspoon fenugreek seeds
- 20 curry leaves, preferably fresh
- 2 tomatoes, chopped
- 2 tablespoons tamarind paste or to taste
- 2 – 3 teaspoons salt
- ½ teaspoon turmeric
- 4 cups water
- pappu rasam podi (recipe follows)
- 2 tablespoons chopped cilantro/coriander

Have cooked toor dal ready. Heat ghee in a saucepan over medium high heat. Add asafoetida and red chilies. When the red chilies begin to darken, add mustard seeds and cover until the spluttering subsides. Uncover and add fenugreek seeds and curry leaves. Fry until curry leaves are crisp. Add tomatoes and cook until they become soft. Add cooked toor dal, tamarind paste, salt, turmeric and water, bring it to boil. Reduce heat to medium and simmer for 5 minutes. Add pappu rasam podi. Garnish with cilantro leaves. Serve with rice.

## Pappu Rasam Podi

- 1 tablespoon pepper corns
- 1 tablespoon cumin seeds
- 2 cloves garlic, minced

Using a spice grinder, grind pepper corns and cumin into coarse powder. Add garlic and mix well.

# Tapioca Pudding

## (Payasam)

*Serves 4 - 6*

- 1 cup big tapioca pearls
- 3 cups water, divided
- 1 cup sugar
- 2 cups warm whole milk
- 1 cup half and half
- 1 teaspoon green cardamom seed powder
- 2 tablespoons ghee
- ¼ cup chopped raw cashew nuts
- mango and papaya pieces for garnishing (optional)

Soak tapioca in 1 cup of water for an hour. Bring 2 cups of water to a boil in a saucepan over medium high heat. Add tapioca and cook for about 10 - 12 minutes until pearls become clear and transparent, while stirring often. Stir in sugar. Let the sugar melt for about 2 - 3 minutes. Stir in milk and half and half. Bring it to boil and reduce heat to medium and simmer for another 5 - 7 minutes. Stir in cardamom powder. Remove from the heat.

Heat 2 tablespoons of ghee in a small skillet over medium high heat. Add cashew nuts. Fry until golden while stirring often. Add the nuts along with ghee to the tapioca pudding. When pudding is warm, transfer to individual serving dishes and garnish with mango and papaya.

# Thali

Thali is a traditional Indian meal, served in a round metal-edged plate with rice and/or bread in the middle and an assortment of curries served in small cups called katoris around the rice. Usually, the round plate and cups are made of stainless steel. This style of serving food is known as "thali". In India, usually thali represents the characteristics of the region you are in, featuring the dishes native to the region. Usually thali includes rice, chappatis, yogurt, meat, vegetables and dal. Typically, the restaurant menu offers a choice of vegetarian or non-vegetarian thali.

## The Menu

# CABBAGE CHENA DAL FRY

*By combining cabbage with chena dal, this dish has enough flavor to satisfy any vegetarian palate.*

*Serves 4 - 6*

- ½ cup chena dal
- 2 tablespoons vegetable oil
- 2 dry whole red chilies, such as chile de arbol
- 1 teaspoon black mustard seeds
- 1 teaspoon cumin seeds
- 1 teaspoon white urad dal
- 10 fresh curry leaves
- 1 - 2 minced fresh green chilies such as serrano
- 1 ½ pounds cabbage, finely shredded
- 1 teaspoon salt or to taste
- ½ teaspoon turmeric

Soak chena dal in boiling water for a couple of hours and drain well.
Heat oil in a skillet over medium high heat. When the oil is hot, add red chillies and mustard seeds and cover until the spluttering subsides. Uncover and add cumin seeds and urad dal. As soon as the urad dal turns golden, add curry leaves. When curry leaves are crisp, add green chili, shredded cabbage, salt and turmeric. Stir fry for 1 minute. Add chena dal, cover with the lid for 2 - 3 minutes. Uncover and fry until cabbage is wilted and cooked through while stirring occasionally. Season to taste. Serve with chappati or rice.

**Cook's Note:** *Red chilies are added for flavor only and are not meant to be eaten.*

# KHAIMA

*Ground lamb or goat meat is often referred to as khaima in Southern states as opposed to Northern kheema. This dish is popular all over India, especially with children when you serve it with pooris. You can substitute peeled and chopped potatoes with peas for variation.*

*Serves 4 - 6*

- 2 tablespoons vegetable oil
- 6 cloves
- one 2-inch stick cinnamon
- 5 cardamom pods, slightly crushed to open the shell
- 1 bay leaf
- 1 cup chopped onion
- 2 tablespoons ginger garlic paste
- 1 - 3 minced fresh green chilies, such as serrano
- 1 tablespoon kashmiri mirch or paprika
- 1 teaspoon coriander powder
- 1 teaspoon roasted cumin powder
- ½ - 1 teaspoon cayenne
- 2 medium tomatoes, chopped
- 1 ½ teaspoons salt or to taste
- 1 ½ pounds ground lamb
- 2 cups frozen peas
- 1 teaspoon garam masala powder
- 1 teaspoon lime juice
- 1 tablespoon finely chopped mint
- 1 tablespoon finely chopped cilantro

Heat oil in medium saucepan over medium high heat. When the oil is hot, add cloves, cinnamon, cardamom pods and bay leaf. When the cloves plump up, add onions and fry until edges begin to brown. Add ginger garlic paste and green chili and stir fry for 2 minutes. Stir in paprika, coriander powder, cumin powder and cayenne and fry for about one minute until all the spices are fried. Add tomatoes and cook until they are soft and some of the moisture evaporates. Add salt. Stir in ground lamb. Fry for 5 - 7 minutes while breaking up the lumps. Add ½ cup of water. Reduce heat to medium and simmer for 30 minutes. Stir in peas. Add another ½ cup of water. Continue to simmer for another 15 - 20 minutes until peas are tender and most of the moisture evaporates. Add garam masala powder and lime juice and mix well. Season to taste. Stir in mint and cilantro. Serve with pooris, parathas, or rice.

**Cook's Note:** *Whole spices are added to flavor the dish and are not meant to be eaten.*

# GHEE RICE

*The rice is fried in ghee before it is cooked.  This not only makes the rice grains separate, but also adds a nutty flavor to the cooked rice.*

*Serves 4 - 6*

- ½ cup ghee
- ¼ cup raw cashew nuts
- ¼ cup golden raisins
- 10 cloves
- 1 - 2 inch stick cinnamon
- 6 cardamom pods, slightly crushed to open the shell
- 2 bay leaves

- 1 star anise
- 1 tablespoon ginger garlic paste
- 1 teaspoon green chili paste (page 303)
- 2 cups basmati rice
- 2 teaspoons salt
- 3 ½ cups water

- ½ cup caramelized onions (page 308)

Heat ghee in a medium saucepan over medium heat.  When the ghee is hot, add cashew nuts and fry until golden.  Using a slotted spoon, remove the nuts to a bowl. Add raisins to the same pan and fry until they plump up.  Remove them into the bowl with the nuts and reserve for later use.

To the same pan, add cloves, cinnamon, cardamom pods, bay leaves and star anise.  Fry until the cloves plump up.  Add ginger garlic and green chili paste and stir fry for about 1 minute.  Add basmati rice and fry for about 3 - 5 minutes until rice turns white.  Stir in salt and water.  At this point, you can transfer the rice mixture to an automatic rice cooker and finish cooking.

Alternately, bring the rice mixture to a boil over medium high heat.  Reduce heat to lowest setting and cover with the lid.  Cook for about 20 - 25 minutes until rice is done.  Let the rice rest for 10 minutes.  Fluff up the rice with a spoon or fork.  Transfer to a serving platter and garnish with the reserved cashews, raisins and caramelized onions.

***Cook's Note:*** *Whole spices are added to flavor the dish and are not meant to be eaten.*

# SORAKAYA PACHADI (LOKI RAITA)

*Opo squash, called loki in Hindi and sorakaya in Telugu, is available at Indian and well-stocked supermarkets. Pachadis are cooked and cooled vegetables and fruits mixed with yogurt, which is the Southern version of the Northern raita.*

*Serves 4 - 6*

- 2 pounds opo squash, peeled, seeded and cut into ½-inch pieces
- 1 teaspoon salt
- 1 tablespoon vegetable oil
- 1 teaspoon black mustard seeds
- ¼ teaspoon fenugreek seeds
- 1 tablespoon minced fresh ginger
- 1 minced fresh green chili, such as serrano
- 10 fresh curry leaves
- 2 cups plain yogurt

Place opo squash and salt in a small saucepan. Cover with a lid and cook over medium heat while stirring occasionally until the squash is tender. Let it cool. To season, heat oil in a small skillet. Add mustard seeds, and cover until the spluttering subsides. Add fenugreek seeds. When the fenugreek seeds turn one shade darker, add ginger, green chilies and curry leaves. Stir fry for 1 minute. Add this seasoning to cooked squash. Stir in yogurt and season to taste.

# PALAKURA PAPPU (SPINACH DAL)

*Roasting dals before cooking is an age old technique from my mother's kitchen. By roasting, not only do dals loose some of their starch, but they add another dimension of flavor and aroma to the dish.*

*Serves 4 - 6*
- ½ cup toor dal
- ½ cup mung dal
- 3 - 5 cups water
- 1 medium onion, chopped
- 2 medium tomatoes, chopped
- 3 - 5 minced fresh green chilies, such as serrano
- 2 teaspoons salt
- ½ teaspoon turmeric
- 9 ounces spinach, shredded
- 2 - 3 tablespoons tamarind paste

*Seasoning*
- 2 tablespoons vegetable oil
- 2 dry whole red chilies, such as chile de arbol
- ⅛ teaspoon asafoetida
- 1 teaspoon black mustard seeds
- 1 teaspoon cumin seeds
- 10 fresh curry leaves
- 2 tablespoons chopped onion

Dry roast both the dals over medium heat in a skillet until one shade darker. Place dal with 3 cups of water in a large saucepan. Bring it to a boil over medium high heat for 5 minutes. Reduce heat to medium and simmer for 10 minutes. Add onions, tomatoes, green chilies, salt and turmeric and continue to simmer. Add more water as needed. Cook until dal is cooked and almost creamy. Add spinach and tamarind. Cook for another 10 minutes.

To season, heat oil in a small skillet over medium high heat. Add red chilies, asafoetida. When chilies are turning darker, add mustard seeds and cover until the spluttering subsides. Uncover and add cumin seeds. After cumin seeds sizzle add the curry leaves. As soon as they are crisp, add onions and fry until onions turn golden brown. Add the seasoning to cooked dal and mix well. Season to taste.

*Cook's Note: Red chilies are added for flavor only and are not meant to be eaten.*

# RASAM

*Serves 4 - 6*

- ½ cup cooked toor dal (page 309)
- 1 tablespoon rasam podi (recipe follows)
- 1 tablespoon ghee
- 2 dry whole red chilies, such as chile de arbol
- ⅛ teaspoon asafoetida
- 1 teaspoon black mustard seeds
- 1 teaspoon cumin seeds
- 20 fresh curry leaves
- 3 cloves garlic, crushed
- 1 cup tomato sauce
- 1 ½ teaspoons salt or to taste
- ¼ teaspoon turmeric
- 4 cups water
- 1 tablespoon coarsely grated ginger
- 1 tablespoon lime juice or to taste
- 2 tablespoons chopped cilantro leaves (optional)

Have toor dal and rasam podi ready. Heat ghee in a medium saucepan over medium heat. When the ghee is hot, add asafoetida and red chilies. When red chilies turn darker, add mustard seeds, and cover until the spluttering subsides. Uncover, and add cumin seeds, curry leaves and garlic cloves. Fry for 1 minute. Stir in tomato sauce, salt, turmeric, water, toor dal, and grated ginger. Bring it to a boil. Reduce heat to medium and simmer for 5 minutes and stir in rasam podi and lime juice and cilantro leaves. Serve with plain rice or serve as soup.

*Cook's Note: Red chilies are added for flavor only and are not meant to be eaten.*

## RASAM PODI

- 5 dry whole red chilies, such as chile de arbol
- ⅓ cup coriander seeds
- ¼ cup cumin seeds
- 2 tablespoons toor dal
- 3 tablespoons black pepper corns
- ½ tablespoon fenugreek seeds
- 2 tablespoons chena dal

Dry roast all the ingredients together in a small skillet until both the dals turn one shade darker, while shaking and stirring the pan. Let it cool. Using a spice grinder, grind into fine powder. Store in an airtight container in a cool, dark place. Use as needed.

# Kerala Feast

Kerala, India's spice trade center, is located on the South West coast of India. This land is a tropical paradise known for its enchantingly beautiful lush rivers and exotic coconut palms.

Over the centuries, Kerala's exotic spices have attracted many foreigners. The Portuguese discovered a sea route to Kerala, followed by the Dutch, the French and finally the British. History helped Kerala's society to become more cosmopolitan with different religions, including Christianity, Islam and Hinduism.

The most fundamental ingredient of Kerala's cuisine is coconut. In every home, the first task in the cooking ritual begins with grinding the coconut, which is then used in an array of dishes prepared during the course of the day.

12

*Bronze urulis are unique to the Kerala region. Traditionally they are meant to be used as cooking vessels, which gives that antique patina to the dish. In the present days, urulis are used in many alternative ways such as to float candles, flowers and even as a small water garden pool.*

## The Menu

# Appam

*Appam is a lacy pancake that is a specialty of Kerala. It is more like a French crepe, except that the batter is made with rice and coconut. You need a special two-handled concave pan to make appam. These pans are available at Indian stores. If you don't have an appam pan, you can use a Chinese wok instead. This is a very traditional recipe for making appam. The most popular way to eat appam is with thick coconut milk mixed with finely ground sugar. Appam can be eaten as a bread with gravy curry. It pairs well with fish molle.*

*Serves 4 - 6*
- 2 cups long grain rice
- 1 cup freshly grated coconut
- ½ teaspoon baking soda
- 1 teaspoon salt

Wash rice with several changes of water. Add enough water to cover 2 inches above the rice and soak it overnight. Drain the rice and transfer it to a grinder along with the coconut. Grind rice and coconut to a smooth batter using 1½ cups of water. Transfer ½ a cup of batter and 1½ cups of water into a small saucepan. Cook over medium heat for about 3 – 5 minutes until it becomes a translucent white dough, while stirring often. Let it cool and mix it with the original batter. Make sure there are no lumps in the batter. Let the batter ferment overnight at room temperature. On the next day, add baking soda and salt and mix well.

To make appam, heat appam pan or wok over medium high heat. When the pan is hot, add about ⅓ cup of batter in the middle of the pan. Immediately using the hot pads, pick up the pan or wok with both hands and swirl the pan and make a 6 - 7 inch circle. Cover the pan and cook for about 3 - 4 minutes until the edges of the appam turn golden brown. The center of the appam should look spongy. Remove with the spatula and serve.

# AVIAL

*Every state in India has its own signature dishes. Avial is an authentic dish of Kerala.*

*Serves 6*

- 1 bell pepper
- 3 Indian or Japanese eggplants
- 2 drumsticks* or 10 frozen pieces
- ¼ pound green beans
- 1 cucumber
- ½ pound banana squash, peeled and seeds removed
- 1 plantain
- 1 chayote squash
- 1 raw mango, peeled and cut around the pit into 1-inch pieces
- 2 tablespoons salt
- 20 curry leaves

*Coconut Paste*

- 1 ½ cups grated coconut
- 2 - 6 chopped fresh green chilies, such as serrano
- ½ tablespoon cumin seeds

- 1 cup yogurt

*Seasoning*

- 1 tablespoon coconut oil or vegetable oil
- 10 curry leaves

Cut bell pepper into strips. Cut eggplant into 1 x 3 inch pieces. Cut drumsticks into 3-inch pieces. Trim both ends of the beans and cut in the middle. Peel and cut cucumber, banana squash, plantain and chayote squash into 1 x 3 inch pieces. Add all the vegetables to shallow heavy bottomed pan along with ½ cup of water. Add salt, turmeric and curry leaves and cook over medium high heat until tender and almost cooked. Meanwhile prepare coconut paste by grinding coconut, green chilies and cumin seeds along with half a cup of water. Add coconut paste to the vegetables and cook for another 5 minutes. Cool vegetables until they are lukewarm. Add yogurt and stir gently to combine.

To season, heat 1 tablespoon of oil in a small frying pan. Add curry leaves and fry until they are crisp. Add this seasoning to vegetables and mix.

*Cook's Note: *Drumsticks are available at Indian stores, fresh or frozen. To eat drumsticks, scrape the flesh with the teeth and discard the fibrous shell.*

# FISH MOLLE

*Kerala's cuisine or any regional cuisine for that matter evolves based on native ingredients. This dish represents the region's abundant supply of fish and coconut.*

*Serves 4 - 6*

- 1 ½ pounds fish fillet such as catfish or sea bass
- 1 cup coconut milk, home made (page 302) or canned, divided
- ¼ cup vegetable oil
- 4 green cardamoms, slightly crushed to open the shell
- 10 curry leaves
- 1 cup sliced onions
- 1-inch piece ginger, julienned

- 1 - 4 green chilies such as serrano, cut lengthwise into two
- 2 teaspoons ginger garlic paste
- 1 teaspoon black pepper corns, slightly crushed
- 1 tomato, finely chopped
- 1 teaspoon salt
- ¼ teaspoon turmeric
- 1 teaspoon lime juice

Clean the fish under cold running water, pat dry with paper towels, cut into large chunks, and set aside. Dilute ½ a cup of coconut milk with ¾ cup of water and set aside until needed.

Heat oil in a wide 10-inch skillet over medium high heat. Add cardamom and curry leaves and fry for a minute. Add sliced onions, green chilies and julienned ginger and sauté until the onions are translucent. Add ginger garlic paste and pepper corns. Sauté for 2 minutes. Add tomatoes, salt and turmeric and cook until the tomatoes are soft for about 2 - 3 minutes. Add diluted coconut milk. Reduce heat to medium and simmer for 5 - 7 minutes. Add the pieces of fish in a single layer and cook for 8 – 10 minutes or until the fish is cooked. Stir in the rest of the ½ a cup of coconut milk in and heat through. Stir in lime juice. Season to taste. Serve with appam, or with plain white rice.

*Cook's Note: Green cardamoms and whole green chilies are added for flavor only and are not meant to be eaten.*

# PLANTAIN CHIPS

*Plantains are green bananas widely used in Kerala cuisine. Traditionally, these chips are fried in coconut oil. Salt is added to the hot oil so that the chips are flavored as they cook.*

- 4 plantains
- 1 teaspoon salt
- 20 curry leaves

- ½ teaspoon cayenne
- oil for deep frying

Peel the skin from the plantain and slice into thin, even rounds. I use a mandoline for this job. Heat oil in a deep fryer to 350 - 360º F. Add sliced plantain in batches, as many as you can fit in a single layer, in the hot oil. Fry until golden brown and crisp, while stirring often. Sprinkle a pinch of salt as soon as you remove from the oil. Once you fry all the chips, add curry leaves to the same oil, fry until crisp and add to the chips. Sprinkle rest of the salt and cayenne, and mix. Store them in an airtight container for up to a week.

# PINEAPPLE PACHADI

*This dish is similar to the fruit raita from North India. Like any pachadi from the South, the fruit is cooked before it is added to the yogurt. This dish combines all the elements of taste - sweetness of the pineapple, tanginess from the yogurt, pungency of the mustard seeds, and bitterness of the fenugreek seeds.*

*Serves 6*
- 3 cups finely chopped ripe pineapple
- 1 teaspoon salt
- 1 chopped fresh green chili, such as serrano
- ⅓ cup freshly grated coconut
- 1 teaspoon black mustard seeds, coarsely ground

*Seasoning*
- 1 tablespoon vegetable oil
- 1 dry whole red chili, such as chile de arbol
- 1 teaspoon black mustard seeds
- ¼ teaspoon fenugreek seeds
- 10 curry leaves
- 1 cup yogurt

Place pineapple and salt in a small saucepan. Add ½ a cup of water and cook for 10 minutes over medium heat, while stirring occasionally. Meanwhile, grind coconut and green chili into a paste, using 2 – 3 tablespoons of water. Add the coconut mixture and the mustard seeds to the pineapple. Cook for another 5 minutes.

To season, heat oil in a small saucepan over medium heat. When the oil is hot, add the red chili. When the red chili turns darker, add the mustard seeds and fenugreek seeds and cover until the spluttering subsides. Uncover and add curry leaves. As soon as they are crisp, pour this seasoning over the cooked pineapple and mix. Let the pineapple mixture come to room temperature and stir in yogurt and serve.

*Cook's Note: Whole red chilies are added for flavor only and not meant to be eaten.*

# Shrimp with Green Mango

*Serves 4*
- 1 ½ pounds shrimp

*Marinade*
- 2 tablespoons coriander powder
- 1 teaspoon roasted cumin powder
- 1 teaspoon cayenne
- 4 cloves garlic
- 1 cup chopped red onions
- 1 teaspoon salt
- ¼ teaspoon turmeric

*Seasoning*
- 2 tablespoons vegetable oil
- ½ teaspoon black mustard seeds
- 10 curry leaves
- 2 cups sliced red onions
- 1-inch piece ginger, julienned
- 1 - 3 fresh green chilies such as serrano, cut lengthwise into two
- 1 raw green mango, peeled and grated around the pit

Peel and de-vein the shrimp. Place all the ingredients for the marinade in a blender and grind into a paste. Combine shrimp with the marinade. Marinate for ½ an hour in the refrigerator.

To season, heat oil in a wide skillet over medium high heat. Add mustard seeds and cover until the spluttering subsides. Uncover and add curry leaves, onions, ginger and green chilies. Sauté until the onions are soft and edges begin to brown. Add shrimp with marinade and cook for 7 - 8 minutes while stirring occasionally, until the shrimp is cooked. Add grated mango and cook for another 3 - 4 minutes. Season to taste. Serve with plain white rice.

*Cook's Note: Whole green chilies are added for flavoring only. They are not meant to be eaten.*

# VEGETABLE KOOTU

*Serves 4 - 6*

- ½ cup chena dal

*Coconut Paste*
- ¾ cup grated coconut
- 2 - 4 dry whole red chilies, such as chile de arbol
- 1 teaspoon black pepper corn

- 2 chayote squash
- 2 medium zucchini squash
- 1 teaspoon salt or to taste

*Seasoning*
- 1 tablespoon coconut oil or vegetable oil
- 1 dry whole red chili, such as chile de arbol
- 1 teaspoon black mustard seeds
- 1 teaspoon white urad dal
- 10 curry leaves
- ¼ cup grated coconut

Soak chena dal in 3 cups of boiling water for two hours and drain.

Meanwhile, grind grated coconut, red chilies and black pepper into a coarse paste using ¼ cup of water and set aside.

Peel chayote squash. Cut in the middle to remove the seed. Cut chayote squash and zucchini squash into 1-inch cubes. Cook vegetables along with salt in a medium saucepan for about 10 - 12 minutes over medium high heat until tender covered and stirring occasionally. Add soaked dal and coconut paste to the vegetables and cook for about 5 minutes.

To season, heat oil in a small sauce pan over medium high heat. Add the red chili. When the red chili turns dark, add mustard seeds, and cover until the spluttering subsides. Uncover and add white urad dal and curry leaves. Fry until white urad dal turns golden and curry leaves are crisp. Add grated coconut and fry until golden brown. Add this seasoning to the vegetables and mix well.

*Cook's Note: 1. Whole red chilies are added for flavor only and are not meant to be eaten. 2. Frozen grated coconut is available at Indian stores.*

# VERMICELLI PAYASAM

*This dish is made with vermicelli, also known as seviyan, which are very thin, long noodles. These are available at Indian stores. If you are using long, thin vermicelli, break them into 2-inch long pieces before you cook. There is another variety available called Bambino vermicelli. You can use either variety to make the payasam.*

*Serves 4 - 6*

- ¼ cup ghee
- 2 tablespoons raw cashews
- 2 tablespoons golden raisins
- 1 cup vermicelli

- 4 cups hot milk
- ½ cup sugar
- ½ teaspoon green cardamom seed powder
- pinch of salt

Heat ghee in a heavy bottomed skillet over medium heat. Add cashews and raisins to the pan. Fry until the cashews are golden and raisins are plump. Using a slotted spoon, remove cashews and raisins to the bowl and set aside. To the same pan, add the vermicelli pieces. Stir fry until they turn golden brown. It takes only 1 - 2 minutes. Not all the pieces will have the same color, which is alright. Add milk and increase heat to medium high. Cook while stirring occasionally for 5 minutes or until vermicelli is soft and cooked. Stir in sugar and cook for another 5 minutes. Add cardamom powder, salt and stir to combine. Transfer to a serving bowl. Garnish with cashews and raisins. Serve warm.

# MANGO LASSI

*This is similar to the Western fruit smoothie and is a popular drink all over India during the summer.*

*Serves 4*

- 2 cups canned sweetened mango pulp or well ripened mango pieces
- 2 cups plain yogurt

- 2 tablespoons sugar
- ¼ teaspoon salt
- 1 cup crushed ice

Place all the ingredients in the blender and process until frothy.

*Detail: In place of a traditional charger, use beautifully shaped leaves to add an exotic touch to the table setting.*

# Regional Cuisines of India

A common denominator for all regional Indian cuisines is the imaginative and innovative use of spices and herbs. Although most of the spices are grown in the southern part of India, their use is common all over the subcontinent. Some dishes are flavored with only one spice while others use a mixture of spices. There are the standard spices such as ginger, garlic, cinnamon, cardamom, and cloves that are common to all the regions. Certain others, such as tamarind, sesame seeds and curry leaves are more commonly used in the South, whereas spice blends such as the garam masala powder are a specialty of the North. Another distinguishing feature of Indian cuisine is the abundant use of vegetables.

Despite these similarities, each region has its own traditions and its own distinctive cuisines. In the Punjabi kitchens, there is a strong influence of the Moghul cuisine. Fish is a dominant presence in Bengali cuisine. Kitchens in the coastal regions make ample use of coconut and seafood. In Rajasthan and Gujarat, one sees a variety of dals and achars. Tamarind is an integral part of Tamil cooking whereas the typical Andhra cuisine is known for avakaya - raw mango pickle and gongura – a sour leaf vegetable chutney. Both these dishes make generous use of chili powder.

In the North, a variety of flours are used to make chappati, roti and naan with the exception of Kashmir, which is a rice eating region much like the South and East of India.

No matter what the dominant ingredient is in each regional cuisine, it is the varied and creative use of spices that make Indian food so distinctly delectable.

# HYDERABAD

For North Indians, Hyderabad is a South Indian city, although many in the South consider it to be the "North" of the South. The region has a strong Muslim influence which is readily evident in its culture and cuisine and gives Hyderabad its own distinct identity. Thus, even though it is the capital of the Telugu-speaking Andhra Pradesh, the dominant language here is Urdu.

Hyderabad developed around the Golkonda Fort in the Telangana region. The fort was originally built by the Kakatiya rulers of Warangal. The Kakatiya Dynasty ruled southern India from the 12th to 14th century A.D. After repeated attacks by the Muslim invaders, it finally succumbed to the Bhahmani kingdom.

In the 16th century A.D., Sultan Quli, a Persian Shia adventurer and the Bhahmani governor of Telangana, proclaimed independence and became the ruler of this region. Thus began the Qutub Shahi Dynasty. Mohammed Quli, the fifth sultan of this Dynasty, built and named Hyderabad in the 1580s.

He fell in love with and married a very beautiful and popular Hindu woman named Bhagmati. He named the city Bhagnagar in her honor. Later, when Bhagmati was chosen to be his queen, she was given the name Hyder Mahal and the city was renamed Hyderabad. Mohammad Quli was a great builder. The famous Charminar in the city center was built by him. It is made in the *tazia* style, *tazia* being a sacred symbol, a replica of the tomb of the revered Imam Hossain that Shia Muslims carry during the procession of Moharrum.

The Moghul emperor Aurangazeb invaded Golkonda in the 17th century and defeated the Qutub rulers, establishing this as the southernmost extent of the Moghul empire. A Nizam (governor) was appointed to rule under the Moghul regime. Later, in the early 18th century, as the Moghul Empire entered its twilight in Delhi, the governor of Hyderabad, Qamruddin, declared his independence and launched the Asaf Jahi dynasty. The city of Hyderabad continued to be ruled as an independent state until India's independence when the seventh Nizam, Osman Ali Khan, signed an agreement for the state to become a part of the Indian democracy. Later, the city of Hyderabad became the capital of Andhra Pradesh. Nizam Osman Ali Khan was considered to be the world's richest man of his time. He had his own railway system and currency.

Hyderabad is known for diamonds, pearls, silver, bangles and finely embroidered clothing. The world's biggest diamond, the Kohinoor, which adorns Queen Victoria's crown, originally came from this region. Hyderabadi women are passionate about wearing bangles. Hands without bangles are described as unattractive bamboo sticks. Streets around the Charminar shimmer with stores abundantly stocked with beautiful multicolored bangles glistening under the fluorescent lights, almost dazzling the eyes of those walking in the streets.

Hyderabadi cuisine is a fusion of the elegance of the North with the spice of the South. Most amazingly, it has flourished in this Muslim community in the middle of Hindu South India. The cuisine relies heavily on meat, a predominantly Muslim influence, and has evolved into an array of exotic dishes that can be quite hot and spicy, a local Telugu influence. Here you will find the best of Moghul dishes such as kabobs, pulaos and biryanis, flavored with the typical South Indian ingredients like curry leaves, tamarind, mustard seeds, coconut, peanuts and hot chilies. Biryani is a dish of rice and meat partially cooked separately, layered together and then baked in the oven or cooked on the stove-top. Pulao on the other the hand is rice cooked along with a spicy meat mixture to absorb the flavors.

Evolving out of the rich Arabic, Persians and Turkish influences on the ancient Hindu heritage of the Kakatiyas, the Hyderabadi cuisine is a highly seductive and tantalizing feast for the discerning palate.

# Nawab's Daawat

*Nawab's Daawat means "the feast of aristocrats".*

# MANGO KA PANNA

*This drink is supposed to have a cooling effect on the body in the hot summer.*

*Serves 4 - 6*

- 2 medium, very firm raw mangoes
- ½ cup sugar
- 3 - 4 cups water
- 10 mint leaves
- 1 teaspoon freshly ground black pepper
- ½ teaspoon black salt
- salt to taste
- 1 tablespoon roasted cumin powder
- ½ fresh green chili such as serrano, seeds removed
- mint sprig for garnishing

Preheat oven to 425º F. Cover mangoes with aluminum foil and roast them in the oven for 40 - 45 minutes. Remove from the oven and let them cool. When they are cool enough to handle, peel the skin and squeeze pulp from the seed. Cool the pulp completely in the refrigerator.

Alternately, you can grill them on a barbeque while turning occasionally until soft. Or, you can boil the mangos in 4 cups of water until soft and squeeze the pulp.

Combine sugar and water in a saucepan and boil for 10 minutes. Let it cool. Add mango pulp, sugar syrup and the rest of the ingredients to the blender and blend until smooth. Adjust the seasoning. Transfer to a pitcher and cool in the fridge for 2 - 3 hours. Serve over ice cubes and garnish with mint sprigs.

# SHAAMI KABOBS (DEEP FRIED LAMB KABOBS)

*The creamy filling of paneer complements the spicy meat mixture.*

*Yield 12*

- 1 pound boneless leg of lamb, fat removed and cut into small cubes
- ½ cup onion, chopped
- ¼ cup chena dal
- 1 tablespoon ginger garlic paste
- 1 teaspoon salt
- 1 cup water
- 1 - 3 minced fresh green chilies, such as serrano
- ¼ cup ground roasted cashew nuts
- 1 egg
- 1 teaspoon freshly ground black pepper
- ¼ cup chopped cilantro and/or mint leaves

*Filling*
- ¾ cup crumbled paneer
- oil for deep frying

Combine lamb, onion, chena dal, ginger garlic paste, salt and water. Place the meat mixture in a pressure cooker. Close with the lid and cook over medium high heat. Cook for a minute at high pressure and decrease heat to medium temperature. Cook for another 5 minutes. Turn off the heat and let the pressure drop on its own. Open the lid and cook the meat on the stove-top until meat is completely dry. Turn off the heat and let the meat mixture come to room temperature.

Alternately, you can cook the meat on the stove-top instead of a pressure cooker. Combine the first 6 ingredients in the pan. Cook over stove-top at medium high heat. Bring it to a boil, reduce heat to medium and cook until the meat and dal are soft, cooked, and completely dry.

Transfer the cooled meat mixture to the food processor, along with minced chilies, ground cashew nuts, egg, black pepper and cilantro leaves. Process until it becomes a dough. Make sure it does not become a paste. Instead, the dough should have a little texture. Divide the dough into 12 portions. Take each portion into the palm of your hand. Flatten into 3-inch rounds. Make a dent in the middle of the dough with your thumb. Place 1 tablespoon of paneer in the dent, close the dent by folding the dough to the center and seal. Flatten again into 2 ½-inch patties. Pour oil into a wok or heavy bottomed saucepan until it is ⅓ full (oil should be at least 2 - 3 inches deep). Heat oil until the temperature reaches 350º - 375º F. Fry 2 - 3 kabobs at a time, turning with the a slotted spoon until crispy on both sides. Serve with cilantro chutney.

***Cook's Note:*** *Don't try to fry too many kabobs at once. When you add too many at a time, the temperature of the oil drops, causing the kabobs to disintegrate in the oil.*

# HYDERABADI CHICKEN BIRYANI

*This is an elegant Indo-Persian dish. This might seem like an elaborate preparation but the end result is a spectacular party dish, usually served with onion chutney.*

*Serves 6 - 8*

- 3 cups basmati rice
- 3 tablespoons salt, divided
- 1 teaspoon lightly packed saffron
- ½ cup hot milk
- ½ cup + ⅓ cup oil, divided
- ¼ cup sliced almond
- ¼ cup golden raisins
- 2 medium onions, halved lengthwise, sliced thinly and cut in the middle
- 3 - 4 pounds chicken leg quarters or whole chicken
- 3 bay leaves
- 1 - 2 inch cinnamon stick
- 10 whole cloves
- 10 green cardamoms, lightly crushed to break the skin
- 1 tablespoon cumin seeds
- 1 onion, chopped
- 3 tablespoons ginger garlic paste
- ½ - 1 teaspoon cayenne

- 2 – 4 minced fresh green chilies, such as serrano
- 1 teaspoon freshly ground black pepper
- 2 teaspoons roasted cumin powder
- ½ teaspoon shea jeera powder (black cumin seed powder)
- 2 cups whole milk yogurt, whisked until smooth
- 3 tablespoons lime juice
- ½ cup roughly chopped cilantro/ coriander leaves
- ½ cup roughly chopped mint leaves
- 1 teaspoon Moghul garam masala powder (page 86)
- extra cilantro and mint leaves for garnishing
- 4 - 6 hard-boiled eggs

Wash the rice with several changes of water and soak for 2 - 3 hours with 1 teaspoon of salt and enough water to cover 2 - 3 inches above the rice.

In a small skillet, over low flame, fry the saffron threads for a few seconds until they become a shade darker. Crumble saffron over hot milk and let it steep for ½ an hour to one hour.

Heat ½ cup of oil in a shallow pan over medium high heat. When the oil is hot, add the sliced almonds. Fry them until golden brown. Using a slotted spoon, remove from the oil and reserve for garnishing. Add raisins to the same pan and fry until they plump up. Remove them from the oil and reserve for garnishing. To the same pan, add sliced onions and fry while stirring occasionally at the beginning and often at the end, until they turn golden brown evenly. Remove onions with the a slotted spatula and with another spatula gently press the onions to release excess oil. Spread them on a sheet pan to crisp up and cool. Reserve the leftover oil for later use. Once the fried onions are cooled, reserve half the fried onions for garnishing. Using the spice grinder, powder the rest of the fried onions.

Remove the skin from the chicken and cut into serving size pieces.

Heat ⅓ cup of oil in a large heavy bottomed skillet over medium high heat. When the oil is hot, add bay leaves, cinnamon stick, cloves, and cardamom. Stir once and add the cumin seeds. When the cumin seeds sizzle, add the chopped onions and fry until the edges begin to brown. Add ginger garlic paste and fry for a minute. Add the chicken pieces. Fry for about 5 minutes until chicken turns white. Stir in 2 teaspoons of salt and cayenne. Add green chilies, black pepper, and cumin powder, shea jeera powder, and stir fry for 2 minutes. Add yogurt 2 tablespoons at a time. Make sure the first 2 tablespoons are incorporated before adding the next 2 tablespoons. This will prevent it from curdling. Add lime juice, fried onion powder, cilantro and mint leaves. Cook the chicken until the sauce is thick. Add ½ a cup of water if necessary. It takes about 30 - 40 minutes. Stir in Moghul garam masala powder. Transfer the cooked chicken to large oven-proof casserole dish.

Preheat oven to 375º F. Bring 10 cups of water to a boil in a large saucepan. Add 2 tablespoons of salt. Drain the rice and slowly add to boiling water and boil for 5 minutes. Drain the rice immediately into a colander.

Spread the rice evenly on top of the chicken. Drizzle saffron milk and leftover oil from fried onions over the rice. Cover the casserole dish tightly with aluminum foil first and then with the lid and bake for 45 minutes. Let it rest for 15 minutes. Gently mix the biryani before serving. Transfer to a serving platter and garnish with almonds, raisins, fried onions, mint and cilantro leaves and halved hard-boiled eggs. Serve with onion chutney.

# Mirchi Ka Saalan

*Mirchi Ka Saalan is usually accompanied by biryani along with yogurt chutney. Traditionally, in India this dish is made with long hot chilies. Yellow banana peppers or Anaheim peppers are good substitutes. Keep in mind that, depending on the maturity of the chilies, this dish can become quite hot. If you prefer a milder version, substitute green bell peppers for chilies.*

Serves 6 - 8

- 1 ½ pound Anaheim peppers, cut lengthwise into 2, seeds removed and cut in the middle
- ⅛ cup tamarind
- 1 cup hot water
- ⅓ cup dry-roasted sesame seeds
- ¼ cup grated unsweetened dry coconut
- 2 onions
- 2 tablespoons ginger garlic paste
- 1 tablespoon coriander powder

- 2 teaspoons jaggery/brown sugar
- 1 teaspoon turmeric
- ½ - 1 teaspoon cayenne
- 1 tablespoon paprika
- 2 teaspoons salt

- ⅓ cup vegetable oil
- 1 teaspoon black mustard seeds
- 10 - 20 fresh or dry curry leaves

Soak tamarind in hot water for 30 minutes. Using your fingers, mash the tamarind to release as much pulp as possible. Pass it through a fine mesh strainer to extract tamarind water. Discard the fibrous remains.

Grind sesame seeds and coconut to fine powder in a spice grinder. Cut onion into ¾-inch thick rounds and brush each round with oil and roast on a hot griddle pan until golden brown on both sides. Alternately, you can roast them in the oven at 425º F for 5 - 7 minutes on each side. Once the roasted onion is cooled, using a blender, grind onion with tamarind water, sesame - coconut powder, ginger garlic paste, coriander powder, jaggery/brown sugar, turmeric, cayenne, and salt into paste and set aside.

Heat oil in a large nonstick frying pan over medium high heat. When the oil is hot, add peppers and fry until they are slightly wilted and acquire a few brown spots all over. Remove them from the oil using a slotted spoon and set aside. To the same pan, add curry leaves and 1 teaspoon mustard seeds. Cover the pan until the spluttering subsides. Uncover and add ground masala paste and fry for 5 - 10 minutes while stirring often. Add 1 cup of water and bring the sauce to a boil, stirring occasionally. Add peppers and reduce heat to medium. Cook until the oil floats to the surface. Adjust seasoning and transfer to a serving dish. Serve with biryani or with plain rice.

*Cook's Note: If you have sensitive skin, it is important to use kitchen gloves when you are handling chilies of any kind.*

# Rumaali Roti

*Rumaali means handkerchief. This roti is supposed to be as thin as a handkerchief. Traditionally in India, these paper-thin rotis are cooked over a convex shaped pan, meant to be used especially for rumaali roti.*

Yield 20

*Dough*
- 4 ½ cups all-purpose flour
- ½ cup vegetable oil
- 1 egg, slightly beaten
- 2 tablespoons sugar
- 1 tablespoon salt
- 1 cup water

*Paste*
- ¼ cup melted ghee
- 4 tablespoons all-purpose flour

- extra flour for rolling
- extra oil for basting

In a bowl combine all the ingredients for the dough except water. Mix until it resembles bread crumbs. Add water and mix to form a pliable dough. If the dough seems sticky, add flour 1 tablespoon at a time. If the dough seems dry, add water 1 tablespoon at a time. Let the dough rest for ½ an hour.

Meanwhile, make the paste by mixing ghee with all-purpose flour.

To make the roti, divide dough into 24 balls. Work with 1 ball at a time. Keep the rest of the them covered to prevent drying. Roll out each ball into 3-inch round roti. Spread 1 teaspoon of paste onto one roti. Place the second roti on top of the first one to make a sandwich with the paste in the middle. Roll the sandwiched roti into 9 - 10 inch rounds.

Meanwhile, heat a griddle pan over medium high heat. When the griddle is hot, cook roti on both sides until dough turns white and acquires a few golden brown spots. Baste with a teaspoon of oil on both sides. Remove from the griddle and separate 2 rotis by pulling them apart (be careful not to burn your hands with the steam when you separate). Fold it 2 times to make a triangle. Cover them with a foil or kitchen towel to prevent from drying. Proceed with rest of the dough.

# BAGHARE BAINGAN (EGGPLANT/BRINJAL CURRY)

*This is a very popular vegetarian dish from Hyderabad. It is also popular with people who are traveling because of its long-lasting quality at room temperature.*

*Serves 6 - 8*

- ⅛ cup tamarind
- 1 cup hot water
- 2 tablespoons coriander seeds
- 2 tablespoons sesame seeds
- ½ teaspoon fenugreek seeds
- 1 teaspoon cumin seeds
- ⅛ cup + ⅓ cup vegetable oil, divided
- 2 cups chopped onion
- ¼ cup roasted peanuts

- 4 cloves garlic
- 1 teaspoon turmeric
- 1 teaspoon – 1 tablespoon cayenne
- 1 tablespoon paprika
- ¼ cup grated unsweetened dry coconut
- 1 teaspoon jaggery/brown sugar
- 1 tablespoon salt
- 2 pounds Indian or Japanese eggplants
- 10 - 20 fresh or dry curry leaves

Soak tamarind in 1 cup of water for ½ an hour. Using your fingers, mash the tamarind to release as much pulp as possible. Pass it through a fine mesh strainer to extract tamarind water. Discard the fibrous remains.

Dry roast coriander seeds, sesame seeds, fenugreek and cumin seeds in a small skillet over medium heat, while stirring and shaking the skillet until spices turn one shade darker. Once it cools, grind them into a powder using a spice grinder. Heat ⅛ cup of oil over medium high heat in a heavy bottomed pan. Add onions and fry until they are soft and translucent. Remove from the pan. Add ground spices along with peanuts, garlic, turmeric, cayenne, paprika, coconut, jaggery, salt, and tamarind water. Transfer contents to the grinder. Grind them into a fine masala paste.

Cut eggplant into 4 sections lengthwise, keeping the pieces intact at the bottom.

Heat ⅓ cup of oil in a large skillet over medium high heat. When the oil is hot, add the curry leaves. When they are crisp add eggplants in a single layer. Fry them, stirring occasionally until the eggplant is soft and wilted. Add masala paste. Cook for 10 minutes while stirring often. Add 1 cup of water and bring the sauce to a boil. Reduce heat to medium low and simmer until the sauce is thickened and oil floats to the surface. Season to taste. Serve with any roti or rice.

# DALCHA (LAMB LENTIL CURRY)

*Dalcha is another speciality of Hyderabad. It is basically cooked lentils, flavored with succulent marrow bones and a small amount of cubed meat. Traditionally, tamarind is used as a souring agent. Here I have replaced tamarind with sour green mango. Depending on the sourness of the mango, adjust the seasoning of the final dish with a little lime juice if necessary.*

*Serves 6 - 8*

- 1 ½ cups masoor dal (red split lentils)
- 6 cups water
- ½ teaspoon turmeric
- one green raw mango,
  peeled and cut around the pit into 1-inch pieces
- ¼ cup ghee or vegetable oil
- 1 cup chopped onion
- 1 ½ pounds lamb (marrow bones and meat pieces)
- 1 tablespoon ginger garlic paste
- 2 - 3 minced fresh green chilies, such as serrano
- 2 teaspoons salt
- 1 teaspoon turmeric
- 1 teaspoon cayenne
- 1 cup water
- 1 teaspoon garam masala powder

*Seasoning*

- ⅛ cup ghee or vegetable oil
- 2 - 4 dry hot red chilies such as chile de arbol
- 1 teaspoon mustard seeds
- 1 teaspoon cumin seeds
- ¼ teaspoon fenugreek seeds
- 4 cloves garlic, minced
- ¼ cup chopped onion
- 20 curry leaves

Wash dal with several changes of water. Boil the dal with 6 cups of water with turmeric in a large heavy bottomed stock-pot over medium high heat. Bring it to a boil and reduce heat to medium low. Simmer for an hour until lentils are almost cooked. Add green mango pieces and cook for another 15 - 20 minutes.

Prepare the meat while lentils are boiling. Heat ¼ cup oil in a pressure cooker over medium high heat. Add the onion and fry until it is soft and edges begin to brown. Add meat and fry until it is browned, while stirring often. Add ginger garlic paste and stir fry for a minute. Add chilies, salt, turmeric and cayenne. Fry everything together for few minutes. Add 1 cup of water to the meat mixture. Cover with the lid and cook at high pressure for a minute. Reduce heat to medium and cook for another 10 - 12 minutes. Turn off the heat. Let the pressure drop on its own.

Alternately, you can cook this meat on the stove-top over medium heat until the meat is tender while adding more water if necessary. This will take 1 - 1 ½ hours.

Stir in garam masala powder and cooked dal into meat mixture and simmer together for 10 - 15 minutes. Adjust the seasoning and transfer to serving dish.

To season, heat ghee or oil in a small sauce pan over medium high heat. When the oil is hot, add red chilies and mustard seeds, and cover until the spluttering subsides. Uncover, add cumin seeds and fenugreek seeds. Stir once and add garlic and onion. Fry until the onions are browned at the edges. Add curry leaves and fry until they are crisp. Pour the seasoning over the lentil meat mixture. Mix in just before serving.

*Cook's Note: Whole red chilies are added for flavor only and are not meant to be eaten.*

# ONION CHUTNEY

*Serves 6 - 8*

- 2 onions
- 1 ½ teaspoons salt
- 4 cups yogurt
- 2 sliced fresh green chilies, such as serrano

Cut the onions in the middle lengthwise. Slice them thinly and cut in the middle. Transfer these sliced onions to a colander. Sprinkle with 1 teaspoon of salt. Let it rest for 15 - 20 minutes. When it's ready, squeeze as much water as possible from the onions. Add onions to yogurt along with sliced chilies and ½ teaspoon salt. Mix everything together. Serve with biryani.

# DOUBLE KA MEETHA (INDIAN BREAD PUDDING)

*This is an Indian version of bread pudding.  This dish is flavored with exotic spices such as saffron and cardamom.*

*Serves 4-6*

- 1 cup saffon-cardamom syrup (page 308)
- 1 pound any rich egg bread, sliced
- ½ cup ghee
- 4 cups half and half
- ½ cup sliced almonds

Trim off the crust from all the slices of bread.  Cut each slice diagonally to make 2 triangles.  Brush all the slices with ghee on both sides.  Heat a griddle over medium heat and fry all the slices until golden brown on both sides.

Meanwhile, heat half and half in a medium saucepan, over medium heat and bring it to a simmer.  Brush one 13 X 9 inch pan or two 9-inch round pans with ghee.  Arrange bread slices in a single layer.  First pour the syrup evenly over the bread.  Pour half and half over it  and let the bread slices soak in the sugar syrup and half and half for ½ an hour.

Preheat oven to 350º F.

Heat leftover ghee in a small frying pan over medium heat.  Add sliced almonds and fry until light brown.  Sprinkle almonds along with ghee on top of the bread slices and bake for ½ an hour.

# PUDINA TEA (MINT TEA)

*It is a tradition of the Hyderabadi Muslim community to drink Pudina tea after every meal. This tea is not only light and refreshing but also acts as a digestive aid after heavy meals such as biryani.*

Serves 2

- 2 cups water
- ⅛ cup chopped fresh mint leaves
- ½-inch piece ginger, sliced
- 1 teaspoon tea leaves
- honey or sugar to taste

In a small saucepan, bring water, mint leaves and sliced ginger to a boil over medium high heat. Boil for 2 minutes and add tea leaves and turn off the heat. Cover the pan and let it steep for 2 - 3 minutes. Strain through a tea strainer into serving cups. Serve with sugar or honey.

*Detail: The aarathi plate shown above is an integral part of Indian culture. It signifies an auspicious beginning to all special moments.*

# GUJARAT

Gujarat is the land of Lord Krishna and Mahatma Gandhi with its history dating back to 2000 B.C. The name Gujarat originates from "Gujjar Rashtra", the Gujjars being members of a migrant tribe who came around the time when the Huns invaded India in the 5th century.

Gujarat is known for its many festivals and fairs. These celebrations usually revolve around the changing of seasons, a new harvest, or a religious event drawn from the mythological traditions of Hinduism. Song, dance and drama are an integral part of all these celebrations.

According to Hindu mythology, Lord Krishna spent his childhood days dancing and playing the flute, much to the enjoyment of the villagers of Gokul. It is said that after he became the king of Dwarka, he promoted folk dance and music throughout his kingdom. The Gujaratis are the bearers of a great tradition of folk dance and music which they have preserved very well.

Three of the most popular forms of dance performed in Gujarat are Raas, Dandia-Raas and Garba. The Raas involves the dancers making measured steps in a circle while others sing and play instruments. The Dandia-Raas, or stick dance, involves hitting dandia sticks together while dancing in circles. Garba is a dance for women, where they dance around a garbo or earthenware pot, filled with water. A betel nut, silver coin and coconut are placed within the pot. The dancers perform around the pot while a singer sings the melodies and a drummer provides the beat.

A majority of Gujaratis are strict vegetarians with the exception of the Muslim and Parsi communities that have settled in Gujarat. Their food is based on grains, beans and vegetables and is usually not very spicy. What sets the Gujarati cuisine apart from the rest of India is their combination of sugar with salt in many recipes.

# Farsan and Mistan

*Farsan are savory snacks and Mistan are sweet dishes. Gujaratis excel in the art of making snacks.*

# DHOKLA

*Dhoklas are savory, steam-cooked cake pieces that are a signature dish of Gujarat. Dhoklas can be served as an appetizer accompanied by cilantro chutney, or they can be served as a part of a meal. Advanced preparation is needed to make dhoklas. Dhoklas are made in a dhokla maker, available at Indian supermarkets.*

*Serves 4 - 6*
- 1 cup chena dal
- ¼ cup white urad dal
- 2 tablespoons long grain rice
- 1 ¼ cup yogurt
- 1 teaspoon salt
- 1 tablespoon finely minced ginger
- 1 minced fresh green chili, such as serrano
- ½ teaspoon turmeric
- ½ tablespoon lime juice
- 1 tablespoon vegetable oil
- 1 teaspoon sugar (optional)
- 1 ½ teaspoons ENO* fruit salt or ¾ teaspoons of each baking soda and citric acid

*Seasoning*
- 2 tablespoons oil
- ¼ teaspoon asafoetida
- 1 teaspoon black mustard seeds
- 1 - 2 fresh green chilies, such as serrano, cut lengthwise into four
- 10 curry leaves
- freshly grated coconut for garnish
- fresh cilantro leaves for garnish

Wash both dals and rice with several changes of water. Soak them overnight with enough water to cover 2 inches above the surface. When ready, drain the dal mixture and transfer to a grinder. Add yogurt and grind into a grainy paste, stopping in between and pushing with a wooden spoon. Transfer the batter to a bowl. Cover with the lid and let it ferment overnight at room temperature. When you are ready to make dhoklas, add salt, ginger, chilies, turmeric, lime juice, vegetable oil and sugar (if you are using) and mix in.

Meanwhile, add enough water to cover 1 inch above the bottom of a pot, large enough to hold a dhokla maker and boil over medium high temperature. Prepare the dhokla pans by greasing the pans or spraying them with nonstick cooking spray. Add ENO fruit salt (or baking soda and citric acid) to the batter and mix well. As soon as you mix in the ENO, the batter will become foamy. Add batter to the dhokla pans until it is ⅔ full. Cover and steam for about 10 - 15 minutes until a wooden skewer inserted in the middle comes out clean. Remove from the heat and let it rest for 5 minutes.

Meanwhile to prepare the seasoning, heat oil in a small saucepan over medium heat. Add asafetida and black mustard seeds and cover until the spluttering subsides. Uncover and add green chilies. Fry for 1 minute. Add curry leaves. When curry leaves are crisp, spread the seasoning over the dhokla cakes. Cut the cakes into diamond shapes and transfer to a serving platter. Garnish with grated coconut and cilantro leaves. Serve with cilantro chutney.

*Cook's Note:*
*1. * ENO is the brand name for an antacid, available at Indian stores. It is commonly known as fruit salt, composed of baking soda and citric acid. ENO, however is widely used ingredient to fluff up the steam cakes such as Dhokla.*
*2. Dhokla batter can be stored in the refrigerator for 2 - 3 days.*
*3. Whole green chillies are added for flavor and not for eating.*

# KACHORI

*These bite-sized snacks have a flaky crust and a delectable filling inside. The kachori exemplifies the typical characteristics of Gujarati cuisine, which specializes in mixing salt and sugar. These can be fried at low temperature to ensure the flakiness of the crust. Kachoris can be stored at room temperature for up to a week and are best served warm.*

*Yield 24*

*Crust*
- 2 cups all-purpose flour
- ½ cup fine-grain semolina
- 1 tablespoon chickpea flour/besan
- 1 teaspoon salt
- ¼ teaspoon black pepper
- ¼ cup vegetable oil
- 1 tablespoon lemon juice
- ½ cup water

- oil for deep frying

*Filling*
- ½ cup green split peas, soaked overnight
- 16 ounces frozen green peas
- 1 - 3 green chilies such as serrano, cut into pieces
- ¼ cup fresh ginger pieces
- ¼ cup vegetable oil
- ⅛ teaspoon asafoetida
- 1 tablespoon fennel seeds
- 1 ½ tablespoons amchoor powder
- ½ tablespoon garam masala powder
- ¼ teaspoon clove powder
- ¼ teaspoon cinnamon
- 1 ½ tablespoons sugar
- ½ tablespoon cayenne
- 1 tablespoon coriander powder
- ½ teaspoon turmeric
- 1 teaspoon salt
- ½ cup finely chopped cilantro leaves

In a bowl, mix all-purpose flour, semolina, besan, salt and black pepper. Add oil and lemon juice. Using your fingers, work until oil and lemon juice are incorporated into the flour mixture. Add water and knead to make stiff dough. If the dough feels dry, add 1 tablespoon of water at a time and knead. If the dough feels sticky, add 1 tablespoon of flour and knead into the dough.

Alternately, you can also make this dough in the food processor. Fit the metal blade in the work bowl. Add flour, semolina, besan, salt and black pepper. Pulse a few times to mix everything together. Add oil and lemon juice and pulse a few times to incorporate into the flour mixture. While the motor is running, add water 1 tablespoon at a time to make stiff dough. The dough should feel firm without sticking to your hands.

Transfer the dough to a bowl and cover with plastic wrap. Let it rest for an hour at room temperature.

Mix in soaked split peas, frozen peas, chilies and ginger pieces together in a bowl. Using a food processor fitted with a metal blade process 1 or 2 cups of peas mixture to a paste. This paste does not have to be very fine. Repeat with the rest of the mixture.

Heat oil in a nonstick wok or skillet over medium high heat. When the oil is hot, add asafoetida and fennel seeds. When the fennel seeds sizzle, add the peas paste and cook while stirring often with a wooden spoon until the paste does not stick to the spoon any more. The mixture should not be dry but it should have the consistency of a dough. This takes about 25 - 30 minutes. Add the rest of the powders and stir fry for 2 minutes. Turn off the stove and let it cool. Stir in cilantro leaves. Divide the filling into 24 portions and roll each portion into a ball.

Both the dough and filling can be made a day ahead. When you are ready to make kachoris, pinch off a tablespoon of dough and roll into 2 ½-inch circle. Place 1 portion of filling in the middle. Gather the edges and cover the filling with the dough by slowly stretching and covering the filling. Pinch off the extra dough and seal the dough tightly around the filling. Use wet fingers to moisten the edges to seal, if necessary. Make it into a smooth round ball. Repeat the process with the rest of the dough and filling.

Pour the oil in a wok or a deep fryer until it is ⅓ full (oil should be 2 - 3 inches deep). Heat oil to 325º F. Add few kachoris at a time and fry until golden brown.

Serve warm or at room temperature with tamarind/sweet chutney.

# KHAJOOR GUJIA

*Most Gujaratis are devotees of Lord Krishna, who is one of the many Hindu Gods. This dish is a prasad offering during Krishna Janmastami (Lord Krishna's birthday) in late August. These bite size pastries are perfect to serve with afternoon tea.*

### Yield 48
### Crust

- 2 cups all-purpose flour
- ¼ teaspoon salt
- ¼ cup ghee or vegetable oil
- ⅓ cup + 2 tablespoon water
- extra flour for rolling

### Filling

- 1 cup chopped dates
- ½ cup sweetened coconut flakes
- ½ cup mixed nuts, such as cashews, almonds and pistachios, finely chopped
- ½ cup sugar
- ½ teaspoon green cardamom seed powder
- vegetable oil to deep fry

Sift flour and salt into a bowl. With your fingers, rub oil into the flour mixture until it resembles bread crumbs. Add water, 1 tablespoon at a time, to make firm, pliable dough. The dough should not stick to your hands. Cover the dough with plastic wrap and let it rest for an hour. This will allow the gluten to develop.

Meanwhile, mix all the ingredients for the filling and set aside.

Divide the dough into 4 quarters and each quarter into 12 pieces. Shape each piece into a ball. Roll out each ball into 2½ – 3 inch circles. Take each circle. Moisten edges of the circle with water. Place 1 tablespoon of filling onto one ½ of the circle. Fold the other half over the filling to make a half-circle. Press the edges with your finger to seal. Crimp the edges using the back of your fork. Repeat with the rest.

Heat oil in a wok or a deep fryer to 325º F. It is important to fry these pastries at a lower temperature to ensure the crispness of the shell. Add pastries to the wok without crowding and fry until pastries turn light golden while turning occasionally. Remove from the oil with a slotted spoon and cool and store them in an airtight container for up to a week.

# MATHRI

*Mathri is a flaky, savory pastry usually eaten with a hot cup of tea in the afternoon or munched at any time of the day.  It is important to fry mathris at a low temperature to cook evenly.*

*Yield 48*

- 2 cups + 2 tablespoons flour, divided
- ¼ cup fine-grain semolina
- 1 teaspoon salt
- 1 teaspoon coarsely ground ajwain
- 1 teaspoon coarsely ground black pepper
- ⅓ cup vegetable oil
- ½ cup water
- 2 tablespoons ghee
- oil for deep frying

Fit the metal blade in the food processor bowl and  add 2 cups of all-purpose flour, semolina, salt, ajwain and black pepper.  Process for few seconds to mix all the ingredients.  Add oil in a thin stream while the motor is running.  Now the flour mixture resembles bread crumbs.  Add water in a thin stream through feed tube while the motor is running.  Process until inside of the bowl is clean and the dough gathers into a firm, pliable ball.  Transfer dough to a bowl.  Cover with plastic wrap and let it rest for ½ an hour.

Alternately, you can make the dough manually.  Stir all the dry ingredients (2 cups flour, semolina, salt, ajwain and black pepper) together in a bowl.  Rub oil into the flour mixture till it resembles bread crumbs.  Add water, 1 tablespoon at a time to make pliable dough.  Transfer dough to a work surface.  Knead 5 - 10 minutes.  Let the dough rest for an hour.

Meanwhile, prepare the flour paste by mixing 2 tablespoons all-purpose flour with 2 tablespoons ghee and set aside.

Divide the dough into 4 quarters.  Take each piece of dough and roll it into 8 x 12 inch rectangle and spread ¼ of the flour paste onto rolled dough.  Starting at the long end, roll into a 12-inch log.  Cut each log into 12 pieces.  Using a rolling pin, gently roll out each piece until they are 2-inches long.

Fill a wok or heavy bottomed saucepan with oil until it is ⅓ full.  The oil should be 2 - 3 inches deep.  Heat oil over medium heat to 300 - 325º F on a frying thermometer or when you drop a small piece of dough, it should rise to the surface after 15 seconds.  Add as many pieces as the wok can hold comfortably without crowding.  Fry while turning as needed until they turn a light golden color evenly.  Remove with a slotted spoon and drain on paper towels.  Cool completely.  Store in an airtight container for up to 1 month.

# SAMOSA

*These triangular, savory pastries are one of the most popular snack items in India. Samosas are sold in every street market and snack shop all over North India. In the west, samosas have become popular through Indian restaurants. The filling for samosas differ from region to region. The most popular filling for samosas is made with potato. They are usually served with cilantro and/or tamarind chutney.*

*Yield 32*

### Crust
- 2 cups all-purpose flour
- ½ teaspoon salt
- ¼ cup vegetable oil
- ⅓ cup + 2 tablespoons water

### Filling
- 1 ½ pounds potatoes, preferably red
- 1 tablespoon + 1 teaspoon salt, divided
- 2 tablespoons vegetable oil
- 1 teaspoon cumin seeds
- 1 tablespoon minced fresh ginger
- 1 minced fresh green chili, such as serrano
- 1 tablespoon coriander powder
- ½ - 1 teaspoon cayenne
- 1 teaspoon garam masala powder
- 1 teaspoon amchoor powder

### Flour - glue
- 3 tablespoons all-purpose flour.
- 3 tablespoons water

- oil for deep frying

Sift all-purpose flour and salt into the bowl. Add oil to the flour mixture and mix with your fingers until the flour mixture resembles bread crumbs. Gradually add water 1 tablespoon at a time to make pliable dough. Transfer dough to work surface and knead for 5 - 10 minutes. Cover the dough with plastic wrap and let it rest for ½ an hour.

Meanwhile, prepare the filling. Place the potatoes and 1 tablespoon of salt in a large stockpot. Add enough water to cover 2 inches above the potatoes and boil them over medium high heat until tender enough to be easily pierced with a skewer. Drain them in a colander. When they are cool enough to handle, peel and cut them into half inch pieces.

Heat oil in a wok or nonstick skillet over medium high heat. Add cumin seeds. When cumin seeds sizzle, add ginger and chili and sauté for a minute. Add the rest of the spices along with 1 teaspoon of salt and stir for another minute. Add the potatoes and stir until the potatoes are covered with the spices. Cook for another 3 - 5 minutes while stirring occasionally. Remove from the heat. Let it cool before using to make samosas.

To make the flour-glue, mix 3 tablespoons of flour with 3 tablespoons of water.

Divide the dough into 16 equal parts. Roll out each piece to 5 - 6 inch circle. Cut each circle in the middle to make 2 semi-circles. Pick up one half of the straight edge and moisten the outer edge with the flour-glue. Bring the dry half of the straight edge and overlap ¼-inch onto moistened edge to make a cone. Press along the straight edges to seal. Pinch the point of the cone to seal. To fill, hold the cone between your thumb and forefinger, pointed side down. Fill the cone with 2 tablespoons of filling. Moisten inside edge of the cone with the flour-glue. Press and pinch together to seal.

Fill a wok or heavy bottomed saucepan with oil until it is ⅓ full. The oil should be 2 - 3 inches deep. Heat oil to 350º F on a deep frying thermometer or until a dough added to the hot oil rises to the surface after a few seconds. Gently add samosas to the hot oil as many as the wok can hold comfortably without crowding. Fry them while turning over with a slotted spoon until golden brown. Transfer samosas to a tray lined with a paper towel. Serve with cilantro chutney and/or tamarind/ sweet chutney.

# SHRIKHAND

*This is a very traditional dessert from the state of Gujarat. You can use low fat yogurt for a healthier version. Avoid using non-fat yogurt. You will be surprised to see how simple yogurt can transform into an elegant dessert.*

*Serves 6 - 8*
- 1 recipe strained yogurt (page 307)
- 1 teaspoon loosely packed saffron threads
- ½ cup hot milk, preferably whole milk
- 1 cup confectioner's sugar
- ½ teaspoon green cardamom seed powder
- ½ cup raw pistachio nuts, coarsely chopped

Prepare strained yogurt.

In a small skillet over low flame, fry for a few seconds saffron threads until they become a shade darker. Crumble saffron over hot milk and let it steep for ½ an hour.

Transfer the strained yogurt to a bowl. Add sugar, saffron milk and cardamom powder. Mix thoroughly with a whisk. Transfer to individual serving bowls. Garnish with chopped pistachio nuts. Chill and serve.

# Masala Chai

*The Gujarati community is known for flavoring their tea with various spices. Like every recipe in India, everyone has their own favorite blend of spices. These are the commonly used spices. Experiment with different combinations to suit your palate.*

*Serves 4*
- 1-inch cinnamon stick
- 5 - 6 cloves
- 3 - 4 green cardamom pods
- 5 - 6 black pepper corns
- 2 slices ginger
- 4 cups water
- ½ cup milk
- 1 tablespoon Indian black tea leaves, unflavored
- sugar or honey to taste

Using a mortar and pestle, slightly crush cinnamon stick, cloves, cardamom pods and black pepper corns. Transfer spices to a medium saucepan. Stir in ginger, water and milk. Bring it to a boil over medium high heat. Reduce heat and simmer for another 2 minutes for all the spices to steep. Add tea leaves and close with a lid. Turn off the heat and let it steep for 3 minutes. Strain tea through a tea strainer or a mesh strainer into tea cups. Serve hot with sugar or honey.

# PUNJAB

The word "Punjab" is derived from the Sanskrit word "panch", meaning five and the Arabic word "aab", meaning water. "Punjab" literally means five waters (rivers). It is the region where the Indus Valley Civilization flourished over 5000 years ago. This is also believed to be the land of the Mahabharata. This great epic of India, dated approximately from the 5th to the 7th century B.C, contains rich details of this land and its people. Over the millennia, many powers from the Northwest - the Persians, the Greeks, the Arabs, the Mongols – invaded Punjab enroute to the proverbial riches of India. Some stayed and ruled for a while when others were forced to leave. All left their mark in one form or the other. As a result, Punjab is heir to a remarkably composite culture most exemplified by the religion of the Sikhs. In the 15th century, a revolutionary saint, Guru Nanak launched a movement against gender inequality, ritualism, superstitions, and the caste system. This was the beginning of Sikhism that was to eventually become the dominant religion in Punjab.

In our time, the word Punjab brings to mind the exuberance and vitality of the Bhangra dance, and its elegant cuisine comprising mouthwatering ingredients.

Bhangra is the prominent folk dance of this region and in its traditional setting, is performed during the harvest season. The lyrics are a tribute to the rich, cultural traditions of Punjab as well as to the struggles of its people in their long, turbulent history. Many different Punjabi instruments contribute to the sounds of Bhangra. The music centers around the heavy beat of the double-barrel drum called the dhol, accompanied by the flute and string instruments. The costumes sport beautiful, vibrant colors for both men and women. Traditionally, the men wear a lungi, a colorful piece of cloth worn around the waist, and a kurta, a long, stylish shirt over which is worn an equally stylish half vest. They cover their heads with bold-colored turbans. The typical women's dress is the salvar kameez, a long colorful shirt with baggy pants in vibrant colors. The dupatta, a flowing, colorful scarf wrapped around the neck adds flair to a woman's dress. Today, as a result of the global Punjabi influence, Bhangra has evolved from a folk dance of the region to a popular style of music and dance that people perform for all occasions such as weddings, receptions and parties in various parts of the world.

When it comes to its cuisine for the most part, Punjab is a wheat-eating region. Rice is cooked on special occasions and is always seasoned with either jeera (cumin) or fried onions. A specialty of the region is kheer made with rice, sugar and milk cooked together on very slow fire for hours. Also indigenous to the region are the tandoors, clay ovens that can be heated to very high temperatures. The breads are placed on the inner walls of the oven to be cooked rapidly. Marinated meats are skewered and dropped in the middle of the oven for optimum cooking. Punjab's great contribution to the culinary world includes the naan, tandoori chicken, the roti and shish kabobs.

# Punjabi Khaana

*Punjabi Khaana means "the food of Punjab".*

# CHICKEN TIKKA

*Serves 6*
- 2 pounds boneless skinless chicken breast meat

*Marinade*
- 1 tablespoon lime juice
- ½ teaspoon salt or to taste
- 1 teaspoon cayenne
- ½ cup strained yogurt (page 307)
- 2 tablespoons cream

- 1 tablespoon ginger garlic paste
- 1 teaspoon garam masala powder
- ½ tablespoon paprika
- few drops red food color

- metal or bamboo skewers
- 2 tablespoons ghee for basting

Cut chicken into 2-inch cubes. Mix all the ingredients for the marinade. Add chicken cubes to the marinade and mix thoroughly to make sure all the pieces are coated completely. Cover with plastic wrap and marinate in the refrigerator for 4 - 12 hours.

If you are using bamboo skewers, make sure to soak them in water for ½ an hour. Preheat oven to 375º F. Thread chicken pieces onto the skewers. Place them on a baking sheet lined with a metal rack. Transfer them to the oven and roast for 20 - 25 minutes.

As soon as you remove pieces from the oven, baste them with ghee. Serve with lime wedges.

# Dal Makhani

*Serves 6*

- 1 cup whole urad dal
- ¼ cup chena dal
- ⅛ cup kidney beans
- 2 teaspoons salt
- ⅛ cup minced fresh ginger
- 2 tomatoes, chopped and pureed in blender

*Seasoning*
- 4 tablespoons vegetable oil
- ⅛ teaspoon asafoetida
- 1 onion, finely chopped
- 2 minced fresh green chilies, such as serrano
- 1 teaspoon cumin powder
- 1 tablespoon coriander powder
- 1 teaspoon kashmiri chili powder or paprika
- 1 teaspoon turmeric
- 1 teaspoon amchoor powder

- ¼ cup plain yogurt
- ¼ cup butter
- ½ teaspoon garam masala powder
- ½ tablespoon paprika

Soak both dals and beans overnight with 6 - 8 cups of water. Wash and drain dals and beans and transfer them to a pressure cooker with 3 - 4 cups of water. Add salt, minced ginger, and pureed tomatoes. Close with the lid and cook over high heat. Once it reaches high pressure, cook for 2 minutes. Reduce heat to medium and cook for another 30 minutes. Turn off the heat and let the pressure drop on its own. It takes about 15 minutes. Open the lid and see if the beans are soft and creamy. If not, add 1 - 2 cups of water and cook over medium heat while stirring occasionally until beans are soft and creamy. Alternately the dal can be cooked over medium heat in a large saucepan stirring occasionally until beans and dal are soft and creamy. It will take 1 - 2 hours.

Heat oil in a small saucepan over medium high heat. Add asafoetida. After a few seconds, add onions. Sauté onions until edges begin to brown. Add minced chilies, cumin powder, coriander powder, chili powder, turmeric, and amchoor powder. Fry for a minute and add to cooked dal. Keep cooking the dal over medium low heat. Add yogurt 1 tablespoon at a time, making sure the 1st tablespoon is absorbed into the dal before adding the next (this is to prevent curdling). Cook dal until thick and creamy. Stir in butter. Transfer to a serving dish. Garnish with garam masala powder and paprika.

# KHEEMA KOFTA

*This is a fool-proof recipe from my friend Shobha Kumar.*

**Yield 18 - 20**

**Koftas**
- 1 pound ground lamb
- 1 tablespoon ginger garlic paste
- 1 – 4 minced fresh green chilies, such as serrano
- 1 egg
- ¼ cup plain bread crumbs
- 1 tablespoon minced cilantro
- 1 teaspoon salt
- 1 teaspoon garam masala powder
- 15 - 20 pieces of cashew nuts

**Gravy**
- ¼ cup vegetable oil
- 2 cups finely chopped onion
- 1 tablespoon ginger garlic paste
- 1 tablespoon coriander powder
- 1 teaspoon cayenne
- 1 tablespoon kashmiri chili powder or paprika
- ½ teaspoon turmeric
- 3 - 4 tomatoes, blanched, peeled (page 298), finely chopped
- 4 cups hot water
- 1 teaspoon salt
- 2 tablespoons cashew paste (page 303)
- ½ teaspoon garam masala powder
- 1 tablespoon chopped mint

Mix all the ingredients together for koftas except cashew nuts. Moisten your clean hands and divide the meat into 18 – 20 portions. Shape each portion into kofta ball with a piece of cashew nut in the middle. Keep aside until gravy is ready.

To make the gravy, heat oil over medium high heat in a large skillet. Sauté onion until edges begin to brown. Add ginger garlic paste, coriander powder, cayenne, kashmiri chili powder, and turmeric and fry for a couple of minutes. Add tomatoes and fry until they become soft. Add hot water and salt. When the gravy comes to a boil, gently drop koftas in a single layer. Cover and reduce heat to medium, simmer until koftas are cooked. Add little more water if necessary. At the end, stir in cashew paste and garam masala powder and heat through. Garnish with mint and serve with rice or parathas.

# Gobi Shalgam Gajar Ka Achar
## (Pickled Cauliflower, Turnips and Carrots)

*This is a very authentic Punjabi pickle. Unlike South Indian pickles, vegetables are parboiled first and marinated with sugar, vinegar, and spices. The sugar and vinegar keep vegetables crunchy and the spices make them pungent.*

- 8 cups water
- ¼ cup + 1 ½ tablespoons salt, divided
- 1 head cauliflower, cut into florets
- 5 - 6 carrots peeled and cut into 3 x 1 inch pieces
- 3 - 4 turnips peeled and cut into 3 x 1 inch pieces
- ½ cup mustard oil or vegetable oil
- 10 - 12 cloves

- 2-inch stick cinnamon
- 2 - 3 bay leaves
- 2 tablespoons ginger garlic paste
- 1 cup malt vinegar or apple cider vinegar
- ½ cup packed jaggery or light brown sugar
- ½ cup coarsely ground black mustard seeds
- ¼ cup kashmiri chili powder or paprika
- 1 - 2 tablespoons cayenne

In a large saucepan, bring 8 cups of water to boil with ¼ cup of salt over medium high heat. Blanch all 3 vegetables separately for 1 minute in boiling water. Using a slotted spoon, remove from the water. Spread them on a large tray or cookie sheet. Do not overcook the vegetables. They should be firm to keep the achar crunchy.

Heat oil in a saucepan over medium high heat. Add cloves, cinnamon stick, and bay leaves and fry for a couple of minutes. Add ginger garlic paste and stir fry for about 1 - 2 minutes until a nice aroma arises. Add vinegar, jaggery or brown sugar, 1 ½ tablespoons salt, mustard seed powder, kashmiri chili powder, and cayenne. Cook only until sugar dissolves. Turn off the heat and let the marinade come to room temperature. Once it reaches room temperature, add vegetables, stir together, and transfer to any wide mouth ceramic or glass container. Cover the container with muslin or 3 - 4 layers of cheesecloth and secure with a rubber band. Leave it in the Sun for 2 - 3 days (bring it inside in the evening). Every day before leaving it in the sun, open the jar and stir with a clean spoon. It stays fresh in the refrigerator for one month.

# PALAK PANEER

*Serves 6*

- 1 recipe fried paneer pieces (page 304)

- 1 pound spinach, finely chopped
- ⅓ cup vegetable oil
- 1 bay leaf
- 1 teaspoon cumin seeds
- 1 large red onion, finely chopped
- 2 tablespoons ginger garlic paste
- 1 tablespoon coriander powder
- 1 teaspoon cayenne
- 1 teaspoon turmeric
- 1 teaspoon amchoor powder (dry mango powder)

- 1 teaspoon fennel seed powder
- 1½ teaspoons salt
- 1 tomato, finely chopped
- ½ cup tomato puree
- 1 teaspoon sugar
- 1 tablespoon milk

*Seasoning:*
- ½ tablespoon ghee
- ¼ teaspoon garam masala powder

- 2 tablespoons chopped cilantro

Have paneer ready, set aside until ready to use. Blanch half of chopped spinach in boiling water for 1 minute and grind into puree in the blender.

Heat ⅓ cup of oil in a medium sauce pan over medium high heat. Add bay leaf and cumin seeds. When cumin seeds sizzle, add onion and sauté until translucent. Add ginger garlic paste and fry for a minute. Add coriander powder, cayenne, turmeric, amchoor powder, and fennel seed powder. Fry all the spices with the onions for 1 - 2 minutes. Add chopped tomato and tomato puree. Add salt and cook for about 5 minutes until tomato is soft and some of the moisture evaporates. Add both pureed and chopped spinach. Cook for 10 minutes, stirring occasionally. Stir in sugar and milk. Add fried paneer pieces to cooked spinach and heat through.

To season, heat half a tablespoon of ghee, in a small skillet over medium heat. Add ¼ teaspoon of garam masala powder to hot ghee. Add seasoning to the cooked spinach. Garnish with cilantro and serve.

## PUNJABI KADHI

*Kadhi chaval (yogurt curry and rice) is an ultimate comfort food from Punjab. Traditional kadhi does not use curry leaves or green chilies. Being a South Indian, I like my kadhi with curry leaves and minced green chilies. You can avoid them completely if you choose to.*

*Serves 6*

*Pakoras*

*These are chickpea flour fritters which are called pakodas in South India. You can eat them plain with cilantro chutney or simmer them in kadhi. They are delicious either way.*

- ¾ cup chickpea flour/besan
- ¼ cup minced onion
- ¼ cup grated potato
- 1 teaspoon minced fresh ginger
- 1 teaspoon minced fresh green chili, such as serrano

- ¼ teaspoon baking soda
- ½ teaspoon salt
- ¼ teaspoon garam masala powder

- oil for deep frying

Sift chickpea flour/besan into a bowl. Add rest of the ingredients and mix thoroughly. Fill wok or heavy bottom sauce pan with oil until it is ⅓ full. Oil should be 2 - 3 inches deep. Heat oil over medium high heat to 350º F. Using a spoon or your fingers, gently drop the batter 1 tablespoon at a time into the hot oil. Add as many pakoras as the pan can hold comfortably in a single layer without crowding them. Turn pakoras from time to time to ensure even frying. Fry until all the pakoras are golden brown. Remove them with a slotted spoon. Proceed with rest of the batter. Reserve until kadhi is ready.

*Kadhi*

- 3 cups yogurt
- 3 cups water
- ½ cup chickpea flour/besan
- 2 tablespoons vegetable oil
- 2 - 3 dry whole red chilies, such as chile de arbol
- ⅛ teaspoon asafoetida
- 1 teaspoon black mustard seeds
- 1 teaspoon cumin seeds

- 1 teaspoon fennel seeds
- 1 teaspoon coriander seeds (slightly crushed)
- 10 curry leaves, fresh or dry
- 1 tablespoon ginger, minced
- 1 minced fresh green chili, such as serrano
- ½ teaspoon turmeric
- ½ teaspoon paprika
- 1 ½ teaspoons salt

Place yogurt, water, and chickpea flour in a blender, process until smooth.

Heat oil in a large saucepan over medium high heat. When the oil is hot, add red chilies and asafoetida. When the chilies turn darker, add mustard seed and cover the saucepan until the splattering subsides. Uncover, and add cumin seeds, fennel seeds, and coriander seeds. As soon as cumin seeds sizzle, add curry leaves, minced ginger, and green chili. Stir fry for a minute. Add turmeric, paprika, and salt. Stir to combine. Slowly add yogurt mixture while stirring constantly. Continue to stir until it boils. Reduce heat to medium low and simmer uncovered for 10 - 15 minutes. Add pakoras and simmer for 5 - 10 minutes more. Serve with plain basmati rice.

# MOOLI KA PARATHA (DAIKON RADISH PARATHA)

*Yield 8*

*Stuffing*

- 2 cups grated daikon radish
- 1 teaspoon salt
- ½ cup grated carrots
- 1 teaspoon dry mint leaves
- ½ teaspoon ajwain
- 1 teaspoon coriander powder
- 1 teaspoon black pepper
- 1 teaspoon anardhana (pomegranate seed powder)
- 1 tablespoon minced fresh ginger
- 1 tablespoon minced fresh green chilies, such as serrano

*Dough*

- 2 cups chappati flour (atta)
- ½ teaspoon salt
- 2 tablespoons vegetable oil or ghee
- ¾ cup water or squeezed out water from radish mixed with enough water to make ¾ cup liquid

- extra flour for rolling
- ¼ cup oil for basting

To make the stuffing, sprinkle salt over the grated radish and let it sweat for 15 - 20 minutes. Using a cheese cloth, squeeze out as much water as you can. Reserve squeezed out liquid to make the dough. Mix in radish with the rest of the ingredients for the stuffing.

To make the dough, mix flour, salt, and oil or ghee in a bowl until oil or ghee mixes evenly into the flour. Add ¾ cup of liquid to the flour mixture. Knead until you have soft, pliable dough. If dough feels dry, add 1 tablespoon of water at a time. If dough looks sticky, add 1 tablespoon of flour at a time until you have soft, pliable dough that does not stick to your fingers. Transfer dough to a work surface. Knead for 3 - 5 minutes. Cover the dough with plastic wrap. Let it rest for ½ an hour allowing the gluten to develop.

To roll, divide the dough into 8 balls. While working with one ball of dough, make sure to cover the rest with plastic wrap to prevent drying. Take one ball of dough and roll it into a 5 - 6 inch circle. Place 2 tablespoons of stuffing in the middle. Gather edges together and pinch them to seal and make a ball again. Flatten the ball into 2 - 3 inch disc. Using extra flour to dust, roll out each disc into 7 - 8 inch circles. Sometimes, due to extra moisture in the stuffing, the paratha develops a hole, it will squirt liquid while rolling. If it happens, dust with extra flour over the hole and roll.

Heat a griddle on top of the stove over medium high heat. When the griddle is hot, place stuffed paratha and cook until it acquires a few brown spots. It takes about a minute or so. Flip to the other side. Cook until other side also covers with brown spots and baste with oil on each side. Remove from the griddle. Wrap in kitchen towel and proceed with the rest of the parathas.

# JEERA RICE

*Jeera means cumin. This rice is flavored with cumin seeds.*

*Serve 6 - 8*

- ¼ cup ghee
- 1 tablespoon cumin seeds
- 1 cinnamon stick
- 2 bay leaves

- 2 cups basmati rice
- 3 ¾ cups water
- 2 teaspoons salt

Heat ghee over medium high heat in large, heavy-bottomed saucepan. Add cumin seeds, cinnamon stick and bay leaves. Heat until cumin seeds sizzle. Stir in rice and mix until all the grains of rice are coated with ghee. Add water and salt and bring it to a boil. Reduce heat to the lowest setting. Cover with the lid and cook for about 20 - 25 minutes until rice is cooked and surface is covered with steam holes. Let it rest for 5 - 10 minutes. Fluff up the rice before serving.

# RED ONION, CUCUMBER & TOMATO SALAD

*Serve 6 - 8*

- 1 medium red onion, finely sliced into rings
- ½ teaspoon salt
- 2 - 4 tomatoes, sliced
- 1 English cucumber, peeled and sliced

- ½ teaspoon roasted cumin powder
- ¼ teaspoon cayenne
- 1 - 2 tablespoons lime or lemon juice
- salt and black pepper to taste

Sprinkle salt over onion. Allow it to drain in strainer or colander for 10 minutes. Rinse under cold water and dry with a paper towel. Arrange tomato slices on a platter. Top with a layer of cucumber and then a layer of onion. Sprinkle with cumin powder and cayenne. Drizzle with lime or lemon juice. Season with salt and black pepper to taste.

# Stuffed Okra

*Serves 6*

- 1 pound okra

*Stuffing*
- 1 tablespoon coriander powder
- 1 teaspoon amchoor powder (dry mango powder)
- 1 teaspoon cumin powder
- 1 teaspoon dry ginger powder
- ½ teaspoon turmeric
- 2 tablespoons chickpea flour/besan

- ¼ teaspoon funnel seed powder
- 1 tablespoon vegetable oil
- ½ teaspoon garam masala powder
- ¼ - ½ teaspoon cayenne
- ½ teaspoon black pepper
- 1 teaspoon salt

*Seasoning*
- 3 tablespoons vegetable oil
- 1 teaspoon cumin seeds
- pinch of asafoetida
- ¼ teaspoon garam masala powder to garnish

In a small bowl, mix together all the ingredients for the stuffing. Rinse okra and dry with a paper towel and trim the cone part. Using a sharp paring knife, make a long slit, leaving ¼-inch top and bottom. Make sure you don't cut through the okra. With your thumb, open the slit and stuff 1 teaspoon of stuffing.

To season, heat 3 tablespoons of oil in a large shallow nonstick skillet, over medium high heat. When oil is hot, add cumin seeds with a pinch of asafoetida. As soon as the cumin seeds sizzle, add okra in a single layer. Reduce heat to medium. Cook uncovered, turning okra gently from time to time, until lightly browned. It takes about 15 - 20 minutes. Garnish with garam masala powder. Serve with any Punjabi meal.

# SALT LASSI

*Lassi is a cool refreshing drink that is popular all over India, especially during summer.*

*Serves 4*
- **2 cups yogurt**
- **½- 1 teaspoons salt**
- **1 ¼ cups water**
- **½ teaspoon roasted cumin powder**

Add yogurt, salt and water to a blender. Blend for few seconds. Pour it into glasses. Garnish with cumin powder and serve.

# KHEER

*Kheer is the primary dessert, not only in Punjab, but at most Indian wedding banquets and restaurant buffets. The base for this dessert is rice and milk, simmered on the stove-top at medium low heat while stirring often to prevent scorching. Garnish with nuts and dried fruits.*

*Serves 6*

- 1 cup basmati rice
- ½ teaspoon saffron
- 12 cups + ½ cup (hot) whole milk
- one 14 ounce can sweetened condensed milk
- ½ cup sugar

- ½ cup slivered almonds
- ½ teaspoon green cardamom seed powder

*Garnishing*
- 4 tablespoons ghee
- ½ cup slivered almonds
- ¼ cup golden raisins

Soak basmati rice in 2 cups of water for 2 hours.
In a small skillet over low flame, fry saffron threads for a few seconds until they become a shade darker. Crumble saffron over ½ cup of hot milk and let it steep for ½ an hour.

In a large, heavy-bottomed shallow pan, bring milk to a boil at medium high heat. Add rice and reduce heat to medium low. While simmering, stir and scrape the sides down occasionally to prevent from burning. Cook until milk is reduced to half. This takes about 2 hours. Add condensed milk, sugar, almonds, saffron-infused milk, and cardamom powder. Cook for another 10 minutes while stirring occasionally.

Transfer to a serving bowl and let it cool. Refrigerate up to 4 hours before serving. Serve in an individual dessert bowl, topped with 1 tablespoon garnish.

Garnish: Heat ghee in a small pan. Add almonds and raisins. Fry until almonds are golden brown and raisins are plump. Use to garnish the kheer.

**Cook's Note:** *Avoid using non-stick pan to make this dish. If you do, the milk will tend to form a brown layer at the bottom of the pan. While you are stirring the kheer, the brown layer breaks off from the bottom and mixes with the kheer and ruins the taste as well as the appearance.*

*Traditional designs called rangolis are drawn around the house with different colored powders to welcome guests during Deepawali.*

India, a land of many religions and languages, is well known for the numerous fairs and festivals that have colored and animated this hallowed land for centuries. These are occasions for celebration, both private and collective, and as with the rest of the Indian culture, they are a unique blend of tradition with novelty, myth with history, and of the sublime with the profane.

These festivals have evolved over the long and colorful history of India. Some are observed throughout the country while others are associated with specific regions. As in any old civilization many of these festivals, such as Deepawali and Navratri, have religious associations while others, such as Sankranthi, mark the important times of the year in the life of a farmer. Each festival has its own unique significance and its own traditions.

Sankranthi, also known as Pongal, is mainly a South India harvest festival that is celebrated with high spirits and joyfulness, particularly by the farmers in the villages of Andhra Pradesh and Tamil Nadu.

Navratri is the festival of goddess worship, celebrated over nine nights ending with Dussehra. It is popular throughout India in various forms and is celebrated with distinct color, opulence, and majesty among Hindu families in the region of Tamil Nadu.

Deepawali, also known as Diwali is the festival of lights. It is popular all over India and is celebrated by Indians living throughout the world. Festivals play many roles. The rituals provide a connection with the past and strengthen our identity. It is thus that the Gayatri hymn, composed in the Vedic era thousands of years ago, is still the most commonly recited mantra in Hindu households. Likewise, festivals are very important for the community. They reinforce the commonly cherished values of interdependence, love, mutual sharing, and respect for others. From a social point of view, if these festivals appear to be a riot of conformity, taken altogether, they are also a recurring affirmation of diversity. Most of all, though, festivals and fairs in India are an expression of the people's irrepressible spirit for the enjoyment of life.

*Navratri Kolu*

# NAVRATRI

Navratri which means nine nights, is one of the most celebrated festivals of India. According to Hindu mythology, the Asura, the demon king Mahishasuran, prayed to the Almighty for power. He asked for a special boon, a wish that only the Almighty could bestow. The Almighty granted his boon, rendering him immortal to all humans and living beings other than women. Mahishasuran, with his newfound powers, wreaked havoc upon all human beings on earth. Believing himself to be immortal, he did not consider any woman to be powerful enough to kill him.

As the sufferings of the human race increased, the people prayed to Sakthi in hopes of relief. Sakthi, the consort of Lord Shiva, took the form of Durga, a composite symbol of holy and divine forces, and challenged the demon Mahishasuran. The epic fight between Durga and the demon Mahishasuran lasted for nine days and nights, ending with Durga eventually vanquishing her foe. This is the legend of Navratri. The festival of Navratri celebrates the victory of the forces of good, namely Durga, against the treachery of evil, lasting the same nine days when the battle took place. The festival is concluded on the tenth day, Vijayadasami, with a special puja or prayer.

It is also a social and cultural festival in Tamilnadu. During this time, idols of Hindu gods, goddesses and mythological characters are arranged on a step-like setting (with an odd number of steps) called kolu, which means "display". Kolu is the essence and spirit of Navratri in the Hindu families of Tamilnadu. The themes featured are scenes from epic stories like Mahabharat, Ramayan or the landscape of a village or a garden. Park scenes and temple models can be seen on the floor on the sides and front of the steps.

It is a tradition for a bride to receive dolls known as "Marapachi Bommai" from her parents during the wedding. From the day the married girl receives her first marapachi bommai, she starts collecting dolls for her own kolu.

On this occasion, all friends, relatives and neighbors are invited to view and enjoy the kolu. Each day, a dish of delicious, mouth-watering sundal, which consists of cooked pulses seasoned with mustard seeds, curry leaves and freshly grated coconut, is prepared as an offering to God. In the evening, when people come to see the kolu, the host offers Thambulam, a welcoming gift consisting of betel leaves, areka nuts, turmeric, kumkum (red powder that Hindu women use to make a dot on their forehead), flowers and fruit. The Thambulam is offered with the sundal and traditional sweets. Offering Thambulam is an integral part of kolu.

# Navratri Thambulam

*Tambulam is a welcoming gift offered to guests by the hostess. It usually consists of betel leaves, areca nuts, flowers, and fruits . Depending on the occasion, thambulam can be elaborate or simple.*

# PULIYODARAI (TAMARIND RICE)

*Every state in South India has its own variety of tamarind rice. This recipe is from Tamil Nadu, and is a popular dish with all the festivals and auspicious occasions.*

*Serve 4 - 6*

- 1 recipe plain rice (page 305)

*Tamarind Paste*
- ¼ cup tamarind
- ¾ cup hot water, divided
- 1 teaspoon turmeric
- 1 tablespoon salt

*Masala Powder*
- ½ tablespoon vegetable oil
- 2 tablespoons coriander seeds
- 2 dry whole red chilies, such as chile de arbol
- ½ teaspoon pepper corn
- 1 teaspoon cumin seeds
- ¼ teaspoon fenugreek seeds
- 1 tablespoon chena dal
- 1 teaspoon white urad dal
- 1 tablespoon sesame seeds
- 2 tablespoons grated dry coconut

*Seasoning*
- ⅓ cup vegetable oil
- ⅛ teaspoon asafoetida
- 3 - 5 dry whole red chilies, such as chile de arbol
- 2 teaspoons black mustard seeds
- 1 teaspoon white urad dal
- 1 tablespoon chena dal
- ¼ cup raw peanuts with skin on
- 20 curry leaves, fresh or dried

Prepare rice using only 3 ½ cups of water and set aside until ready to use.

To make tamarind paste, soak tamarind in ½ a cup of hot water for an hour. Using your fingers, mash tamarind to release as much pulp as possible. Pour the mixture into a mesh sieve set over a bowl. Extract as much pulp as possible by pushing it through the sieve. Transfer fibrous remains to the bowl and add rest of the hot water. When it is cool enough to handle, mash with your fingers again to extract any remaining pulp. Pour the mixture through the sieve again. Discard fibers left in the sieve.

Transfer all the pulp into a small saucepan. Add turmeric and salt. Cook over medium heat for 7 - 8 minutes until sauce is thick. Remove from the heat and set aside.

To make masala powder, heat ½ tablespoon of oil in a small frying pan over medium high heat. When the oil is hot, add coriander seeds, red chilies, pepper corns, cumin seeds, fenugreek seeds, chena dal, and urad dal. Fry until urad dal is light golden brown, while stirring often. Set aside to cool. Meanwhile, dry roast sesame seeds and the coconut over medium high heat for 2 minutes and add to the rest of the spices to cool. Transfer all the spices to the spice grinder and grind into a fine powder and set aside until ready to use.

To season, heat oil in a small saucepan over medium high heat. Add asafoetida and red chilies. As the chilies turn darker add mustard seeds and cover until the spluttering subsides. Stir in urad dal, chena dal and peanuts. When dals and nuts are golden brown, add the curry leaves. As soon as they are crisp, add this seasoning to the tamarind paste along with masala powder and stir to combine. Now add this mixture to the cooked rice and mix everything together. Let it rest for ½ hour, taste and adjust the seasoning. Transfer to a serving dish and serve at room temperature.

*Cook's Note: Whole red chilies are added for flavor only and are not meant to be eaten.*

# SUNDAL

*This is another signature dish for prasad offering to God during the Navratri season. Traditional sundal is made with kaala chena. Kaala chena is a variety of beans similar to garbanzo beans. They are smaller in size and have dark brown skin. Kaala chena is as common in the South as garbanzo beans are in the North.*

*Serves 4 - 6*

- 1 cup kaala chena (black chickpeas)
- 1 teaspoon salt
- 2 tablespoons vegetable oil
- ⅛ teaspoon asafoetida
- 1 dry whole red chili, such as chile de arbol
- 1 teaspoon black mustard seeds
- 1 tablespoon chena dal
- 1 teaspoon white urad dal
- 1 teaspoon minced fresh ginger
- 1 teaspoon minced fresh green chilies, such as serrano
- 20 fresh or dry curry leaves
- ½ cup freshly grated coconut

Place kaala chena and 1 teaspoon of salt with 4 cups of water in a saucepan over medium high heat. Bring it to a boil, reduce heat to medium and simmer until the chickpeas are cooked and tender but not mushy. Add more water if necessary to cook. Drain cooked chickpeas into a colander. To season, heat oil in a wok or skillet over medium high heat. When the oil is hot, add asafoetida and red chili. When the chili turns darker, add mustard seeds and cover until the spluttering subsides. Uncover and add chena dal and urad dal. Fry until urad dal turns golden brown. Add ginger and green chili and fry for a minute longer. Add the curry leaves. As soon as they are crisp, add grated coconut and fry for 2 more minutes. Stir in cooked kaala chena and heat through. Check for the seasoning and add salt to taste. Transfer to a serving dish and serve.

# PURANPOLI (STUFFED SWEET POORIS)

*Yield 16*

*Dough*
- 1 cup all-purpose flour
- ⅛ teaspoon salt
- ¼ cup vegetable oil
- ⅓ cup cold milk

*Stuffing*
- 1 cup chena dal
- 4 cups water
- 2 tablespoons ghee
- ¾ cup grated packed jaggery or 1 ¼ cups light brown sugar
- 1 teaspoon green cardamom seed powder
- ¼ - ½ cup ghee for basting

To make the dough, stir in all-purpose flour and salt in a bowl. Add oil. Rub oil into the flour mixture with your fingers. Add milk and mix into flour mixture to make a soft pliable dough. Work with the dough for 2 - 3 minutes until the dough no longer sticks to your hands. Let the dough rest for 1 - 2 hours at room temperature.

Meanwhile, prepare the stuffing. Heat chena dal with 4 cups of water in a saucepan over medium high heat. Bring it to a boil, reduce heat to medium and simmer until dal is tender. Add more water if necessary. Cook until dal is completely cooked and almost all the moisture evaporates. Let it cool to room temperature. When it is ready, transfer dal to the food processor, process into a puree. Heat 2 tablespoons of ghee in a wok or skillet over medium high heat. When the ghee is hot, add pureed dal from the food processor and stir fry for 5 minutes. Add jaggery or brown sugar. Reduce heat to medium to medium high and cook for another 10 - 12 minutes while stirring often. Add cardamom powder and stir in. Let the stuffing cool to room temperature.

Divide the dough and stuffing into 16 portions. Take each portion of the stuffing and make them into balls. Work with one portion of the dough at a time. Spread the dough into 2 ½-inch round, in the palm of your hand. Place one ball in the middle. Wrap the dough around the ball by stretching it. Gather edges together and pinch them to seal. Flatten stuffed balls into 3-inch disks.

Take two 10 x 10 inch sheets of wax paper and place stuffed disk on one paper. Cover with another paper. Using a small rolling pan, gently roll into 5 - 6 inch round pooris.

Heat a griddle on the stove over medium heat. Gently peel off the wax paper and place the poori onto the hot griddle. When the bottom is cooked and dotted with golden brown spots, turn it over with a spatula and cook the other side until it is cooked and covered with golden brown spots. Before removing from the griddle, baste both sides of the poori with ½ teaspoon of ghee. Proceed with rest of the pooris the same way. You can store them at room temperature for 2 days or for 1 week in the refrigerator. Before serving, you can warm them on the griddle.

# Rava Kesari (Semolina Halwa)

*This dish is a popular prasad offering during ceremonial pujas, which is when one offers prayers to God.*

*Serves 6*

- 3 cups whole milk
- ¼ teaspoon loosely packed saffron
- ¾ cup ghee
- ¼ cup raw cashew nuts

- 1 cup medium-grain semolina
- 1 cup sugar
- 1 teaspoon green cardamom seed powder

Heat milk in a saucepan over medium high heat until it reaches its boiling point. Add saffron, and turn the heat to the lowest setting and keep the milk hot until ready to use.

Heat ghee in a nonstick skillet over medium heat. When the ghee is hot, add cashew nuts and fry until golden brown. Using a slotted spoon, remove cashews from hot ghee and transfer to a bowl and reserve. Add semolina to the same pan, stir fry until lightly golden brown. Stir in sugar and fry for a minute. Slowly add the milk while stirring constantly. Once the milk is added, cook for another 20 - 25 minutes, while stirring often until most of the moisture evaporates and starts pulling away from the sides and forms a big lump. Stir in nuts and cardamom powder. Transfer to a serving dish and serve.

# Deepawali

Deepawali is the combination of two Sanskrit words, "deep" meaning light and "awali" meaning rows. Thus, the name of this festival translates to rows of lights or festival of lights. Deepawali is considered to be the most well-known of all the Indian festivals. Deepawali is celebrated throughout India as well as in Indian communities all over the world. Celebrating Deepawali is as important to Hindus as Christmas is to Christians, and it usually takes place eighteen days after Navratri.

The ancient story of Deepawali evolved into a widely celebrated festival in India. Deepawali signifies different things to people across the country. In North India, Deepawali celebrates King Rama's return home to Ayodhya after his epic war with Ravana, the demon king of Lanka. In Gujarat, the festival honors Lakshmi, the goddess of wealth; and in Bengal, people worship Kali, the goddess of strength. Wherever it is celebrated, Deepawali universally signifies the renewal of life.

Traditional designs called rangolis are drawn in the house with different colored powders to welcome guests. Also, it is a practice in India to light small oil lamps (called diyas) and place them in and around the house, as well as on outer walls, verandahs and gardens. In celebrating the festivities, friends and families visit each other and exchange sweets.

The day ends with brilliant fireworks at each house which last for several hours illuminating the night skies. As children we always looked forward to this ceremony with so much anticipation. Deepawali is enthusiastically enjoyed by the people of all religions and its splendor and grandeur create an atmosphere of joy and festivity.

# Deepawali Vindu

*Vindu means "feast". Deepawali is celebrated all over India. Hence, the menu represents different parts of India.*

Drink:

Falooda (page 237)

Main Course:

Poori (page 232)

Potato Curry (page 232)

Grated Coconut Rice (page 234)

Dahi Vada (page 232)

Deepawali Sweets:

Carrot Halwa (page 234)

Ricotta Burfi (page 236)

Kajji Kaya (page 235)

# POORI

*Poori is one of my children's favorite breads. When they were young, they loved to watch the pooris puff up in hot oil.*

### Yield 16
- 1 cup chappati flour
- ¼ cup all-purpose flour
- ¼ cup fine-grain semolina
- ½ teaspoon salt
- 2 tablespoons vegetable oil
- ⅓ cup warm water
- extra flour for rolling
- oil for deep frying

In a bowl, combine chappati flour, all-purpose flour, semolina and salt. With your fingers, rub oil into the flour mixture. Add water 2 tablespoons at a time to make pliable dough that does not stick to your fingers. If the dough feels sticky, add flour 1 tablespoon at a time. If the dough feels dry, add water 1 tablespoon at a time. Cover the dough with plastic wrap and let it rest for an hour to allow the gluten to develop.

To make the pooris, divide the dough into 16 portions. Make each portion into a ball. Roll out each ball into 4 - 5 inch circles, dusting often with flour to prevent from sticking. Pour oil into a wok or a deep fryer until it is ⅓ full (the oil should be 2 - 3 inches deep). Heat oil over medium high heat until it reaches 360° F or until a piece of dough dropped into the hot oil can rise to the top in a couple of seconds. When the oil is ready, gently slide the poori into the oil. Within a few seconds, the poori will rise to the top. Gently push it down with the back of a slotted spatula. Keep the poori submerged in hot oil to puff up. When the poori is puffed and the underside is cooked (it takes about 5 - 10 seconds), turn it over and cook the other side. Cook for another 15 - 20 seconds. Remove poori from the hot oil using a slotted spatula onto a tray lined with a paper towel. Proceed with the rest of the pooris. Serve with potato curry or any curry with gravy.

# POTATO CURRY

### Serves 4 - 6
- 1 ½ pounds red potatoes
- 1 tablespoon + 1 teaspoon salt, divided
- 2 large tomatoes, chopped
- 2 tablespoons vegetable oil
- 2 teaspoons cumin seeds
- 10 fresh or dry curry leaves
- 1 tablespoon ginger garlic paste
- 1 tablespoon coriander powder
- ½ - 1 teaspoon cayenne
- ½ teaspoon turmeric

Place potatoes and 1 tablespoon of salt in a medium stock-pot. Add enough water to cover 2-inches above the potatoes. Boil them over medium high heat until tender enough to be easily pierced with a fork or skewer. Drain them into a colander. When they are cool enough to handle, peel and cut them into small pieces and set aside until ready to use.

Place tomatoes in the blender and grind them into puree and set aside.

Heat oil in a wok or nonstick skillet over medium high heat. When the oil is hot, add cumin seeds. As the cumin seeds sizzle, add the curry leaves. As soon as they are crisp, add ginger garlic paste and fry for a minute. Add coriander powder, cayenne, and turmeric powder. Stir fry for another couple of minutes. Add 1 teaspoon of salt and tomato puree. Cook for 5 minutes, while stirring occasionally. Reduce heat to medium and simmer for 5 minutes. Stir in potatoes and 1 cup of water. Simmer for another 15 - 20 minutes and serve with pooris.

# DAHI VADA
## (URAD DAL CROQUETTES IN YOGURT SAUCE)

*This is a typical North Indian dahi vada recipe. I must admit, while growing up, I have never eaten dahi vadas combined with sweet chutney. Unlike the North Indian recipe, South Indian dahi vadas are made with yogurt seasoned with ginger, green chilies, mustard seeds, fenugreek seeds, and curry leaves. Traditionally, these vadas are soaked in water first. The water is then squeezed out before adding it to the yogurt. I feel that the vadas lose their flavor when you soak them in water. I prefer to add the fried vadas directly to the yogurt mixture. However, if you prefer to soak vadas in water, do so.*

### Yield 20 - 24
- tamarind/sweet chutney (page 303)

### Vadas
- 1 cup white urad dal
- 1 teaspoon salt
- 1 teaspoon cumin seeds
- 3 - 4 tablespoons water
- ½ tablespoon minced fresh ginger
- ½ tablespoon minced fresh green chilies, such as serrano
- ¼ teaspoon baking soda

- oil for deep frying

### Yogurt Sauce
- 6 cups plain yogurt
- 2 teaspoons salt
- 2 cups milk

Prepare the tamarind/sweet chutney
Soak white urad dal overnight with enough water to cover 2 - 3 inches above the dal. When ready, wash dal with several changes of water and drain. Transfer to a blender along with one teaspoon of salt and cumin seeds. Using 3 - 4 tablespoons of water, grind into a smooth paste by stopping and pushing it down with a wooden spoon. Transfer the dough to a bowl and mix with ginger, chilies and baking soda.

Mix yogurt with 2 teaspoons of salt and milk, whisk to smoothen and set aside.

Pour oil into a wok or a deep fryer until it is ⅓ full (oil should be 2 - 3 inches deep). Heat oil to 350º F or until a tiny bit of dough dropped into hot oil can rise to the top in 10 - 15 seconds. I use 1 ½-inch ice cream scoop to drop dough into hot oil to make all vadas similar in size. Alternately, wet your fingers with water, pick up 2 tablespoons of batter with your fingers and gently drop into the oil. Add as many vadas as the wok can hold comfortably without crowding. Fry, turning and stirring with the slotted spoon until they are crisp and golden brown evenly. With a slotted spoon, transfer vadas to yogurt mixture directly. Proceed with the rest of the dough. Let vadas soak in yogurt mixture at room temperature for 1 hour. To serve, place 2 - 3 vadas with yogurt in an individual serving bowl. Drizzle with sweet chutney.

# GRATED COCONUT RICE

*This recipe is from Tamil Nadu. This is a popular item served during festivals.*

*Serves 4 - 6*

- 1 recipe plain rice (page 305)
- ⅓ cup vegetable oil
- 2 dry whole red chilies, such as chile de arbol
- 1 teaspoon black mustard seeds
- 1 tablespoon white urad dal
- 2 tablespoons chena dal
- ¼ cup raw cashew nuts
- 10 - 20 curry leaves
- 1 tablespoon minced fresh ginger
- 1 tablespoon minced fresh green chili, such as serrano
- 1 cup coarsely grated fresh coconut
- 2 teaspoons salt

Prepare the rice according to the directions and set aside. Heat oil in a wok over medium high heat. When the oil is hot, add red chilies. When chilies turn darker, add mustard seeds and cover until the spluttering subsides. Uncover and add white urad dal and chena dal. Stir fry until they turn golden brown. Stir in cashew nuts and curry leaves. As soon as the cashew nuts turn golden brown and the curry leaves are crisp, add minced ginger and green chili and fry for a couple of minutes. Add coconut and stir fry for 2 - 3 minutes. Stir in salt and rice. Mix everything together and heat through. Remove from the heat and transfer to a serving dish.

# CARROT HALWA

*This recipe is from Delhi, where carrot halwa is made with bright pink carrots.*

*Serves 4 - 6*

- ¼ cup ghee
- ¼ cup raw cashew nuts
- 6 cups grated carrots
- 1 cup sugar
- 2 cups grated khoa*
- 1 teaspoon green cardamom seed powder

*Garnishing*
- Two 4-inch squares silver leaves

Heat ghee in a wok or heavy bottomed saucepan over medium high heat. Add cashew nuts and fry until golden brown, while stirring constantly. Using a slotted spoon, remove the nuts and set aside for garnishing. Add carrots to the same pan. Cover and cook for another 5 - 7 minutes while stirring occasionally. Reduce heat to medium and add sugar. Fry until the sugar melts. Increase heat to medium high and stir in khoa. Cook for about five minutes until halwa is ready. Stir in cardamom powder and transfer to a serving bowl. Garnish with silver leaves and nuts and serve.

*Cook's Note: *Khoa is available at Indian stores.*

# KAJJI KAYA

*This recipe is from Andhra Pradesh. Even though there is an array of fillings used to make this dish, this is my favorite choice.*

### Yield 16

#### Crust

* 2 cups all-purpose flour
* ¼ cup vegetable oil or ghee
* ¼ teaspoon salt
* ⅓ cup water + 2 tablespoons water

#### Filling

* ¼ cup ghee
* 3 cups finely grated fresh coconut
* ¾ cup jaggery, grated and firmly packed
* 1 cup water
* 1 teaspoon green cardamom seed powder

* oil for deep frying

To make the crust, sift flour and salt into a medium bowl. Add oil. With your fingers, rub oil into the flour mixture till it resembles bread crumbs. Add water, 2 tablespoons at a time, to make a firm, pliable dough that does not stick to your fingers. Transfer the dough to the work surface and knead for 5 minutes. Cover the dough with plastic wrap and let it rest for an hour to allow the gluten to develop.

Meanwhile, prepare the filling. Heat ghee in a skillet over medium high heat. Add grated coconut and fry until golden brown, while stirring constantly for about 10 - 15 minutes. Add jaggery along with 1 cup of water. Cook while stirring occasionally until most of the moisture evaporates and forms a thick lump and the mixture starts becoming white and bubbly underneath. It takes about 10 - 12 minutes. Turn off the heat and stir in the cardamom powder. Let the filling come to room temperature.

Divide the dough and filling into 16 portions. Take 1 piece of dough and roll it into a 4 ½-inch circle. Moisten the edges of the circle with water. Place one portion of filling on to one half of the circle. Fold the other half over the filling. Press the edges with your fingers and then use back of the fork to seal and crimp or fold edges like a rope.

Pour oil into a wok or deep fryer until it is ⅓ full (the oil should be 2 - 3 inches deep). Heat oil until 325° F or until a piece of dough that is dropped into the hot oil can rise to the top in 15 - 20 seconds. When the oil is ready, add as many prepared kajji kayas as the wok can comfortably hold without crowding. Fry while turning and stirring as needed, until golden brown on both sides. Remove from the oil with the slotted spoon onto a tray lined with a paper towel. When they are cool, store in an airtight container for up to a week. Serve at room temperature.

# RICOTTA BURFI

*Yield 32 - 40 pieces*

- ½ cup butter
- one 32 ounce container ricotta cheese
- 1 cup instant nonfat dry milk
- one 14 ounce can sweetened condensed milk
- 1 teaspoon green cardamom seed powder
- 3 - 4 (4 inch) squares silver leaves

Melt butter in a small heavy bottomed shallow pan (avoid using nonstick pan) over medium high heat. Add ricotta cheese and cook for 5 minutes, while stirring often. Reduce heat to medium and cook for another 20 - 25 minutes until most of the moisture evaporates, while stirring occasionally. Stir in the milk powder and cook for another 5 minutes. Now the mixture should look dry. Add condensed milk and cook for about 20 - 25 minutes until the mixture pulls away from the sides. In the end, add cardamom powder and stir in. Transfer to a buttered sheet pan, spread it with a spatula and let it cool. When the burfi is cool, garnish with silver leaves and cut into diamond shapes. Alternately, when the mixture is lukewarm, press into individual molds to desired shapes and garnish with silver leaves. Store in the refrigerator for a month.

# FALOODA

*Serves 6*

- rose syrup (page 308)
- 2 tablespoons basil seeds
- 1 package dried falooda noodles or cellophane noodles*
- 4 cups whole milk
- 2 tablespoons sugar
- 1 cup crushed ice
- 1 pint good quality vanilla ice cream
- rose petals to garnish

Prepare the syrup and cool. Soak basil seeds in water for 1 - 2 hours to bloom. Soak noodles in warm water for 15 - 20 minutes. Drain the noodles, and chop them into 2 - 3 inch pieces and set aside.

To assemble, add 2 tablespoons of rose syrup to each of the 6 glasses. Add 2 - 3 teaspoons of basil seeds, topped with 2 tablespoons of noodles into each glass.

Add milk, sugar, crushed ice to the blender and process until frothy. Distribute milk mixture into all six glasses. Top with a scoop of ice cream. Garnish with rose petals and serve.

*Cook's Note: *Falooda noodles are available at Indian stores and cellophane noodles are available at Asian stores and at some supermarkets.*

*The muggu is a decorative pattern traced with lime powder that is usually drawn on the floor in front of the house. It is decorated with pumpkin flowers, kumkum and turmeric during Sankranthi season.*

# SANKRANTHI

*Detail: My grandmother Rajamma's prayer dishes take center stage, filled with marigolds during Sankranthi celebrations.*

Being from a farming family, I have the most cherished childhood memories of Sankranthi. This is a harvest festival celebrated in all Southern states of India and is the most important festival for farmers. It typically falls on the 14th or 15th day of January and is observed over a period of three days. During this festival, farmers not only celebrate the bountiful harvest but also thank Mother Nature for giving us the cycles of life.

The first day of Sankranthi is called Bhogi. On this day, homes are cleaned and decorated to prepare for the festival. Amongst the Hindu households in the villages, there is the tradition of making a muggu also known as kolam in other regions. The muggu is a decorative pattern traced with lime powder that is usually drawn on the floor in front of the house. It is decorated with pumpkin flowers, kumkum and turmeric powder. There is a great deal of good-natured rivalry as women compete with each other to show off their artistic talents in making the most elaborate and intricate designs of muggu. Doorways are decorated with torans of mango leaves and garlands of marigolds to welcome family and friends. Bonfires are lit at street corners and old household articles and agricultural waste are thrown into them in a ceremony symbolizing cleansing. Girls dance around the bonfire singing folk songs and thanking nature for providing ample grain. One of my husband's fondest memories of Sankranthi is that of him and his siblings making the biggest bonfire in his village.

The second day of the festival is called Pongal, and it is the most important day of the entire festival. Pongal means "boiled over". Freshly harvested rice is boiled with milk and sugar in new terra-cotta pots and is symbolically offered to the Sun God. This is the day for performing the puja, an act of ceremonial worship. Ariselu, traditional rice cakes, are served as part of a big traditional feast and are enjoyed by all the families. In the evening, men carry idols of Hindu Gods and Goddesses on a chariot in procession through the streets, stopping in front of every house and offering blessings.

The third day of the festival is called Kanuma, the festival of cattle. The cattle are washed and their faces and horns painted with an array of colors. Farmers hang multi-colored bead chains, tinkling bells and flower garlands around the neck of their cattle. They are then taken to the village center to parade. Cock fights are another tradition of this day. The joyful atmosphere and fun-filled events make it an exciting experience for all.

As with any other festival, delicious food is an integral part of Sankranthi. On the day of Kanuma, meat is eaten by Hindus who are not vegetarians. For Sankranthi, I follow my mother's traditional menu. These are the dishes I cook when I celebrate Sankranthi with my family and friends. For an ethnic touch, I like to set the table with banana leaves on a charger plate and incorporate traditional Indian fabrics and accessories into the table-scape.

# Sankranthi Bhojanam

*Sankranthi Bhojanam means Sankranthi meal. This is the traditional menu served in the country side in the state of Andhra Pradesh.*

Prasadam:

## Paramannam (page 251)

Bhojanam:

## Gaarelu (page 246)

## Andhra Chicken Kurma (page 242)

## Chikkudu Kaya Vepudu (page 244)

## Dappalum (page 245)

## Gongura Chutney (page 248)

## Nimmakaya Pulihora (page 249)

## Pappu (page 250)

## Plain Rice (page 305)

## Masala Majjiga (page 248)

Sweet:

## Poornam (page 250)

*Doorways are decorated with torans of mango leaves and garlands of marigolds to welcome family and friends, during the Sankranthi season.*

# ANDHRA CHICKEN KURMA

*While I was growing up in my village, all marriages were arranged by the parents. When a girl got married and left her home to live with her in-laws in a different town, the girl's parents longed to see her and her family. Even though they would visit from time to time, it was not often enough, owing to the poor transportation facilities. Whenever a daughter came home with her husband for a visit, the mother-in-law lovingly and affectionately made gaarelu and chicken kurma for a feast to welcome her daughter and son-in-law. As opposed to classic Moghul kormas, South Indians have their own version of kormas. Southern kormas are pronounced as kurma, usually made with coconut. Traditional Andhra chicken kurma is made with coconut and poppy seeds. In India, the poppy seeds are ground on a stone to make a paste. Unfortunately, most American blenders are not suitable for grinding poppy seeds unless you make it into a powder in a spice grinder and add it to the rest of the spices. Another option is to soak the poppy seeds in warm water for 1 hour and grind with coconut and chilies in a blender. This curry will be equally delicious even if you decide to leave out the poppy seeds.*

*Serves 6 - 8*

- 4 - 5 pounds, whole chicken, skin removed, cut into serving size pieces

*Coconut paste*
- ¾ cup grated fresh coconut
- 2 tablespoon white poppy seeds, soaked in warm water for 1 hour
- 2 - 4 chopped fresh green chilies, such as serrano

*Masala powder*
- 3 tablespoons coriander seeds
- 8 cloves
- 1-inch piece cinnamon stick
- ½ teaspoon green cardamom seeds

- ¼ cup vegetable oil
- 20 curry leaves
- 3 cups chopped onions
- 4 tablespoons ginger garlic paste
- ½ teaspoon turmeric
- 1 - 2 teaspoons cayenne
- 1 ½ teaspoons salt or to taste
- 1 tablespoon lime juice

To make the coconut paste, grind coconut, poppy seeds and green chilies with ¼ cup of water in a blender. Set aside until ready to use.

To make the masala powder, dry roast coriander seeds, cloves, cinnamon stick, and cardamom seeds, in a small skillet over medium heat about 3 - 4 minutes while stirring and shaking the skillet, until spices are one shade darker. When spices are cooled, transfer them to a spice grinder and grind into powder.

Heat oil in a large wide nonstick saucepan over medium high heat. When the oil is hot, add curry leaves. When the curry leaves are crisp add onions and fry until edges begin to brown. Stir in ginger garlic paste and stir fry for 1 minute. Add turmeric and cayenne and fry for another minute. Stir in coconut paste and fry for 2 - 3 minutes. Add masala powder and fry for about 3 - 4 minutes until all spices are fried until they release a nice aroma. Stir in the salt. Now add the chicken and fry for about 10 minutes until the chicken turns white, while stirring often without covering with the lid. Reduce heat to medium. Stir in 1 cup of water. Cover with the lid and cook for 30 - 35 minutes or until chicken is cooked, while stirring occasionally. Stir in lime juice and transfer to a serving dish. Serve with plain rice, gaarelu, dosa, or chappati.

# CHIKKUDU KAYA VEPUDU (BEANS FRY)

*Chikkudu kaya is a South Indian variety of green beans, available at Indian supermarkets. If they are not available, substitute with regular green beans.*

*Serves 6*

- 1 ¼ pounds chikkudu kaya
- 2 tablespoons vegetable oil
- 2 dry whole red chilies, such as chile de arbol
- 1 teaspoon black mustard seeds
- 1 teaspoon cumin seeds
- 1 teaspoon white urad dal
- 1 tablespoon chena dal

- 10 - 20 fresh or dry curry leaves
- 1 onion, chopped
- 2 tomatoes, chopped
- 1 teaspoon salt
- ¼ teaspoon turmeric powder
- ½ - 1 teaspoon cayenne

Wash and trim the ends of chikkudu kaya and remove any stringy fiber from the sides. Cut into 2-inch pieces. Heat oil in a wok or skillet over medium high heat. Add red chilies. When the red chilies turn darker, add mustard seeds and cover until the spluttering subsides. Uncover and add cumin seeds. When the cumin seeds sizzle, add white urad dal and chena dal. As soon as white urad dal turns golden, add curry leaves. As the curry leaves turn crisp, add onions and fry until edges begin to brown. Add tomatoes and cook until soft. As soon as the tomatoes soften, stir in chikkudu kaya, salt, turmeric and cayenne. Cover and reduce heat to medium and cook until the beans are tender and almost all the moisture evaporates, while stirring occasionally. Season to taste. Serve with plain rice.

*Cook's Note: Whole chilies are added for flavor only and are not meant to be eaten.*

# DAPPALUM (SWEET AND SOUR VEGETABLE STEW)

*You can make dappalum with any assortment of vegetables. My mother used to save one piece of vegetable in a basket everyday before she prepared vegetable curries. By the end of the week, she would have enough vegetables to make dappalum. This is a typical practice in the villages where women always save up for the rainy day.*

*Serves 6 - 8*

- 1 ½ pounds butternut squash, peeled, seeded, and cut into 1-inch pieces
- 2 pounds assorted vegetables such as Japanese or Indian eggplants, *drum sticks (fresh or frozen), bell peppers (seeded), opo squash ( peeled and seeded), and okra, cut into 1 ½-inch pieces.

- ¼ cup vegetable oil
- 2 - 3 dry whole red chilies, such as chili de arbol
- 1 teaspoon black mustard seeds
- ¼ teaspoon fenugreek seeds
- 10 - 20 fresh or dry curry leaves

- 1 large onion, cut into 1-inch chunks
- 1 - 3 fresh green chilies, such as serrano, cut lengthwise in two
- 2 medium tomatoes, chopped
- 2 - 2 ½ teaspoons salt or to taste
- ½ teaspoon turmeric
- 1 - 2 teaspoons cayenne
- 2 - 3 tablespoons tamarind paste (page 300)
- 2 cups water
- 1 teaspoon jaggery or brown sugar

Heat oil in a large saucepan over medium high heat. When the oil is hot, add red chilies. When the red chilies turn darker, add mustard seeds and cover until the spluttering subsides. Uncover and add fenugreek seeds. As soon as fenugreek seeds turn a shade darker, add curry leaves. When the curry leaves are crisp, add onions and green chilies. Sauté until onions are translucent and soft. Add the butternut squash and stir fry for 3 minutes. Add the tomatoes and cook until soft. Add rest of the vegetables, salt, turmeric and cayenne and fry for 5 - 7 minutes, while stirring occasionally. Add tamarind paste and stir in 2 cups of water. Cook until vegetables are tender and the sauce is thick. Stir in jaggery or brown sugar. Serve with white rice.

*Cook's Note: 1. Whole red chilies and green chilies are added for flavor only and are not meant to be eaten.*
*2. * To eat drumsticks, scrape the flesh with the teeth and discard the fibrous shell*

# GAARELU
## (URAD DAL VADA)

*We call these vadas "gaarelu" in my mother's house. This recipe is very traditional to the countryside. I don't remember any festival, celebration or auspicious occasion in my childhood without these gaarelu. The recipe has not changed much over centuries.*

*Traditionally, these are made by soaking urad dal with skin and removing the skin before grinding by washing several times. In this recipe, some of the flavor is lost when we use skinned white urad dal. To bring back the sweetness, I have included chena dal, although the traditional recipe does not include chena dal.*

### Yield 12

- 1 cup white urad dal
- ¼ cup chena dal
- 1 teaspoon salt
- ¼ teaspoon baking soda
- ½ cup finely chopped onion
- 1 tablespoon minced fresh ginger
- 1 minced fresh green chili, such as serrano
- 1 teaspoon cumin seeds, slightly crushed
- 10 fresh curry leaves, finely shredded

Wash both the dals with several changes of water. Soak the dals overnight in water by covering 2 inches above the surface. Drain the dal. Reserving ¼ cup of dal, transfer rest of the dal to food processor fitted with a metal blade. Add salt and baking soda. Process into a sticky paste by stopping and pushing it down with a spatula. It is important not to add any water to make crunchy vadas. At the end, add the rest of the soaked dal and pulse a few times. The idea is to keep a portion of the dal coarsely ground. Transfer to a bowl. Add onions, ginger, green chilies, cumin seeds and curry leaves. Mix into the batter. Divide the batter into 12 portions.

Pour oil into a wok until it is ⅓ full (oil should be 2 - 3 inches deep). Heat oil to 350º F or until a pinch of dough dropped into the oil rises to the top in 5 - 10 seconds. Meanwhile, have a small bowl of water ready to wet your fingers. Line the back of a dinner plate with plastic wrap or a quart size freezer bag. Wet the surface with a little water. Transfer one portion of the dough onto the plastic surface. Using your wet fingers, spread the dough into 3 ½-inch round. Using your forefinger, make a one inch hole in the middle. Dip your fingers in water. Gently lift plastic wrap to flip the doughnut shaped dough onto your forefingers. Immediately slide it into the hot oil carefully. Add as many as the wok can hold without crowding. Fry until bottom is golden brown. Use tongs to turn them to the other side. Remove them onto a tray once both sides are evenly golden brown. Serve them plain or with orange bell pepper chutney.

# GONGURA CHUTNEY

*Gongura is to Andhra Pradesh what dhokla is to Gujarat and tandoor is to Punjab. Gongura is often referred to as Andhra matha, which means mother of Andhra Pradesh. This chutney is known for its outrageously hot and sour flavor. This book would be incomplete if I do not mention gongura, my father's favorite leafy vegetable. Even though it is not very common, gongura leaves are available at Indian stores during summer. I grow these leaves in my kitchen garden during the summer and preserve them for the entire year in my freezer. It is a very versatile leafy vegetable. You can make dal, chutney and curry with gongura.*

### Serves 8 - 10
- 2 tablespoons + 2 teaspoons vegetable oil, divided
- 1 teaspoon fenugreek seeds
- 1 tablespoon black mustard seeds
- 1 tablespoon cumin seeds
- 12 - 15 dry whole red chilies, such as chile de arbol
- 1 pound gongura leaves, washed and dried
- 2 teaspoons salt or to taste

### Seasoning
- 1 tablespoon vegetable oil
- pinch of asafoetida
- 1 teaspoon black mustard seeds
- 1 teaspoon cumin seeds
- 1 teaspoon white urad dal
- 10 - 12 fresh curry leaves

Heat 1 teaspoon of oil in a skillet over medium heat. Add fenugreek seeds, mustard seeds and cumin seeds. Fry until all the spices turn one shade darker. When you fry these spices, the mustard seeds will splutter. Remove them and place in a bowl and set aside. Add another teaspoon of oil to the same pan. Add chilies and fry until 1 shade darker and let it cool.

Transfer all the spices and chilies to the spice grinder. Grind them into a powder.

Heat 2 tablespoons of oil in a medium skillet over medium high heat. Add gongura leaves. Fry until leaves are wilted and cooked. Add the spice powder and salt to the cooked gongura. Mix in thoroughly.

For seasoning, heat oil over medium high heat. Add asafoetida and mustard seeds and cover until the spluttering subsides. Uncover and add cumin seeds. As soon as the cumin seeds sizzle, add white urad dal. When the white urad dal turns golden, add curry leaves. When curry leaves are crisp, add this seasoning to the gongura chutney and mix thoroughly. Serve with generous portion of plain rice.

**Cook's Note: It is important to fry the spices in a well-ventilated space.**

# MASALA MAJJIGA (SPICY BUTTERMILK)

*Buttermilk and yogurt are consumed all over India in many forms. This drink is a speciality of Andhra Pradesh and is even served at weddings, especially during the hot summer.*

### Yield 6 cups
- 2 cups plain yogurt
- 4 cups water
- ½ teaspoon green chili paste or to taste
- ½ teaspoon dry ginger powder
- 2 teaspoons salt
- 10 - 12 fresh curry leaves, shredded
- 1 tablespoon lime juice

Whisk together yogurt and water. Stir in the rest of the ingredients. Season to taste. Serve in tall glasses.

# NIMMAKAYA PULIHORA

## (LEMON RICE)

*Lemon rice is a South Indian dish. It is made with limes as lemons are not available in the South. Limes are tarter in flavor than lemons. The tartness of limes balances the spicy chilies and ginger in this recipe. Mustard seeds add crunchiness and pungency to the dish. It is not only simple to make, but also looks colorful, grand, festive and good enough to serve at banquets. Lemon rice gets its bright and vibrant lemon color from turmeric, a spice widely used in Indian cooking.*

*It is a contemporary version of traditional pulihora (Andhra tamarind rice). Lemon rice is usually served at room temperature. Lime juice, ginger, chilies, and turmeric preserve this rice and keeps it from spoiling. It can be left at room temperature for a day, loosely covered. It is a popular choice for kid's school lunches, picnics and train journeys.*

*I like to garnish lemon rice with pomegranate seeds, which shimmer like fine jewels against the vibrant yellow colored bed of rice.*

- one recipe plain rice (page 305)
- ⅓ cup vegetable oil
- ⅛ teaspoon asafoetida
- 2 - 3 dry whole red chilies such as chile de arbol
- 1 tablespoon black mustard seeds
- 2 tablespoons chena dal
- 1 tablespoon white urad dal
- ½ cup raw cashew nuts
- 1-inch piece ginger, minced
- 1 - 3 minced fresh green chilies, such as serrano
- 20 fresh or dry curry leaves
- ½ teaspoon turmeric
- 2 ½ teaspoons salt
- ⅓ cup + 2 tablespoons lime juice
- pomegranate seeds to garnish (optional)

Prepare the rice according to the directions using only 3 ½ cups of water. Heat oil in a saucepan over medium high heat. Add asafoetida and red chilies. When the red chilies turn one shade darker, add the mustard seeds and cover until the spluttering subsides. Uncover and add white urad dal and chena dal. When the white urad dal turns golden brown, stir in the cashews. As soon as cashew nuts turn one shade darker, add curry leaves. As curry leaves turn crisp, add ginger, chilies, turmeric, and salt. Fry for one minute, and turn off the heat. Let it cool for 3 minutes and add lime juice. Now add lime juice mixture to cooked rice, and mix thoroughly. You must let the rice rest for at least ½ an hour for flavors to mingle before serving. Garnish with pomegranate seeds.

*Cook's Note: 1. If you taste the rice as soon as you make it, it tastes very lemony. But after it sits for ½ an hour, the rice absorbs the lime juice and the flavors mingle. Then you can adjust the seasoning if necessary.*
*2. Red chilies are added for flavor. They are not meant to be eaten.*

# POORNAM

*Poornam means "full moon". Since this dish looks like a round ball, it was named after the full moon.*

### Yield 16

**Coating**
- ¾ cup white urad dal
- ¾ cup long grain rice
- ½ teaspoon salt
- ⅔ cup water
- pinch of baking soda

**Filling**
- one recipe for stuffing from puranpoli (page 228)

Wash dal and rice with several changes of water. Add enough water to cover 2 - 3 inches above the surface and soak for 6 - 8 hours.

Meanwhile follow the directions for stuffing from the recipe for purunpoli, prepare the filling. Divide the filling into 16 portions and make them into round balls.

Drain the rice mixture and transfer it to a grinder. Add salt and grind into a fine paste using ⅔ cup of water. Transfer to a bowl, add a pinch of baking soda and mix in.

To make poornam, pour oil into a wok or deep fryer until it is ⅓ full. The oil must be 2 - 3 inches deep. Heat oil to 350º F or until a small amount of batter in the hot oil rises to the top immediately. Dip each prepared filling ball in the batter. Gently remove using a fork, making sure that the filling is completely covered with batter, and add it to the hot oil. Add as many balls as wok can hold without crowding. Fry while stirring and turning when necessary until golden brown. Using a slotted spoon, remove from the hot oil and place onto a tray lined with a paper towel. Serve warm or at room temperature.

# PAPPU

*Pappu in this menu acts as a joker piece in the card game. It can be mixed and eaten with paramannam, pulusu, chutney or eaten with plain rice and ghee.*

- 1 recipe cooked toor daal (page 309)
- 1 teaspoon salt or to taste

Follow the instructions for cooked toor dal and stir in salt.

# PARAMANNAM (SWEET RICE)

*Religious festivals dot the Indian calendar throughout the year. In the South, this sweet rice is a part of prasad offerings to God during festivals.*

- 1 cup long grain rice
- ¼ cup mung dal
- ¼ teaspoon salt
- 1 ¾ cups water
- 6 cups hot whole milk
- 1 cup grated, packed jaggery
- 1 teaspoon green cardamom seed powder
- ⅓ cup ghee
- ½ cup raw cashew nuts

Combine rice, dal, salt and water in a medium heavy bottomed saucepan (avoid using nonstick pan). Bring it to a boil over medium high heat. Stir once. Reduce heat to lowest setting, cover with the lid and simmer for 10 - 12 minutes or until almost all the water is absorbed.

Stir in milk and increase heat to medium high and bring it to a boil. Reduce heat to medium and simmer for 30 - 35 minutes or until rice is very soft, while stirring often. Stir in jaggery and cook for about 10 minutes until jaggery is thoroughly incorporated into the rice mixture. Stir in cardamom powder.

Meanwhile, in a small skillet, heat ghee over medium heat. Add cashews and fry until golden brown. Add fried cashews along with the ghee to the cooked rice and stir in. Serve warm.

*Detail: Using leaves as disposable plates is an age old tradition in India.*

# Holiday Entertaining

There is no other time of the year like the holiday season, when tradition and fashion go hand-in-hand. Even with all the commercialisation of holiday shopping, gift exchange, and the never ending busy schedules between Thanksgiving and New Year, people still make time to gather and share the holiday cheer with family and friends. Grandmothers' recipes, the fine china and silver and family traditions take center stage during this season.

There are some traditions that we want to follow, and some which we create uniquely to suit our own family needs. Whatever the reason behind these traditions, they give us a comforting sense of continuity in our lives and we look forward to experiencing them year after year.

When I came to America, there were some holidays I had never heard of, such as Thanksgiving, and others that I had never taken part in, such as Christmas. Today, my children cannot imagine life without either one of these celebrations. As an immigrant, it is important to hold on to our cultural heritage to give us strength and foundation for our future but it is equally important to embrace the surrounding culture and customs to keep us moving forward. In keeping with the tradition, roasting the turkey for Thanksgiving and decorating a tree for Christmas perpetuates the tradition. As a result, hosting an elaborate traditional Thanksgiving dinner and celebrating Christmas with glamour and splendor has become my repertoire. Thanksgiving and Christmas have become beloved and enduring traditions in my family. Holiday traditions are enriching when we share them with the people we love.

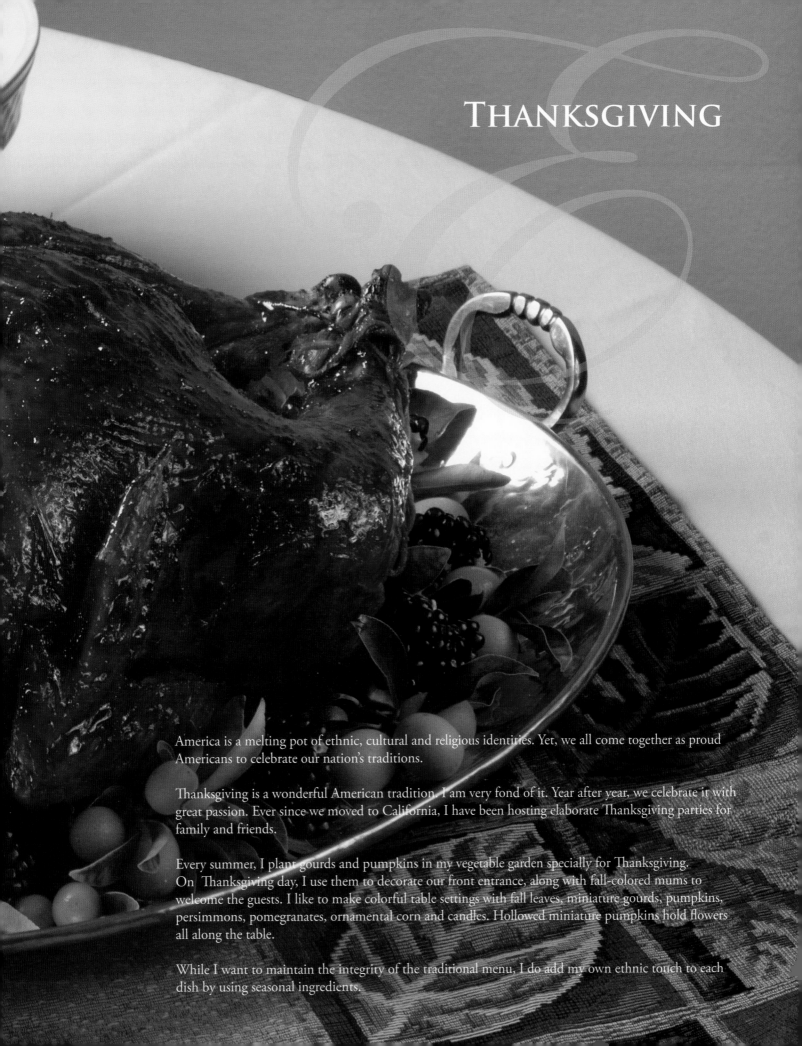

# THANKSGIVING

America is a melting pot of ethnic, cultural and religious identities. Yet, we all come together as proud Americans to celebrate our nation's traditions.

Thanksgiving is a wonderful American tradition. I am very fond of it. Year after year, we celebrate it with great passion. Ever since we moved to California, I have been hosting elaborate Thanksgiving parties for family and friends.

Every summer, I plant gourds and pumpkins in my vegetable garden specially for Thanksgiving. On Thanksgiving day, I use them to decorate our front entrance, along with fall-colored mums to welcome the guests. I like to make colorful table settings with fall leaves, miniature gourds, pumpkins, persimmons, pomegranates, ornamental corn and candles. Hollowed miniature pumpkins hold flowers all along the table.

While I want to maintain the integrity of the traditional menu, I do add my own ethnic touch to each dish by using seasonal ingredients.

# Thanksgiving Feast

Appetizer:

Kabocha Squash Coconut Soup (page 260)

Main Course:

Brine Roasted Turkey with
    Pomegranate Glaze (page 262)

Mashed Potatoes with Caramelized Onions (page 264)

Green Beans (page 264)

Creamed Corn (page 260)

Roasted Winter Vegetables (page 264)

Cranberry Sauce with Ginger (page 266)

Jeweled Rice with Dry Fruits and Nuts (page 265)

Assorted Breads

Dessert:

Persimmon Date Coconut Pudding (page 266)

# KABOCHA SQUASH COCONUT SOUP

*Serves 8*

- 3 pounds kabocha squash, quartered and seeded
- melted butter for brushing
- 6 cups milk, divided
- 2 tablespoons vegetable oil
- 20 fresh or dry curry leaves
- one 13.5 ounce can coconut milk
- ½ teaspoon cayenne
- ½ teaspoon dry ginger powder
- ½ teaspoon lightly packed saffron
- 2 teaspoons salt

*Garnish*

- fried curry leaves
- paprika

Preheat oven to 400° F. Brush the fleshy side of the squash with the melted butter. Set the squash on a sheet pan, flesh side up. Roast for 35 - 40 minutes or until the flesh is soft.

Scoop the flesh from the squash and puree it in the food processor using 2 cups of milk. Puree in batches if necessary.

Heat oil in a medium stock-pot over medium heat. When the oil is hot, add curry leaves. As soon as the curry leaves are crisp, add pureed squash along with coconut milk and rest of the milk. Bring it to a simmer. Stir in cayenne, ginger, saffron and salt. Continue to simmer for another 5 - 10 minutes. Season to taste. Ladle soup into the soup bowls, and garnish with curry leaves, and a sprinkling of paprika, and serve.

# CREAMED CORN

*Green chilies and fresh ginger jazz up the flavor of sweet cream corn.*
*Serves 8*

- ½ cup ghee
- 4 cups finely chopped onions
- 1 tablespoon minced fresh green chilies, such as serrano
- 1 tablespoon minced fresh ginger
- ¼ cup all-purpose flour
- ½ cup cornmeal
- 1 tablespoon salt
- 4 cups half and half
- 4 cups frozen corn
- 2 cups grated sharp cheddar cheese

Preheat oven to 400° F. Heat ghee in a heavy bottomed skillet over medium high heat. When the ghee is hot, add onions. Sauté for about 15 - 18 minutes until cooked and translucent. Add green chilies and ginger. Stir fry for 2 minutes. Stir in all-purpose flour, cornmeal and salt, fry for 2 more minutes. Add half and half and cook until thickened. Stir in corn and 1 cup cheddar cheese. Transfer whole corn mixture to 13 x 9 inch casserole dish. Sprinkle with the remaining cheese. Bake for 25 - 30 minutes and serve hot.

# Brine Roasted Turkey with Pomegranate Glaze

*Serves 8 - 10*

*Brine*
- 2 gallons water
- 1 cup light brown sugar
- 1 cup salt
- ⅛ cup crushed cloves
- ¼ cup crushed black pepper corn
- ¼ cup grated fresh ginger
- 6 bay leaves
- 6 dry whole red chilies, such as chile de arbol
- one 10 - 12 pound whole fresh turkey

- 4 cups turkey stock (recipe follows)
- pomegranate glaze (page 306)

*For the roasting pan:*
- 1 large onion, cut into chunks
- 2 carrots, cut into 2-inch pieces
- 2 stocks celery, cut into 2-inch pieces
- 2 bay leaves

*For the turkey:*
- ½ cup butter, softened
- 2 tablespoons masala spice blend (page 301)
- 1 yellow onion, cut into 1-inch pieces
- 2 carrots, cut into 1-inch pieces
- 1 stock celery, cut into 1-inch pieces
- 1 lemon, cut into quarters
- 2 sprigs thyme
- 3 bay leaves
- ¼ cup butter, melted
- gravy (recipe follows)

To make the brine solution, add sugar and salt to water in a large wide stock-pot (big enough to accommodate the turkey and the brine). Bring the water mixture to a boil over medium high heat until sugar and salt dissolve. Stir in the rest of the ingredients. Reduce heat to medium temperature and simmer for 5 minutes. Turn off the heat. Allow the solution to cool to room temperature.

Remove the neck and giblets from the turkey and reserve for the stock. Rinse turkey under the cold running water inside and outside. Set the turkey in the brine. Place a weight on top of the turkey to make sure the turkey is fully immersed in the brine. Soak turkey in the brine, covered, in the fridge for up to 24 hours.

Meanwhile prepare turkey stock and pomegranate glaze.

Preheat oven to 425º F with oven rack at the lowest position. In a shallow roasting pan, spread vegetables and place a metal rack on top of the vegetables. Add 1 cup of water to the roasting pan.

Remove turkey from the brine. Pat dry inside and outside with paper towels. Using your fingers, gently loosen the skin from the breast meat without tearing. Mix softened butter with masala spice blend to make compound butter. Rub the compound butter underneath the skin. Stuff the turkey cavity with onion, carrots, celery, lemon, thyme and bay leaves. Drizzle melted butter on top of the bird and rub all over the skin. Use kitchen twine to tie the legs together. Fold the neck skin under the body, fold the wing tips under the body or secure with small metal skewers. Place the turkey, breast side up, on the rack in a prepared roasting pan. Roast turkey uncovered in the oven for 15 minutes and reduce oven temperature to 325ºF. Baste the turkey every half an hour with ½ a cup of turkey stock or pan juices. If the turkey is browning too quickly, cover loosely with aluminum foil. Continue roasting until an instant meat thermometer registers 160ºF when inserted in the thickest part of the breast or thigh. It takes about 3 - 3½ hours of total roasting time. Transfer the turkey to a platter. Cover with aluminum foil for 15 minutes. After 15 minutes, start glazing the turkey with pomegranate glaze. Meanwhile, prepare the gravy.

## Turkey Stock

- 2 tablespoons vegetable oil
- giblets and neck from turkey, discard liver
- 1 bay leaf
- ½ cup chopped onion
- ½ cup chopped carrots
- ½ cup chopped celery
- ½ teaspoon pepper corns
- 1 teaspoon salt

Heat oil in a medium saucepan. When the oil is hot, add neck and giblets. Cook for about 8 - 10 minutes until browned evenly, while stirring occasionally. Add bay leaf, onion, carrots, celery, pepper corn and salt. Cook until vegetables are soft. Add enough water to cover 4 - 5 inches above and bring it to boil. Reduce heat and simmer for 1½ - 2 hours. Skim off any scum that rises to the surface. Strain the stock and discard the solids. Add enough water to make it 4 cups. *Cook's Note: You can make this stock for up to 2 days in advance.*

## Gravy

- pan juices from the roasting pan
- left over turkey stock
- water
- 2 tablespoons vegetable oil
- 4 tablespoons all-purpose flour
- salt and pepper to taste

Using a fine mesh sieve, strain the juices from the pan into 4 cup glass measuring cup. Skim off any visible fat from the top with a spoon. Add enough leftover turkey stock or water to make it 3 cups total volume. Add 1 cup of water to the roasting pan. Place it over 2 burners over medium high heat and scrape the bottom of the pan to release any remaining brown bits. Bring it to a boil. Reduce heat to medium and simmer for 10 minutes. Pour it through the mesh sieve into the glass measuring cup with pan juices and stock.

Heat oil in a medium saucepan over medium low heat and add flour. While stirring constantly with a wooden spoon, cook until light brown. It takes about 5 - 7 minutes. Add stock mixture in a stream while whisking constantly to prevent lumps. Increase heat to medium high and bring it to a boil, then reduce heat to simmer. Simmer for 5 minutes. Season with salt and pepper if necessary.

# MASHED POTATOES WITH CARAMELIZED ONIONS

*Serves 8*
- 1 recipe caramelized onions (page 308)
- 2 ½ pounds russet potatoes
- 1 tablespoon salt
- ¾ cup warm whipping cream
- salt and pepper to taste

Prepare caramelized onions according to the directions, and reserve the leftover oil.

Place potatoes with 1 tablespoon of salt in a large stock-pot. Add enough water to cover 2 - 3 inches above the potatoes. Boil them over medium high heat until tender enough to be easily pierced with a fork or skewer. When potatoes are ready, drain them into a colander. Once they are cool enough to handle, peel them. Using a potato ricer, or potato masher, mash the potatoes into the mixing bowl. Stir in warm cream while the potatoes are still warm. Season with salt and pepper. Stir with a wooden spoon to blend.

Transfer mashed potatoes to a serving bowl. Garnish with caramelized onions, and drizzle with reserved oil. Serve warm.

# GREEN BEANS

*Serves 8*
- 1 ½ pound green beans, ends trimmed and cut in the middle
- 1 ½ teaspoons salt, divided
- 2 tablespoons vegetable oil
- 2 dry whole red chilies, such as chile de arbol
- 1 teaspoon black mustard seeds
- 1 teaspoon cumin seeds
- 20 fresh curry leaves
- 1 teaspoon white urad dal
- 2 tablespoons chena dal
- ½ teaspoon cayenne

Boil 6 cups of water with 1 teaspoon salt in a medium stock-pot over medium high heat. Add green beans and boil for 3 minutes until the beans are tender but crisp. Strain the beans into a colander.

Heat oil in a skillet or wok over medium high heat. When the oil is hot, add red chilies. When red chilies turn darker, add mustard seeds and cover until the spluttering subsides. Uncover and add cumin seeds. When the cumin seeds start sizzling, add curry leaves, white urad dal, and chena dal. When white urad dal turns light golden brown, stir in cooked beans and fry for 2 - 4 minutes. Stir in ½ teaspoon salt and cayenne.

# ROASTED WINTER VEGETABLES

*Serves 8*
- 1 pound carrots, peeled and cut in half lengthwise and cut into 2-inch pieces
- 1 pound parsnips, peeled and cut lengthwise and cut into 2-inch pieces
- 1 pound sweet potatoes, peeled and cut into 2 x 1 inch pieces
- 1 pound butternut squash, peeled and cut into 2 x 1 inch pieces
- 4 tablespoons vegetable oil
- 1 ½ tablespoons masala spice blend (page 301)
- ½ teaspoon salt

Preheat oven to 425º F. Toss all the vegetables with oil, spice blend and salt. Transfer to a baking sheet in a single layer and roast them in the oven for 20 - 25 minutes. Season to taste and serve.

# Jeweled Rice with Dry Fruits and Nuts

*Coconut milk adds a sweet taste to the rice. The dry fruits and nuts garnish glimmer like jewels against a white bed of rice.*

*Serves 8*

- ¼ cup ghee
- 2 bay leaves
- 10 cloves
- 1-inch stick cinnamon
- 6 green cardamoms, lightly crushed to open the shell
- 2 tablespoons ginger garlic paste
- 2 teaspoons minced fresh green chilies, such as serrano

- 2 teaspoons salt or to taste
- 2 cups basmati rice
- one 13.5 fluid ounce can coconut milk
- 2 cups water
- ¼ cup dry apricots, cut into ½-inch pieces
- ¼ cup dry cranberries
- ¼ cup pistachio nuts

Heat ghee in a medium sauce pan over medium high heat. When the ghee is hot, add bay leaves, cloves, cinnamon stick and cardamom pods. Fry until cloves plump up. Add ginger garlic paste and green chili and stir for about 1 minute. Add salt and basmati rice. Stir well to coat all the rice grains with a thin film of ghee and spices. Stir in coconut milk and water. At this point, you can transfer the mixture to a rice cooker and finish cooking. Alternately, bring the rice mixture to a boil. Reduce heat to lowest setting. Cover with a lid and cook for about 20 - 25 minutes until rice is done. Let it rest for 10 minutes. Fluff up the rice with fork. Transfer to a serving platter. Garnish with dry fruits and nuts and serve.

*Cook's Note: Whole spices are added for flavoring the dish and are not meant to be eaten.*

# CRANBERRY SAUCE WITH GINGER

*Serves 8*

- 2 apples, peeled, cored, and cut into ½-inch pieces
- 12 ounces fresh cranberries
- 1 tablespoon orange zest
- ½ cup orange juice
- 1 cup sugar
- ¼ teaspoon salt

- 1 tablespoon minced fresh ginger
- 1 teaspoon cinnamon
- 1 teaspoon lemon juice
- one 8-ounce can crushed pineapple, drained
- 1 tablespoon Grand Marnier or other orange liquor

Combine apple pieces, cranberries, orange zest, orange juice, sugar, salt, ginger, cinnamon and lemon juice in a heavy bottomed saucepan. Cook over medium high heat and bring it to a boil while stirring often. Reduce heat to medium low. Cook for about 20 - 25 minutes while stirring occasionally until the sauce thickens. Stir in pineapple and Grand Marnier. Transfer to a serving dish. Press plastic wrap directly onto the surface to prevent the formation of a skin. Refrigerate to chill.

*Cook's Note: This can be made few days in advance.*

# PERSIMMON DATE COCONUT PUDDING

*Persimmons are bountiful during the Thanksgiving season. Use only over ripened fruit for this recipe. This recipe combines 3 of my favorite ingredients: persimmons, dates, and coconut with a touch of cardamom. The end result is absolutely divine.*

*Serves 8*

- 2 cups flour
- 1 teaspoon cinnamon
- 1 teaspoon baking powder
- 1 teaspoon baking soda
- ¼ teaspoon salt
- 1 teaspoon dry ginger powder
- 1 teaspoon green cardamom seed powder
- 3 eggs
- ¾ cup light brown sugar

- ½ cup butter, melted and cooled
- 1 teaspoon vanilla
- 2 cups persimmon puree
- 1 cup whipping cream
- ½ cup sweetened coconut
- 1 cup chopped dates
- ½ cup chopped pecans

- apricot glaze (page 50)

Preheat oven to 350º F. Spray a 6 cup fluted tube pan with nonstick cooking spray.

In a bowl, stir in flour, cinnamon, baking powder, baking soda, salt, ginger and cardamom and set aside.

Using an electric mixer with a paddle attachment, combine eggs and sugar. Beat until well-blended. Add melted butter and vanilla. Beat until butter is incorporated into the egg mixture. Add persimmon puree and whipping cream and mix until combined. Slowly stir in the dry ingredients until moistened. Add coconut, dates and pecans. Stir to mix. Add batter to the prepared pan.

Set the baking pan in a large roasting pan. Transfer roasting pan to the oven. Pour enough hot water to the roasting pan until water is halfway up to the sides of the baking pan.

Bake for an hour to hour and 15 minutes or until a wooden skewer inserted in the middle comes out clean. Remove the pudding from the oven and water-bath and let it cool completely. Unmold onto a serving plate. Glaze with apricot glaze. Serve either with ice cream or whipping cream.

*The jars of home-made fruit preserves serve as party favors as well as place card holders.*

# CHRISTMAS

Being born into a Hindu family, I don't have any childhood memories of Christmas, except that it was a school holiday. When I went to a Catholic college, I was exposed to Christmas celebrations. Christmas and all its festivities were very important at the Catholic college and dormitory. Every year, we had an elaborate Christmas feast served in the dormitory. Special mass was held for all Christian students, but non-Christian students were always welcome to attend.

When I came to America I got the real taste of Christmas. After I saw the Christmas spirit and cheer among people, I realized that I didn't have to be a Christian to celebrate Christmas. I guess it was the traditions behind Christmas I was attracted to. Since Christmas is all about beautiful traditions, I wanted to incorporate these traditions into my life along with other holiday traditions.

It soon became a family tradition to seek the perfect Christmas tree to decorate. We decorate our tree with ornaments collected over the years, while listening to Christmas carols in the background. Decorating the tree has become a treasured family affair every year.

Gift giving during Christmas time is a simple gesture to thank people and appreciate year-long friendship and companionship. My trademark homemade Christmas gift baskets have become a tradition. The real preparation for Christmas begins in summer itself by making jams and preserves as part of the Christmas gifts. Three weeks before Christmas my home looks like a pastry shop, filled with aromas from tea cakes, baklava, biscotti, rugulach and Christmas cookies from around the world. My daughter patiently paints each cookie like a piece of art with multi-colored royal icing. My whole family gets involved in making gift baskets with all its delicacies, to give them to teachers, neighbors and friends. This Christmas menu is my family's favorite and I hope it becomes yours too.

*Detail: The traditional Christmas color palate gets a tropical touch with colorful accents of elephants, peacocks and parrots.*

# Christmas Dinner

# Mushroom Daisies

*Yield 18*

- 2 tablespoons vegetable oil
- 1 cup finely chopped onion
- 1 teaspoon ginger garlic paste
- 1 tablespoon coriander powder
- ½ teaspoon salt
- ¼ - ½ teaspoon cayenne
- 3 cups chopped mushrooms
- 2 tablespoons all-purpose flour
- ½ teaspoon garam masala powder
- ¾ cup grated parmagioano-riggiano cheese
- 1 package frozen puff pastry (2 sheets), thawed over night in the refrigerator

**Special equipment needed**
- 3-inch daisy or round cookie cutter
- 1 ½-inch round cookie cutter

Heat oil in a skillet over medium heat. When the oil is hot, add the chopped onions. Sauté onions until edges begin to brown. Add ginger garlic paste, coriander powder, salt and cayenne and stir fry for 1 - 2 minutes. Add the chopped mushrooms. Fry until mushrooms are cooked through and almost dry. Stir in flour and garam masala. Fry until moisture from the mushrooms is absorbed by the flour. Turn off the heat. Stir in the cheese and mix thoroughly to incorporate into the mushroom mixture. Set aside.

Preheat oven to 375º F.
Lay out puff pastry onto the work surface. Roll the pastry gently with a rolling pin to flatten. Using a 3-inch cookie cutter, cut out daisies or rounds from the puff pastry. Without cutting all the way through, push with a small cookie cutter halfway down, in the middle of puff pastry cutouts. Do not pull out the center yet. You have to do this after they are baked. Arrange them on an ungreased sheet pan. Bake for about 20 - 25 minutes until golden brown. Immediately transfer them to a wire rack. Cool to room temperature. Cut around the centers with a sharp knife without cutting through. You have to leave the bottom intact to hold the filling. Pull out the center to make a hollow round in the middle of the pastry. Divide the mushroom filling among the daisies and serve.

# RAAN

*Serves 6 - 8*
- 3 ½ - 4 pounds whole leg of lamb

*Marinade*
- 2 tablespoons vegetable oil
- 2 cups chopped onions
- ¼ cup ginger garlic paste
- 1 tablespoon minced fresh green chili, such as serrano
- ½ - 1 teaspoons cayenne
- 1 teaspoon dry roasted cumin powder
- 2 tablespoons coriander powder
- ½ teaspoon freshly grated nutmeg
- ½ teaspoon green cardamom seed powder

- 1 teaspoon freshly ground black pepper
- 1 teaspoon garam masala powder
- 1 ½ teaspoons salt
- 2 tablespoons lime juice
- ½ cup strained yogurt (page 307)

*Almond Coating*
- 1 tablespoon ginger garlic paste
- 4 tablespoons ground slivered almonds
- 4 tablespoons pomegranate syrup (page 306) or 2 tablespoons sugar
- 1 teaspoon salt
- 1 teaspoon cayenne
- few drops of red food color
- 2 tablespoons ghee for basting

Trim off all the fat and silver membrane of the meat. Using the point of a sharp knife or metal skewer, pierce the meat all over to allow marinade to penetrate into the meat.

To make the marinade, heat oil in a small saucepan over medium high heat. When oil is hot, add onions. Sauté until onions are translucent. Once it is cool place it in a electric blender along with ginger garlic paste, green chili, cayenne, cumin powder, coriander powder. nutmeg, cardamom powder, black pepper, garam masala, salt and lime juice. Grind them into a smooth paste. Transfer this masala paste to a bowl and stir in yogurt.

Add marinade to the lamb. Rub well into the meat, making sure the meat is completely covered with marinade. Cover with plastic wrap and refrigerate for 12 - 48 hours. Just before you are ready to bake, make almond coating.

Preheat oven to 350º F.

Mix all the coating ingredients. Transfer marinated leg of lamb to the shallow roasting pan lined with metal rack. Coat the meat with almond coating all over. Cover loosely with aluminum foil. Bake for 1 ½ hours. Remove the cover and bake for another 1 – 1 ½ hours until the meat is very tender. Just before removing from the oven, baste the meat with ghee. Remove meat from the oven and let it rest for 15 minutes. Transfer meat to a serving platter. Garnish with red onions and mint. Carve at the table for a grand presentation.

# NAVRATAN KORMA

*Navratan means nine gems. This curry is made with nine different vegetables, paneer and nuts, which are compared to nine gems. It is a creamy, rich and colorful dish and is perfect for parties.*

*Serves 6 - 8*

- 2 potatoes, peeled and cut into 1-inch pieces
- 2 carrots, peeled and cut into 1-inch pieces
- 1 cup green beans, cut into 1-inch pieces
- 2 cups cauliflower florets
- 6 ounces paneer, home made (page 304) or store bought
- 2 tablespoons all purpose flour
- ½ cup vegetable oil
- ¼ cup raisins
- ¼ cup raw cashew nuts
- 1 onion, finely minced or chopped
- 2 tablespoons ginger garlic paste
- 1 tablespoon coriander powder
- 1 - 2 teaspoon cayenne
- ½ cup tomato puree
- 2 teaspoons salt or to taste
- 2 bell peppers (mixed colors), cut into 1-inch pieces
- ½ cup frozen peas
- 1 cup canned baby corn, cut into 1-inch pieces
- ½ cup cream
- 1 teaspoon garam masala powder
- 2 tablespoons chopped cilantro/coriander to garnish

Bring 6 cups of water to boil in a medium stock-pot over medium high heat. Boil potatoes and carrots separately for 3 - 4 minutes. Using a slotted spoon, remove them onto a tray. Boil beans and cauliflower separately for 2 minutes. Remove them and place onto a tray. Set aside until ready to use.

Dredge the panner pieces in flour, and shake off excess. Heat oil in a large saucepan over medium heat. When the oil is hot add paneer in batches, if necessary and fry until golden brown. Using a slotted spoon, remove from the oil and place onto a tray lined with a paper towel. Add raisins to the same oil and fry until they plump up. Remove them and place them onto the same tray as the paneer pieces. Fry cashews until golden brown in the same pan. Add to the paneer and reserve for later use. Increase temperature to medium high and add onions, and sauté until edges begin to brown. Add ginger garlic paste, coriander powder and cayenne and stir fry for 2 minutes. Stir in tomato puree, salt and turmeric and cook until the tomato puree is cooked with spices and the oil starts rising to the surface. Add the boiled vegetables along with the rest of the vegetables and cook for 5 minutes. Add 2 cups of water and bring it to a boil and reduce heat to medium. Cover the pan and cook for about 20 - 25 minutes until all the vegetables are tender and the sauce is thick, stirring occasionally.

When the vegetables are cooked and ready, add reserved paneer, raisins and cashews. Stir in cream and garam masala powder and heat through. Season to taste. Garnish with cilantro.

# STUFFED BELL PEPPERS

*Serves 6*

- 1 ½ pounds potatoes
- 1 tablespoon + 1 teaspoon salt, divided
- 1 tablespoon sesame seeds
- 2 tablespoons vegetable oil
- 1 teaspoon cumin seeds
- 1 tablespoon minced fresh ginger
- 2 cloves garlic, minced
- 2 minced fresh green chilies, such as serrano
- ¼ teaspoon turmeric
- 2 teaspoons amchoor powder (dry mango powder)
- 1 teaspoon coriander powder
- 2 tablespoons minced fresh cilantro
- 6 medium colored bell peppers
- ⅓ cup plain bread crumbs
- 2 tablespoons melted butter

Place potatoes with 1 tablespoon of salt in a medium saucepan. Add enough water to cover 2 - 3 inches above the potatoes. Boil them over medium high heat until tender enough to be easily pierced with a fork or skewer. When the potatoes are done, drain them into a colander. When they are cool enough to handle, peel them and cut into small pieces.

In a small skillet, dry roast sesame seeds over medium heat for two minutes. Let it cool to room temperature and grind them into a in a spice grinder. Set aside.

Preheat oven to 350º F. Heat oil in a skillet or wok over medium high heat. When the oil is hot, add cumin seeds. When the cumin seeds sizzle, add ginger garlic and green chilies and stir fry for 2 minutes. Add 1 teaspoon salt, turmeric, amchoor powder and coriander powder and fry everything together for 1 minute. Stir in the potatoes. Mix well until all the spices are blended into the potatoes and stir fry for 5 minutes while stirring occasionally. Sprinkle sesame seed powder and cilantro on top. Stir to combine.

If necessary, you can trim the base of the peppers without making a hole to make it stand. Cut off the tops. Remove seeds and membrane. Fill the peppers with potato mixture.

Mix the bread crumbs with melted butter. Spread 1 tablespoon of buttered bread crumbs on top of potato mixture. Arrange stuffed peppers in a baking dish. Bake in the oven for 40 - 45 minutes. Serve with onion tomato chutney (page 298).

# BHATURA

*This is a very rich bread, usually served at special occasions*

*Yield 20*

- 4 cups all-purpose flour
- 2 eggs
- 2 teaspoons sugar
- 1 teaspoon salt
- 2 tablespoons vegetable oil
- 2 tablespoons baking powder
- 1 cup yogurt or sour cream

- vegetable oil for deep frying

Mix all the ingredients together into pliable dough. You can mix this in a Kitchen Aid mixer using the dough hook. Cover with plastic wrap, and let the dough rest for an hour at room temperature. Divide the dough into 20 portions. Take one piece of dough and roll it into an 8-inch circle. Proceed with the rest of the dough.

Pour oil into a wok or a deep fryer until it is ⅓ full (oil should be 2 - 3 inches deep). Heat oil to 350º F or until a piece of dough dropped into the hot oil rises to the top immediately. Add the bhaturas one at a time to the oil. Fry both sides until done. It takes only a few minutes to fry each bhatura.

*Cook's Note: Bhaturas should be cooked but not browned.*

# DIKON AND POMEGRANATE SALAD

*The colors in this salad truly brings out the spirit of Christmas.*

*Serves 4 - 6*

- 2 cups grated dikon
- 1 teaspoon minced fresh green chilies, such as serrano
- 1 teaspoon chaat masala, homemade (page 301) or store-bought
- ¼ cup cilantro leaves
- salt to taste
- ½ cup pomegranate seeds to garnish

Gently toss grated dikon, green chilies, chaat masala, cilantro leaves and salt together. Transfer to a serving bowl or platter. Garnish with pomegranate seeds.

# MANGO RAITA

*Serves 4 - 6*

- 2 cups whole milk yogurt
- ¼ cup sour cream
- 1 ripened mango, peeled and cut around the pit into ½-inch cubes
- 1 tablespoon finely chopped mint
- 1 teaspoon salt or to taste

Stir all the ingredients together. Transfer to a serving bowl and serve.

# SHRIMP PULAO

*Serves 4 - 6*

- 1 pound medium sized shrimp
- ⅓ cup vegetable oil
- 10 cloves
- 1-inch stick cinnamon
- 5 cardamom pods, lightly crushed to break the shell
- 1 star anise
- 2 bay leaves
- 2 cups chopped onions
- 1 - 2 fresh green chilies such as serrano, cut lengthwise into two
- 2 tablespoons ginger garlic paste
- 1 tablespoon coriander powder
- 2 medium tomatoes, chopped
- 2 teaspoons salt
- ½ - 1 teaspoon cayenne
- ¼ teaspoon turmeric
- 1 teaspoon garam masala powder
- 2 cups basmati rice
- 2 cups milk
- 1 ½ cups water
- 2 tablespoons chopped cilantro
- 2 tablespoons chopped mint

Peel and de-vein the shrimp and refrigerate until ready to use.

Heat oil in a medium sauce pan over medium high heat. When the oil is hot, add cloves, cinnamon stick, cardamom pods, star anise and bay leaves. When the cloves plump up, add onions and green chilies and fry until the onions begin to brown. Add ginger garlic paste and coriander powder and stir fry for 1 minute. Add tomatoes and cook until tomatoes are soft and some of the moisture evaporates. Add salt, cayenne, turmeric and garam masala powder and stir fry for 1 minute. Stir in shrimp and cook for about 5 - 6 minutes until shrimp turns pale, while stirring occasionally. Add basmati rice. Stir well until all the rice grains are coated with the shrimp masala. Add milk and water and sprinkle cilantro/coriander and mint.

At this point, you can transfer the rice mixture into an automatic rice cooker and finish cooking. Alternately, bring the rice mixture to a boil on stove-top. Once it starts boiling, reduce heat to the lowest setting. Cover with the lid and cook for about 20 - 25 minutes until the rice is done. Let it rest for 10 minutes. Fluff up the rice before serving.

*Cook's Note: Whole spices are added for flavor only and are not meant to be eaten.*

# CASHEW SHORTBREAD

*Serves 4 - 6*

- 1½ cups all purpose flour
- ½ cup ground raw cashew nuts
- 1 teaspoon green cardamom seed powder
- ¼ teaspoon salt
- 1 cup unsalted butter
- ¾ cup confectioner's sugar, sifted

In a bowl, stir together all-purpose flour, cashew nuts, cardamom powder and salt. In a bowl of an electric mixer fitted with pedal attachment, cream butter and sugar until light and creamy. While the mixer is on low speed, slowly add the flour mixture. Mix until well-combined.
Spray a 9-inch shortbread pan with nonstick cooking spray. Press dough evenly into the pan and refrigerate the pan for an hour.

Preheat oven to 325° F.

Remove the pan from the refrigerator and use a toothpick or fork to prick the entire surface to prevent from rising. Using a small knife, score the dough into desired size pieces. Bake the shortbread in the middle of the oven for 35 - 40 minutes or until shortbread is lightly golden. Immediately, re-score the bread and transfer onto a wire rack. Let it cool in the pan for 10 - 15 minutes. Unmold onto a flat surface. Cut into serving size pieces along the scored lines.

*Cook's Note: If you don't have shortbread pan, use 9-inch fluted tart pan with removable bottom.*

Everyone looks forward to bringing in the New Year, be it by throwing a lavish party or a quiet get together at home. It is at this time that people begin to reflect upon the good and the bad of the past year. As everyone remembers their achievements and failures of the past year, the bad somehow seems to outweigh the good.

Regret over what could have been or what could have been prevented often permeates our thoughts on New Year's Eve. At the same time, everyone views the New Year as a clean slate, free from whatever bad mark the past year left on it. To us, the New Year represents a chance to start over and make new beginnings.

As a result, the inevitable New Year's resolutions are made. We resolve to forge new bonds, embrace new experiences, and create new memories. Most of all, we resolve to avoid the mistakes made in the past year. For many, the same resolution is made every year: to lose weight. Hopefully, with the recipes I provide you, this resolution can be kept once and for all.

# New Year's Eve Bash

# BABY POTATO CURRY

*Serves 4 - 6*
- 1 ½ pounds baby potatoes, red or yukon gold
- 1 tablespoon salt

*Marinade*
- 1 tablespoon ginger garlic paste
- 1 teaspoon minced fresh green chili, such as serrano
- ½ - 1 teaspoon cayenne
- ½ teaspoon freshly ground black pepper
- 1 teaspoon coriander powder
- ½ teaspoon fennel seed powder
- 1 tablespoon lime juice
- ¼ cup yogurt
- 1 tablespoon vegetable oil
- ½ teaspoon salt

*Gravy*
- 2 tablespoons vegetable oil
- 2 cups finely minced onions
- 1 tablespoon ginger garlic paste
- 1 tablespoon coriander powder
- ½ - 1 teaspoon cayenne
- ½ teaspoon turmeric
- 1 teaspoon salt
- ½ cup tomato puree
- 1 teaspoon kasuri methi (dry fenugreek leaves)
- 2 cups water
- 2 tablespoons milk
- 2 tablespoons chopped cilantro/ coriander

Place potatoes with 1 tablespoon of salt in a medium stock-pot. Add enough water to cover 2 - 3 inches above the potatoes. Boil them over medium high heat until tender enough to be easily pierced with a fork or skewer. When the potatoes are ready, drain them into a colander. When they are cool enough to handle, peel them. Using a toothpick or a skewer, prick all over the potatoes to allow the marinade to penetrate.

For the marinade, whisk to combine all the ingredients in a bowl. Add the potatoes and gently toss to cover the potatoes evenly with marinade. Cover and marinate for 1 - 2 hours, stirring once or twice in between.

Preheat oven to 375° F.

Line a baking sheet with aluminum foil and spray with nonstick cooking spray. Spread potatoes in a single layer and roast them in the oven for 30 - 35 minutes while stirring once in the middle.

Meanwhile, prepare the gravy. Heat oil in a medium saucepan over medium high heat. When the oil is hot, add onions. Sauté onions until the edges begin to brown. Add ginger garlic paste, coriander powder, cayenne, turmeric and salt and stir fry for 2 minutes. Stir in tomato puree and kasuri methi and cook for 2 - 3 minutes while stirring often. Stir in 2 cups of water. Reduce heat to medium and simmer for about 20 minutes until oil rises to the surface. Stir in roasted potatoes and cook for another 5 minutes. Stir in milk. Transfer to a serving dish. Garnish with cilantro.

# BEETS-CUCUMBER SALAD

*Look for baby beets in an array of colors at the farmer's market and specialty supermarkets.*

*Serves 4 - 6*
- 1 pound fresh beets (preferably multi colored), well scrubbed
- 1 English cucumber, peeled and cut into ½ inch pieces

*Ginger Honey Dressing*
- 1 tablespoon ginger juice (page 304)
- 2 tablespoons honey
- 2 tablespoons peanut or vegetable oil
- 1 tablespoon lemon juice

- ½ teaspoon cayenne
- ½ teaspoon salt or to taste
- 1 teaspoon chaat masala, homemade (page 301) or store bought
- 1 tablespoon chopped mint

Preheat oven to 425º F. Wrap the beets individually with aluminum foil and place onto a baking sheet and roast them in the oven for about 1 – 1½ hours, depending on the size of the beets, until tender enough to be easily pierced with a fork or skewer. Remove from the oven and let it cool. When they are cool enough to handle, using a paper towel, gently rub the skin off. Cut the beets into ½-inch pieces.

Alternately, place beets in a stock-pot with 1 tablespoon salt. Add enough water to cover 2 - 3 inches above the surface of the beets. Cook over medium high heat and bring it to a boil. Simmer uncovered for 50 minutes to 1 hour or until the beets are tender. Drain them into a colander. When they are cool enough to handle, peel and dice into ½-inch pieces.

Transfer beets and cucumber into a bowl. In a small bowl, whisk all ingredients together for the dressing and pour it over the beets and cucumber mixture. Gently toss to coat. Let it marinate in the refrigerator for 2 - 3 hours. Mix again before serving.

*Cook's Note: To avoid stained fingers, wear kitchen gloves when handling the beets.*

# BROCCOLI FRY

*Serves 4 - 6*
- 1 ½ pounds broccoli florets
- 2 tablespoons vegetable oil
- 1 - 2 dry whole red chilies, such as chile de arbol
- 2 cloves garlic, sliced
- 10 curry leaves
- ½ teaspoon salt
- ¼ teaspoon turmeric
- ½ teaspoon cayenne or to taste

Wash and drain the broccoli florets and dry with paper towels. Heat 2 tablespoons of oil in a skillet or wok over medium high heat. When the oil is hot, add red chilies. When red chilies turn darker, add garlic and stir for 1 minute. Add curry leaves and when they are crisp, stir in broccoli florets. Sprinkle salt, turmeric and cayenne and stir fry for 1 minute. Reduce heat to medium, cover the skillet and cook until broccoli is tender while stirring occasionally. Serve as a side dish to any Indian meal.

# CUCUMBER RAITA

*This is a refreshingly cool raita, that goes well with almost all Indian menus. Salting cucumbers draws out the moisture, so the raita doesn't end up waterlogged.*

- 2 cups plain yogurt
- 1 large English cucumber, peeled and grated
- 1 teaspoon salt
- 1 tablespoon chopped mint leaves
- salt or pepper to taste

Place grated cucumber with salt in a colander. Set the colander over a bowl to catch the drippings. Refrigerate for 2 – 3 hours. Stir in drained cucumbers, and mint into the yogurt and season to taste with salt or pepper. Serve with any Indian meal.

# FISH FRY

*Serves 4 - 6*

*Marinade*

- 1 medium red onion, finely minced
- 5 cloves garlic, finely minced
- ½ tablespoon salt
- 1 tablespoon paprika
- ½ - 1 teaspoon cayenne or to taste
- 1 teaspoon freshly ground black pepper
- ½ teaspoon roasted cumin powder
- 1 tablespoon vegetable oil

- 1 ½ pounds salmon, cut into 2-inch pieces

- 1 tablespoon vegetable oil

- 2 tablespoons chopped cilantro for garnishing

Mix all the ingredients for the marinade in a bowl. Add fish pieces to the marinade and gently toss to coat the fish pieces. Cover with plastic wrap and let it marinate for 2 - 4 hours in the refrigerator. Heat 1 tablespoon of oil in a wok or skillet over medium high heat. When the oil is hot, add the marinated fish. Fry until the fish is cooked thoroughly, while stirring occasionally. Garnish with cilantro and serve.

# MOTI MUSHROOM PULAO

*"Moti" means "pearl". This earthy pulao is garnished with very elegant pearls, made with paneer, wrapped in silver leaves.*

### Serves 4 - 6
- 8 ounces mushrooms
- ¼ cup vegetable oil
- 1 bay leaf
- 6 cloves
- 1-inch cinnamon stick
- 2 - 3 green cardamom pods, slightly crushed to open the shell
- 1 onion, cut lengthwise, sliced and cut in the middle
- 1 - 2 fresh green chilies such as serrano, cut lengthwise in two

- 1 tablespoon ginger garlic paste
- 1 teaspoon garam masala powder
- 2 cups basmati rice
- 2 teaspoons salt
- 3 ½ cups water
- 2 tablespoons cilantro

- paneer pearls (recipe follows)

Wipe mushrooms with a damp paper towel to clean and slice them.

Heat oil in a medium sauce pan over medium high heat. When the oil is hot, add bay leaf, cloves, cinnamon stick and cardamom pods. When the cloves plump up, add onion and green chili. Sauté until the onion is translucent and edges begin to brown. Add ginger garlic paste and stir fry for 1 minute. Add mushrooms and sauté until mushrooms are slightly wilted. Stir in garam masala powder, basmati rice and salt. Mix thoroughly to coat all the rice grains with a thin film of oil and spices. Stir in 3 ½ cups of water. At this point, you can transfer the mixture to an automatic rice cooker and finish cooking.

Alternately, bring the rice mixture to a boil and reduce heat to the lowest setting. Cover with a lid and cook for about 20 - 25 minutes until the rice is done. Let it rest for 10 minutes. Fluff the rice with fork. Mix in cilantro and garnish with paneer pearls.

*Cook's Note:*

*1. It is important not to wash mushrooms in water to avoid absorbing too much moisture.*

*2. Whole spices are added to flavor the dish, but not meant to be eaten.*

## PANEER PEARLS

- 4 ounces paneer
- salt and pepper to taste
- 4 - 5 silver leaves*, cut into 2 x 2 pieces with paper

Crumble paneer in a bowl. Add salt and pepper to taste and knead for two minutes. Take a teaspoon of the paneer mixture and roll into a ball. Place a paneer ball in the middle of silver paper and wrap the paper around the ball so that the silver foil sticks to the paneer. Peel and discard the paper. Proceed with the rest.

*Cook's Note: *Silver leaves are available at Indian supermarkets.*

# MUNG DAL WITH COCONUT MILK

### Serves 4
- ½ cup mung dal
- ½ cup masoor dal (red lentils)
- 1 teaspoon turmeric
- 1 teaspoon salt or to taste
- ½ cup chopped onion
- 1 - 2 minced fresh green chilies, such as serrano
- 1 medium tomato, chopped
- ½ cup coconut milk, homemade (page 302) or canned

### Seasoning
- 2 tablespoons vegetable oil
- ⅛ teaspoon asafoetida
- 1 teaspoon black mustard seeds
- 1 teaspoon cumin seeds
- ¼ cup chopped onions
- 20 curry leaves

Wash both the dals and place it in a medium saucepan with 4 cups of water. Bring it to a boil over medium high heat. Reduce heat to medium and cook for 10 minutes, uncovered, while stirring occasionally. Stir in turmeric, salt, onions, chilies and tomatoes and cook for about 15 - 20 minutes more, until dal is cooked, soft and creamy, while stirring occasionally. Add more water if necessary. Stir in the coconut milk. Cook for another 5 minutes.

To season, heat oil in a small saucepan over medium high heat. When the oil is hot, add asafoetida and mustard seeds. Cover until the spluttering subsides. Uncover, and add cumin seeds. When the cumin seeds sizzle, add curry leaves. As soon as they are crisp, add onions. Stir fry until the onions are golden brown. Add this seasoning to dal and stir in. Serve with plain rice, chappati or paratha.

# MISSI ROTI

*Missi Roti is popular in Punjabi households for breakfast. It is usually served with yogurt, which makes it a healthy breakfast.*

- 1 ½ cups chappati flour (atta)
- ¾ cup chickpea flour/besan
- ¾ teaspoon salt
- ¼ teaspoon cayenne or to taste
- 1 teaspoon ajwain powder
- 1 teaspoon anardhana (ground pomegranate seed powder)
- 2 tablespoons vegetable oil
- 2 tablespoons finely chopped cilantro/coriander
- ½ - ¾ cup water
- ghee or oil for basting

In a bowl, stir in both flours with salt, cayenne, ajwain powder, and anardhana. Using your fingers, rub oil into the flour mixture. Stir in cilantro. Using ½ - ¾ cup of water, make a soft, pliable dough. If the dough feels sticky, add 1 tablespoon of flour at a time and mix. If the dough feels dry, add 1 tablespoon of water at a time and mix. Transfer the dough to a work surface and knead for 3 - 5 minutes. Place the dough in an oiled bowl. Cover and let it rest for ½ an hour allowing the gluten to develop.

Divide the dough into 8 portions and roll them into balls. Work with 1 piece of dough at a time, keeping the rest covered to prevent drying. Roll out each piece of dough into 6 - 7 inch circles on a floured work surface.

Heat tava or griddle over medium high heat. When it is hot, place one roti at a time. Cook until golden brown spots appear at the bottom. Flip it over and repeat on the other side. Brush lightly with ghee or oil on both sides. Remove from the tava/griddle. Store it covered with a kitchen towel while you prepare the rest of the rotis. Serve with yogurt or with any gravy curry.

*Cook's Note: Tava is a round, slightly concave cast iron griddle. It is an integral part of Indian kitchens to cook roti or paratha. You can find tavas at Indian stores or you can simply use a griddle pan.*

# GINGERED PINEAPPLE WITH PISTACHIO PALMIERS

*Serves 4 - 6*
- ½ a pineapple, peeled, cored and cut into 1-inch pieces

*Syrup*
- 1 cup sugar
- 1 cup water
- ¼ cup grated ginger
- 2 tablespoons lemon juice

- pistachio palmiers (recipe follows)

To make the syrup, stir in sugar, water, ginger and lemon juice in a small sauce pan. Stir over medium heat to dissolve sugar. Increase heat to medium high and bring it to a boil. Reduce heat to medium low and let it simmer for 10 minutes. Remove from the heat and let it steep for ½ hour. Strain the liquid into a bowl and add the pineapple pieces and let it cool. Place it in the refrigerator until ready to use. Serve strained fruit in a bowl with pistachio palmiers on the side.

## PISTACHIO PALMIERS

*Yield 24*
*Filling*
- ⅔ cup ground raw pistachios
- ½ cup sugar
- ½ teaspoon green cardamom seed powder
- ½ teaspoon cinnamon
- pinch of salt

- 1 package frozen puff pastry (2 sheets), thawed over night in the refrigerator

Preheat oven to 450º F. For the filling, stir together pistachio, sugar, cardamom powder, cinnamon and salt and set aside. Work with 1 sheet of puff pastry at a time. Unfold 1 sheet of puff pastry onto floured work surface. Spread ½ the amount of filling onto the surface. Using a rolling pin, press the filling onto the puff pastry. Roll the dough into 10 X 12 inch rectangle. Fold ¼ of the 12-inch side towards the center. Do the same thing with the other side. Then fold both sides again to meet exactly at the middle of the dough. Fold one half over the other like a book. Using a sharp knife, cut the dough into twelve 1-inch pieces. Place the slices cut side up, 3-inches apart, onto a parchment/silpat lined baking sheet. Repeat with the remaining dough. Cover and refrigerate for 1 hour.

Bake palmiers in the oven for 6 minutes until the bottom is caramelized. Turn them over quickly with a spatula and bake for another 3 - 5 minutes or until caramelized on the other side. Transfer palmiers onto a wire rack to cool. Store them in an airtight container for 2 - 3 days. Just before serving, quickly reheat in the oven for better taste.

**Cook's Note:** *Silpat is a reusable silicone liner for baking pans, available at gourmet cooking supply stores. This has become an indispensable tool for baking in my kitchen.*

# Master Recipes

## Cilantro Chutney

*Yield  about1 cup*

- 2 cups cilantro leaves
- 1 green bell pepper, seeded and cut into small pieces
- 1 - 3 fresh green chilies such as serrano, cut into pieces
- 2 cloves garlic, chopped
- 2 tablespoons lime juice, or to taste
- 1 teaspoon salt or to taste

Place all the ingredients in a blender. Grind everything into a smooth paste, while stopping and pushing with the wooden spoon when necessary.

## Onion Tomato Chutney

*Yield  about 1 cup*

- 3 large tomatoes blanched, peeled and ground into puree*
- 2 tablespoons vegetable oil
- ⅛ cup sugar
- ¾ teaspoon salt
- ½ teaspoon cumin powder
- ½ teaspoon cayenne
- 1 tablespoon lemon juice
- 1 tablespoon vinegar
- ½ cup finely chopped shallots or onion

Heat oil in a small sauce pan over medium high heat. Add tomato puree, sugar, salt, cumin powder, and cayenne and cook for about 20 minutes, until it reduces to 1 cup. Stir in lemon juice and vinegar and heat through. Remove from the heat and mix in the shallots or onion. Cool and store in the refrigerator. You can make this one week ahead.

*Cook's note:* Bring enough water to boil in the sauce pan. Using a paring knife, make an X at the bottom of the tomatoes. Gently drop the tomatoes into the boiling water. Boil for a minute. Using a slotted spoon, remove from the water. When they are cool enough to handle, peel and cut into pieces. Transfer tomatoes into the blender and grind into the puree.

## Orange Bell Pepper Chutney

*Yield  about 1 cup*

- 2 tablespoons vegetable oil
- 2 - 4 dry whole red chilies such as chile de arbol
- 1 teaspoon cumin seeds
- 1 tablespoon white urad dal
- 2 orange bell peppers, chopped
- 1 ½ cups chopped tomato
- 1 tablespoon tamarind paste (page 300)
- 1 teaspoon salt or to taste
- 2 cloves garlic

*Seasoning:*

- 1 tablespoon vegetable oil
- ⅛ teaspoon asafoetida
- 1 teaspoon cumin seeds
- 10 curry leaves

Heat oil in a skillet over medium high heat. When the oil is hot add chilies. When chilies turn one shade darker add the cumin seeds. As soon as the cumin seeds start to sizzle add urad dal. Fry until urad dal turns golden. Add bell pepper and stir fry for 2 minutes and add tomatoes. Cook about 4 - 5 minutes, until tomatoes are soft and some of the moisture evaporates. Add salt and garlic and let it cool. Transfer mixture to a blender and grind till smooth. Transfer to the bowl.

To season, heat oil in a small skillet. When the oil is hot add asafoetida and cumin seeds. When cumin seeds sizzle add curry leaves. Once they are crisp add the seasoning to the chutney and mix well.

# Urad Dal Chutney (Minumula Pachadi)

*This is a tongue-scorching hot chutney, a speciality of Nellore. All Andharites are known to devour hot and spicy chutneys and pickles with plain rice. Be wary of the spiciness of this chutney.*

*Serves 10 – 12*

- 4 – 6 tablespoons tamarind paste (page 300)
- 1 tablespoon + 1 teaspoon vegetable oil, divided
- 1 teaspoon fenugreek seeds
- 1 tablespoon cumin seeds
- 1 tablespoon black mustard seeds
- ½ cup urad dal
- ½ cup broken pieces of dry whole red chilies with seeds, such as chile de arbol
- 2 teaspoons salt or to taste

*Seasoning*

- 2 tablespoons vegetable oil
- ⅛ teaspoon asafoetida
- 2 dry whole red chilies, such as chile de arbol
- 1 teaspoon black mustard seeds
- 1 teaspoon cumin seeds
- 10 fresh curry leaves

Prepare the tamarind paste. Meanwhile heat 1 tablespoon of oil in a skillet over medium to medium high heat. When the oil is hot add fenugreek seeds, cumin seeds, mustard seeds and urad dal and fry the spices until urad dal turns golden, while stirring often. When you fry these spices, the mustard seeds will splutter. Remove all the spices into a bowl and set aside. To the same skillet add 1 teaspoon of oil and red chilies and fry until they turn a shade darker, while stirring often. Remove the chilies to the same bowl as the spices and let it cool.

Using the spice grinder, grind all the spices into a coarse powder.

In a bowl, stir in spice powder, salt, tamarind paste and ⅓ cup water.

To season, heat oil in a small sauce pan. When the oil is hot, add asafoetida and red chilies. When chilies turn one shade darker add mustard seeds and cover until the spluttering subsides. Uncover and add cumin seeds. When cumin seeds sizzle add curry leaves. When curry leaves are crisp, add the seasoning to the chutney and mix.

# Tomato Pickle

*This is a variation of my mother's recipe. Traditionally, pickles are made when fruits and vegetable are plentiful in the season. It is done not only to preserve the vegetables and fruits for the rest of the year but also to make them more economical. Large quantities of salt and cayenne are added as preservatives to store at room temperature. Pickles are stored with a layer of seasoned oil on top, which helps to seal the air and bacteria. Since I can store my pickle in the refrigerator, I have reduced the salt and cayenne to moderation without compromising the flavor or texture. If you want to save the pickle for a prolonged period of time, store the pickle free of any moisture. You can serve this pickle with dosa, rice or as a dip. Store in the refrigerator for up to a month.*

*Yield 1 cup*

- 2 teaspoons black mustard seeds
- ½ teaspoon fenugreek seeds
- ¼ cup vegetable oil
- 4 cups chopped tomato
- 1 tablespoon salt
- 2 tablespoons cayenne
- 1 teaspoon turmeric
- 1 tablespoon seedless tamarind, packed
- 4 cloves garlic, sliced

*Seasoning:*

- 2 tablespoons vegetable oil
- ⅛ teaspoon asafoetida
- 2 dry whole red chilies, such as chile de arbol
- 1 teaspoon mustard seeds
- 10 curry leaves

In a small skillet, dry roast mustard seeds and fenugreek seeds over medium heat until fenugreek seeds turn a shade darker. Once it cools, transfer to a spice grinder and grind into a powder. Set aside until ready to use.

Heat oil in a medium sauce pan over medium high heat. When it is hot, add tomatoes, salt, cayenne, turmeric and tamarind. Cook while stirring occasionally until tomatoes are soft and most of the water is evaporated and the mixture becomes thick. Let it cool. Transfer the tomato mixture to the food processor and process until smooth. Transfer the mixture to a bowl and stir in the garlic and reserved powder.

To season, heat oil in a small sauce pan and add asafoetida and red chilies. When red chilies turn darker add mustard seeds and cover until the spluttering subsides. Uncover and add curry leaves; when they are crisp add the seasoning to the tomato pickle and mix.

# TAMARIND PASTE

*Tamarind trees are indigenous to India.  These are evergreen, shady trees that can grow up to 80 feet tall and 25 - 35 feet wide.*

*When we were kids, we used to walk to school. Along the way, there was a pond we passed by every day that was filled with beautiful, bright pink lotus flowers. These lotus flowers bloom at sunrise.  With the gentle breeze, these flowers used to move their heads as though they were smiling and welcoming us to school every morning. When we would leave the school in the evening, all the flowers would close at sunset, as if they were sad because we were leaving. There were six beautiful tamarind trees on the bank of the pond.  We used to take shelter under those trees if it happened to rain along the way, especially during the monsoon season.*

*Tamarind is a traditional souring agent and is quintessential to South Indian cuisine.  I prefer to soak and extract  the pulp as needed. But with our busy lives, when you are short on time, it is nice to have this paste handy whenever you need it. I prefer to make it for a week and store it in the refrigerator.*

*Yield about 1 cup*

- 4 ounces tamarind, without seeds
- 2 cups hot water


Soak tamarind in 1½ cups of hot water for 1 - 2 hours to soften. Using your fingers, mash the tamarind to release as much pulp as possible. Pass it through a fine mesh sieve to extract pulp. Transfer fibers left in the sieve to a bowl and add another ½ cup of hot water. When it is cool enough to handle, mash with your fingers again to extract any remaining pulp. Pass it through the sieve again. Discard leftover fibers.

Transfer pulp to a small sauce pan. Boil until it reduces to 1 cup paste. Store in a sterile container for up to a week in the refrigerator.

*Cook's Note: You can buy tamarind paste from the Indian supermarkets. Be aware that some brands are better than others. I prefer Laxmi  brand natural tamarind concentrate.*

# TAMARIND/SWEET CHUTNEY (IMLI CHUTNEY)

*Tamarind chutney is served with many north Indian snacks and salads along with cilantro chutney*

*Yield about 2 cups*

- 5 ounces seedless tamarind
- 2 cups sugar
- 1 - 3 minced fresh green chilies, such as serrano
- 1 tablespoon minced fresh ginger
- ½ teaspoon black salt
- 1 teaspoon roasted cumin powder
- ½ teaspoon chaat masala powder, home made (page 301) or store bought
- 1 teaspoon salt.

Soak tamarind in 2 cups of hot water for a couple of hours to soften. Using your fingers mash the tamarind to release as much pulp as possible. Transfer to a fine mesh strainer set over a bowl. Using a wooden spoon or rubber spatula push it through the strainer to extract as much pulp as possible. Transfer fibers left in the sieve to a bowl and add another cup of hot water.  When it is cool enough to handle, mash with your fingers again to extract any remaining pulp.  Pass it through the mesh strainer to extract remaining pulp. Discard fibrous remains.

Transfer all the pulp to a medium sauce pan and boil until it reduces to 2 cups. Add sugar, minced chilies and ginger, black salt, cumin powder, chaat masala powder, and salt. Bring it to boil and reduce heat to medium and simmer for 8-10 minutes. If the sauce is too thick add ½ cup of water and heat through. Transfer to a clean container once it has cooled and refrigerate for up to 2 months. You can store for at least 6 months in the freezer.

*Cook's Note: You can use a food mill to extract the pulp instead of a mesh strainer.*

# CHAAT MASALA POWDER

*Chaat masala is a salty, tangy spice blend which is used to jazz up the flavors of fruits, vegetables, snacks and salads.*

*Yield about 1 cup*
- ¼ cup coriander seeds
- ⅓ cup cumin seeds
- ¼ cup amchoor powder (dry mango powder)
- 2 tablespoons anardhana (pomegranate seed powder)
- 1 tablespoon freshly ground black pepper
- 1 teaspoon ajwain seed powder
- 1 tablespoon black salt
- 1 tablespoon salt
- 1 tablespoon dry ginger powder
- 2 teaspoons cayenne
- ½ teaspoon asafoetida

Dry roast coriander seeds and cumin seeds in a small skillet for about 2 - 3 minutes, while shaking and stirring the skillet until aromatic and one shade darker. After they are cool, grind into a fine powder using a spice grinder. Transfer coriander-cumin powder into a bowl and stir in rest of the ingredients. Store in an airtight container in a cool dark place.

# MASALA SPICE BLEND

*This is my all- purpose spice blend, that can be used with vegetables or as a dry rub for chicken, lamb, and sea food.*

*Yield about ½ cup*
- 3 tablespoons paprika
- 2 teaspoons cayenne
- 2 tablespoons coriander powder
- 1 teaspoon roasted cumin powder
- 1 teaspoon amchoor powder (dry mango powder)
- 1 teaspoon garlic powder
- 1 teaspoon dry ginger powder
- ½ tablespoon salt
- 1 tablespoon sugar

Stir all the ingredients together in a bowl. Transfer to an air tight jar and store in a cool dark place.

# GARAM MASALA POWDER

*Garam masala means "hot spice mix". Actually, this is not a tongue-burning hot spice mix; rather, it is an aromatic spice blend. Unlike other spices, garam masala is usually added at the end of the preparation to almost all meat dishes and some vegetable dishes and sprinkled over as a garnish for pulaos and biryanis. Even though every region has its own variation, it is usually made up of 4 main ingredients: cloves, cardamom, cinnamon, and black pepper. Proportions can vary according to individual preferences.*

*Yield about ⅓ cup*
- 2 bay leaves, broken into small pieces
- two 2-inch pieces cinnamon stick, broken into small pieces
- 2 tablespoons coriander seeds
- 2 tablespoons cumin seeds
- 1 tablespoon peppercorns
- 1 tablespoon cloves
- 2 teaspoons green cardamom seeds

Combine all the spices in a shallow skillet over medium heat. Dry roast all the spices for about 2 minutes while shaking and stirring the skillet until aromatic and one shade darker. Let it cool. Using the spice grinder, grind them into fine powder. Store in an air tight container in a cool dark place.

# KADHAI MASALA POWDER

*Yield  about ½ cup*

- ¼ cup coriander seeds
- 1 tablespoon cumin seeds
- 1 tablespoon fennel seeds
- 2 dry whole red chilies, such as  chile de arbol
- 1 teaspoon pepper corns
- ½ teaspoon cloves
- 1 inch stick cinnamon, broken
- ½ teaspoon green cardamom seed powder
- 1 tablespoon kasuri methi leaves (dry fenugreek leaves)
- 1 tablespoon dry mint leaves
- ½ tablespoon dry ginger powder
- 1 tablespoon amchoor (dry mango powder)
- 1 tablespoon anardhana (pomegranate seed powder)
- ¼ teaspoon ground nutmeg
- ½ tablespoon paprika
- ½ teaspoon black salt

Dry-roast coriander seeds, cumin seeds, fennel seeds, red chilies, pepper corns, cloves, and cinnamon stick in a small skillet over medium heat, while stirring and shaking until the spices are one shade darker.  Let it cool to room temperature.  Using a spice grinder, grind into coarse powder.  Add the rest of the ingredients and mix thoroughly.  Store in a covered glass jar in a cool dry place.

*Cook's Note: You can use store-bought kadhai masala instead of home made. I would suggest MDH brand Tava Fry Masala.*

# ROASTED CUMIN POWDER

*Dry-roasting the spices brings out their essential oils and flavors. This is very true with cumin seeds. On rare occasions, I do use cumin powder without roasting. Normally, I always roast a week's supply of cumin seeds and grind them into powder to use as needed.*

*Yield ½ cup*

- ½ cup cumin seeds

In a small skillet, roast cumin seeds over medium high heat, while stirring and shaking the skillet. Fry until aromatic and they turn a shade darker. Remove from the heat let it cool. Transfer to a spice grinder and  grind into powder. Store it in an airtight container in a cool dark place. This stays fresh at room temperature for up to 2 weeks.

# CRACKING THE COCONUT

Using a clean screw driver, pierce the dark colored eyes of the coconut and drain off the liquid. This is not coconut milk. This is coconut water, which you can enjoy as a refreshing drink. Before you drink, make sure the water does not smell foul or rancid. If it does, this is an indication that the coconut is spoiled.

Cover the coconut with kitchen towel, hold it in your left hand, and tap hard with a hammer to break the shell. If you are unable to break it, place the coconut in the preheated oven at 375ºF for 15 minutes. This will cause the coconut shell to crack as it cools. If not, use the hammer once more to crack the shell.

# GRATED COCONUT

Using a sturdy blunt knife, you can release the meat from the shell. Once the meat is out, you can peel the brown skin with a paring knife or a vegetable peeler. Using a box grater, you can grate the coconut either finely or coarsely. Alternately, you can grate the coconut in the food processor, but the texture will be different.

# COCONUT MILK

*Yield 1 cup*

- 1 cup grated coconut

Transfer grated coconut into a blender along with ½ cup water and grind into a smooth paste. Transfer the paste into a bowl and stir in ½ cup of hot water. Let it rest for 5 minutes. Pour the mixture through the strainer. This is thick coconut milk.

Repeat the process by adding ½ cup hot water to the leftover pulp. After 5 minutes, strain the liquid again to collect the thin coconut milk.

# ALMOND PASTE

*Almond paste is used to enrich Moghul sauces*

*Yield 1 cup*
- 1 cup raw slivered almonds

Add enough water to cover one inch above the surface of the nuts and soak them for 2 - 3 hours. Drain and grind in a blender to make a smooth paste, using 2 - 3 tablespoons of water. Store in the refrigerator for up to 3 days.

# CASHEW PASTE

*Cashew paste is used to flavor the curries and to thicken sauces.*

*Yield 1 cup*
- 1 cup raw cashew nuts, coarsely chopped

Add enough water to cover 1-inch above the surface of the nuts and soak them for 2 - 3 hours. Drain the nuts and grind in a blender into a smooth paste using 2 - 3 tablespoons of water and stopping and pushing with the spatula. Store it in a clean air tight container in the refrigerator for up to 3 days.

# GREEN CHILI PASTE

*Yield ½ cup*
- ½ cup chopped green chilies, such as serrano

Process green chilies in a blender or in a food processor, until smooth paste. Add a tablespoon of water if necessary. Stays fresh in the refrigerator up to a week.

# ONION PASTE

*Use this paste when you want to make smooth gravies for curries.*

*Yield approximately 1 cup*
- 2 cups chopped onion

Process onions in a blender or in a food processor, until smooth paste.

# GINGER GARLIC PASTE

*This is a basic ginger-garlic paste that is used in many Indian curries. It is a ritual for many Indian home cooks to grind the ginger-garlic paste in the morning to use in their day to day cooking.*

*Yield about 1 cup*
- 1 cup peeled and chopped ginger
- 1 cup peeled garlic cloves

Transfer ginger and garlic into a blender or food processor and process into a smooth paste, stopping and pushing it from time to time. Add 1 tablespoon of water at a time as needed. It is important not to use too much water. Transfer to a clean container, cover tightly with plastic wrap and then with the lid.

Store in the refrigerator for up to 10 days.

# RED CHILI PASTE

*This chili paste is very intense in color. It adds flavor rather than making the dish spicy.*

*Yield about ½ cup*
- 2 ounces California chili pods or New Mexico chili pods
- ½ cup water for soaking.

Remove stems and seeds from the chilies. Using kitchen scissors, cut the chilies into small pieces and soak them in water for an hour. Transfer them to a blender and grind into a smooth paste. Store in the refrigerator up to a week.

*Cook's Note: If you have sensitive skin, it is important to use kitchen gloves while handling chilies of any kind.*

# PANEER

*This is a traditional North Indian cheese and is a primary source of protein along with dals for many vegetarians. I had never heard of paneer while growing up in the South. It was introduced to me by my North Indian friends after coming to this country. Ever since, this has become a staple in my menus.*

*Paneer is made by simply boiling milk to the boiling point and adding a souring agent such as lemon juice/lime juice or white vinegar. The milk solids coagulate and separate from the whey. Drain the whey using a cheese cloth. Compress the curd using a weight on top. Once it is made you can use it in a variety of curries, desserts and stir-fries with a sprinkle with chaat masala. It can be a terrific addition to any meal.*

*Yield about 12 ounces*
- 12 cups whole milk
- ¼ cup lemon/lime juice or vinegar

Pour milk into a large sauce pan. Bring milk to a boil over medium high heat, while stirring with a wooden spoon to prevent it from boiling over. Stir in lemon juice. Continue to stir until curds and whey are separated and the liquid is clear. Remove from the heat. Line a metal sieve/colander with a cheese cloth large enough to hang over the edges. Pour the curds and whey to a sieve/colander. Drain off the whey and collect the curds. Gather the edges of the cheese cloth tie a knot and gently squeeze out excess moisture. Place the cheese ball on a plate, place another plate on top to weigh it down with any weight, such as canned beans. Let it stand for an hour in the refrigerator. The curds will compress into a solid block. Cut the paneer into desired size pieces and use as needed.

Paneer stays fresh in the refrigerator for up to three days and two months in the freezer.

*Cook's Note: Alternately, you can buy paneer from the refrigerator section of any Indian grocery store.*

# FRIED PANEER PIECES

*Yield about 12 ounces*
- 12 ounces paneer
- 2 tablespoons all purpose flour
- oil for pan frying

Cut paneer into 1½-inch pieces, and dredge the paneer-pieces in all purpose flour, shake off the excess. Add enough oil to cover the bottom of a large skillet. Heat over medium high heat. When the oil is hot add paneer pieces as many as skillet can hold in a single layer without crowding. Fry the pieces until golden brown evenly. Using a slotted spoon, remove them onto a tray lined with a paper towel. Let it cool. Use as needed.

*Cook's Note: You can refrigerate fried paneer for up to a week. You can freeze them for up to a month.*

# GINGER JUICE

*Yield about 2 tablespoons*
- 2 inch piece fresh ginger

Using a fine grater, grate ginger and place it in a small piece of cheese cloth and squeeze the juice.

# PLAIN RICE

*Rice is a staple food in all Indian homes especially in South India. In South India, long-grain rice is used for day to day cooking, whereas in the north Basmati rice is eaten along with Roti. South Indians tend to consume lot more rice compared to North Indians. In the South, almost all curries and chutneys are meant to be eaten as an accompaniment to rice; in the North roti, chappati or parathas are used with their curries. I'm not used to adding salt to plain rice. Most of the chutneys and curries are heavily spiced already. Adding extra salt is not necessary. However, if you choose to do so, add one teaspoon of salt when the rice is boiling.*

*Automatic rice cookers have became very popular in American households. If you own a rice cooker, cooking rice is as simple as snapping a finger. Remember to add 2 cups of water for every cup of rice.*

*Yield  4 cups cooked rice*
- **2 cups long grain rice**
- **3 ¾ cups water**

Wash rice with several changes of water. Place rice and water in a heavy medium sauce pan and bring it to a boil over medium high heat. Reduce heat to lowest setting, cover and cook for about 20 - 25 minutes, until rice is cooked and the surface is covered with steam holes. Let it rest for 5 - 10 minutes. Use a fork to fluff up the rice before serving.

# PLAIN BASMATI RICE

*Popularly known as saada chawal, basmati rice is found all over North India.  The secret to making the perfect, puffy rice is to wash it thoroughly to get rid of excess starch and soak for ½ an hour to 1 hour. Plain basmati rice goes well with any North Indian curry.*

*Yield  4 cups cooked rice*
- **2 cups basmati rice**
- **3 ½  cups water**

Wash rice with several changes of water and soak for ½ an hour to 1 hour. Place the soaked rice and water in a heavy medium sauce pan and bring it to a boil over medium high heat. Reduce heat to the lowest setting, cover and cook for about 20 - 25 minutes until the rice is cooked and the surface is covered with steam holes. Let it rest for 5 - 10 minutes. Fluff up the rice before serving.

# CHAPPATIS

*Chappatis, parathas and rotis are basic flat breads consumed all over North India. All  these breads are made with durum wheat flour, popularly called Atta or chappati flour available at all Indian stores. If you don't have access to chappati flour use equal parts of whole wheat flour (available at regular supermarkets) and all-purpose flour.*

*Yield 10*
- **2 cups chappati flour (atta)**
- **½ teaspoon salt**
- **¾ cup water**
- **extra flour for dusting and rolling**
- **extra ghee or oil for basting**

Stir in flour and salt in a bowl.  Add water to the flour mixture and make a soft, pliable dough.  If the dough feels too dry, add water 1 tablespoon at a time and mix in.  If the dough feels sticky, add flour 1 tablespoon at a time.  The dough should be soft and pliable, but not sticky. Transfer the dough to a work surface,  knead for 3 - 5 minutes.  Cover the dough with plastic wrap.  Let it rest for ½ an hour allowing the gluten to develop.

Divide the dough into 10 equal portions.  Work with 1 piece at a time and keep the rest covered to prevent from drying.  Roll out the dough into 7-inch circles.

Heat a griddle over medium high heat.  When the griddle is hot, place rolled chappati onto it.  When the bottom is cooked and dotted with brown spots, flip to the other side.  Using a flat spatula, apply gentle pressure on top.  This makes the chappatis  puff up. When the other side is also covered with a few brown spots, baste with ghee or oil on both sides.  Remove from the griddle.  Cover the chappatis with a kitchen towel while you prepare the rest.

# POMEGRANATE JUICE

*I am fortunate to have three pomegranate trees in my backyard. I simply love to use these jewel-like seeds in every possible manner. We not only enjoy these fruits fresh but I also use it in salads, to garnish rice dishes, and to make jams as party favors. They are always part of the decoration at my Thanksgiving table. I use pomegranate juice to make drinks and concentrate it to use as glazes for meats. The list goes on and on. I refuse to waste even a single fruit. After reading this book, I hope I inspire you to use more pomegranates in your diet. They are sooo good for you.*

*Yield 1 cup*
- **2 - 3 fresh pomegranates**

Remove the seeds from the pomegranates. Using the food processor pulse seeds 4 - 5 times and pass it through a sieve lined with a cheese cloth set over a bowl to collect the juice. Discard seeds. Alternately, cut pomegranates in half horizontally and juice them using manual or electric citrus juicer. The pomegranate juice can be made a few days in advance.

# POMEGRANATE SYRUP

*Yield 1 cup*
- **1 cup pomegranate juice**
- **1 cup sugar**

In a small sauce pan dissolve sugar in the pomegranate juice. Heat over medium heat about 20 – 25 minutes, until the liquid is thick and reduces to half its volume.

*Cook's note: You can substitute pomegranate juice with ¾ cup water and ¼ cup unsweetened pomegranate molasses, available at gourmet food stores.*

# POMEGRANATE GLAZE

*Yield 1 cup*
- **1 cup pomegranate syrup**
- **1 tablespoon ginger juice**
- **½ - 1 teaspoon cayenne pepper**
- **½ teaspoon salt**

Stir everything together in a small sauce pan. Heat over medium-low heat until heated thoroughly.

# CANDIED FLOWERS

*Making candied flowers is a practice that was popular in the 17th and 18th century Europe. Many flowers like violets, rose petals, scented geraniums, and nasturtiums can be candied. Make sure the flowers you choose are pesticide-free. Once you make these flowers, you can store them in a cool, dry place for months.*

- **1 cup edible flowers**
- **1 egg white**
- **super fine sugar for coating**

Rinse flowers in cold water and gently dry with paper towels. In a small bowl, whisk egg white lightly. Using a small paintbrush, brush flowers with the egg white. Make sure flowers are completely coated with the egg white. Sprinkle sugar on both sides. Let it air dry on a rack. As they dry, these flower petals harden. Store in an airtight container in cool, dark place.

# YOGURT (CURD)

*Yogurt is called curd in India. Yogurt-making has been a common practice throughout India over the centuries. I remember, when I was growing up, a farmer's day began with milking the cows and buffaloes and boiling the milk in a large terra-cotta pot over a wood-burning stove. It was a tradition to use only terra-cotta pots to boil the milk and to set the yogurt. Not only does the yogurt taste better, but it is believed that yogurt from terra-cotta containers have a cooling effect on the body. The tropical weather of Southern India presents an ideal temperature to set the yogurt.*

*My mother would churn the yogurt from the previous night to extract the butter. The liquid that remains is called buttermilk. Buttermilk has all the benefits of the yogurt except the fat, and can be enjoyed as a refreshing drink throughout the day or can be served as part of a meal. The butter was then melted into ghee to use in curries or to make sweets. We used to mix rice with any curry and drizzle some melted ghee on top to give an extra -rich buttery taste to any dish. In the cholesterol-conscious world we live in today, we are moving away from the practice of eating ghee.*

*Homemade yogurt is not only easy to make but is also free of any preservatives found in store-bought yogurt. You can make yogurt with any kind of milk such as whole milk, 2 percent, 1 percent and even with non-fat. Higher milk fat content translates to creamier yogurt.*

*Yogurt is eaten with every meal in India. It acts as a tenderizer in marinades, it is cooked with curries and it thickens gravies. The health benefit of eating yogurt every day surpasses any vitamin pills.*

*Yield 4 cups*
- 4 cups milk
- ¼ cup natural yogurt

Bring the milk to a boil in a heavy bottomed sauce pan over medium high heat. Keep an eye on it to prevent the milk from boiling over. Transfer milk to a ceramic, terra-cotta, or stainless steel container. Let the milk cool to 115ºF -120ºF and stir in the yogurt. Cover tightly with plastic wrap first and then with the lid. If you live in a colder climate, wrap the pot with an old sweater to insulate the pot and to maintain the ideal temperature required for the yogurt to set. Let the milk rest for 3 - 4 hours undisturbed. Check if the yogurt is set. Once the yogurt is set, you might notice some watery liquid on top of the yogurt, which is normal. Refrigerate until ready to use. The yogurt will remain fresh for 3 - 5 days.

# STRAINED YOGURT

*Strained yogurt is popularly called hung curd in India. It is made by putting yogurt in a cheese cloth and tying it over the kitchen faucet to drain off the whey. Strained yogurt is used in marinades, is mixed with vegetables and fruit to make raita, and is also used to make desserts such as shrikhand.*

*Yield 3 cups*
- 6 cups yogurt
- cheese cloth

Place yogurt in a sieve or colander lined with 2 - 3 layers of cheese cloth. Set it over a bowl to catch the whey. Cover with the plastic wrap and refrigerate overnight. The yogurt should reduce to half its original volume. Discard the whey. Transfer to a bowl and use as needed.

*Cook's Note: Cheese cloth is available at any gourmet food shops and in some super markets. Good quality paper towels or unbleached coffee filters can be used in place of cheese cloth.*

# GHEE

*Ghee is often compared to melted butter. Melted butter is where you heat the butter fat and it rises to the top, with the milk solids settled at the bottom. Ghee, however, is clarified butter that is simmered at medium low temperature until the milk solids turn golden brown. In the process it develops a nutty flavor. Then, you strain the milk solids using a fine mesh strainer. Ghee has a higher melting point, which means you can heat it to a high temperature without burning. Traditionally, using ghee to cook curries was a common practice in India. Nowadays, health-conscious Indian cooks replace ghee with vegetable oil. However, some dishes simply cannot do without ghee.*

*Yield 1 ½ - 1 ¾ cups*
- 1 pound unsalted butter

Place butter in a heavy bottomed sauce pan. Heat over medium low heat. At first the butter will start foaming and then it will subside. Continue simmering until all the water is evaporated and the milk solids turn golden brown. Remove from the heat and slowly pass it through a fine mesh sieve. Discard the brown bits.

# SIMPLE SYRUP

*Yield 1 cup*
- 1 cup sugar
- 1 cup water

Place sugar and water in a small saucepan. Stir to dissolve sugar. Bring it to a boil over medium high heat. Reduce heat to medium and simmer for 2 more minutes. Turn off the heat. You can store syrup in the refrigerator for up to a month.

# GINGER SYRUP

*Yield 1 cup*
- 1 cup sugar
- 1 cup water
- 4 tablespoon grated ginger

In a small saucepan, boil sugar, water and grated ginger over medium heat. Stir until the sugar dissolves and boil for two more minutes. Turn off the heat and let it steep for 30 minutes allowing the flavors to infuse. Strain the syrup and use as required. You can store the syrup in the refrigerator for up to a month.

# ROSE SYRUP

*Yield 1 cup*
- 1 cup sugar
- 1 cup water
- ½ teaspoon green cardamom seed powder
- 1 teaspoon rosewater
- few drops of red food color

To make the syrup, boil sugar and water in a medium saucepan. Bring it to a boil for 2 minutes. Turn off the heat. Add cardamom powder, rosewater and food color. Let the syrup come to room temperature. Store in the refrigerator for up to 1 month.

# SAFFRON-CARDAMOM SYRUP

*Yield about 2 cups*
- 2 cups sugar
- 2 cups water
- ½ teaspoon green cardamom seed powder
- 1 teaspoon loosely packed saffron

In a small saucepan, boil sugar and water over medium heat. Stir until the sugar dissolves and boil for two more minutes. Add cardamom powder and saffron. Turn off the heat and let it steep for ½ an hour. You can store this syrup in the refrigerator for up to a month.

# CARAMELIZED ONIONS

*Yield 1-1 ½ cups*

- 2 medium onions, peeled, cut lengthwise, sliced and cut in the middle.
- ½ cup peanut or vegetable oil

Heat oil in a shallow pan over medium high heat. Add onions and fry while stirring occasionally at the beginning and often at the end, until they turn golden brown evenly. Remove onions with a slotted spatula and with another spatula gently press the onions to release the excess oil. Spread them on to a sheet pan to crisp up and cool. Caramelized onions stays fresh in the refrigerator for up to a month. Reserve leftover oil for marinades.

# CARAMELIZED ONION POWDER

*Yield ½ cup*
- **1 cup caramelized onions**

Using a spice grinder, grind fried onions into a powder. This stays fresh in the refrigerator for up to a month.

# PAPRI CHIPS

*You can make papri chips using the traditional method or you can make them using flour tortillas. They can be used interchangeably.*

*Traditional Papri Chips:*
- **1 ½ cups all-purpose flour**
- **½ cup fine-grain semolina**
- **1 teaspoon salt**
- **2 tablespoons vegetable oil**
- **½ cup water**
- **oil for deep frying**

In a bowl, stir in flour, semolina and salt to combine. Using your fingers, mix oil into the flour mixture until it resembles bread crumbs. Add water 2 tablespoons at a time to make a pliable dough. Let the dough rest for an hour allowing the gluten to develop. Divide the dough into 4 sections and make each section into a ball. Roll out each ball into a 9-inch circle. Cut each circle into ½-inch stripes and then into diamonds.

Heat oil in a heavy bottomed saucepan to 325° F. Add enough pieces to cover the oil in a single layer without crowding. Fry until light golden brown, while stirring often with a slotted spoon. Remove them and place onto a sheet pan lined with a paper towel. Proceed with the rest. When they are cool, store in an airtight container until ready to use.

*Papri Chips with Flour Tortillas*

*This is a very quick way to make papri chips. These are a good substitute for traditional papri chips.*

- **twelve 8-inch flour tortillas**
- **oil for deep frying**

Heat oil in a medium saucepan over medium high heat until it reaches 325° F. Meanwhile, cut flour tortillas into 1-inch pieces. Fry tortilla pieces in batches until golden while stirring often with a slotted spoon. Using a slotted spoon, remove them and place onto a sheet pan lined with a paper. Proceed with the rest. Let them cool. Store in an airtight container until ready to use.

# COOKED TOOR DAL

*Yield 3 - 4 cups*

- **1 cup toor dal**

Wash dal with several changes of water. Place dal with 3 cups of water in a pressure cooker. Close and cook for 2 minutes at high pressure over medium high heat. Reduce heat to medium and cook for another 10 - 12 minutes. Turn off the heat and let the pressure drop on its own. It usually takes about 15 minutes. After the pressure drops, open the lid carefully. Stir with a whisk to mash the dal. Cooked dal should be creamy, if not cook on stove top until it is ready, add ½ cup water if necessary.

Alternately, place dal with 3 cups of water in a large saucepan. Bring it to a boil over medium high heat and boil for 5 minutes. Reduce heat to medium. Cover with the lid and cook for about 40 - 45 minutes until dal is soft and creamy. As the dal cooks, you will notice some of the scum rising to the top, simply stir it back in. Add **½ cup water** whenever necessary and cook dal until creamy. Stir with a whisk to mash the dal.

# GLOSSARY

**Ajwain seeds:** Ajwain seeds look like mini cumin seeds. They are used in snacks either whole or ground. They have a very strong flavor. They are known to cure digestive problems and are often added to starchy snacks.

**Amchoor powder:** It is a beige powder made from dried green mango. Used as a souring agent. It is an essential ingredient in chaat masala.

**Anardhana:** Dried ground pomegranate seeds. Similar to amchoor powder. It has a sweet and sour flavor.

**Asafoetida:** Popularly known as "Hing" all over North India. It is a resin extracted from the dried sap of the stem and roots of the Ferula plant, grown in Iran, Afghanistan, and Kashmir. You can buy it in powder form and as a lump. It has a very strong flavor. Use it very sparingly. Used as digestive aid.

**Banana leaves:** Often used as disposable plates to eat in South India. Available at Indian and Mexican super markets. I often use them as plate liners.

**Basil seeds:** These are tiny black seeds, soaked in water until they bloom. Used in drinks such as Falooda. Available at Indian stores.

**Bay leaves:** California bay leaves are similar to Indian bay leaves. Indian bay leaves are from the cassia trees, whereas European bay leaves are from the laurel tree. Both can be used interchangeably.

**Black eyed peas:** These are dried cow peas. You need to soak them before cooking.

**Black salt:** Black salt is used as a flavor enhancer. It is an essential ingredient in chaat masala. Black salt is mined from the underground sulfur deposits of central India, Pakistan, and Afghanistan. Available at Indian stores.

**Cardamom:** Native to India, it is the third most expensive spice after saffron and vanilla. Two different types of cardamom pods are available, green and brown/black. Brown/black ones are earthier in flavor, whereas green ones are more pungent and very aromatic. The three-sided green ones are more commonly used. Whole pods are used in pulaos, biryanis, and meat dishes. Green cardamom seed powder is essential in many Indian desserts, similar to vanilla flavoring in western desserts. It is a home remedy for nausea. Often chewed on as a mouth freshener after meals.

**Cayenne:** It is hot chili powder made from a long, thin variety of hot chilies, called Capsicum frutescens. It is very popular in Indian curries. It is used both for the color and the heat.

**Chaat masala:** Salty, tart spice blend used to season salad-like snacks.

**Chappati flour:** Also called "atta". It is finely ground whole wheat flour. Used in making Indian flat breads such as chappati or paratha.

**Chena dal:** Split Bengal gram, these are hulled, split, black chena peas. These are similar to split yellow peas, used in variety of dishes. In South, these are also used as a spice.

**Chickpeas and Black Chena:** Bengal gram is very versatile in Indian cooking. These come in beige-colored heart-shaped beans or black-brown heart shaped beans known as chickpeas or the black-brown heart shaped small ones called black chena. Beige-colored ones are more popular in the North to make chole, whereas in the South small black-brown beans are readily available. Canned chickpeas are very convenient to use and are sold in all supermarkets. They are also hulled and ground into besan to make pakodas and bajjis.

**Cilantro/Coriander:** Dhania, is the most favorite Indian herb for cooking, garnishing and for making chutney. It is an indispensable part of Indian food.

**Cinnamon:** Inner bark of the cinnamon tree. Sold as rolled up bark. When you use whole bark, it is used for flavoring only and is not meant to be eaten. Ground cinnamon is popular in sweet and savory dishes.

**Cloves:** Unopened flower buds from the clove tree. They have an aromatic spicy flavor and are used whole or ground. Whole cloves are added to enhance the flavor of a dish, especially meat. Ground cloves are part of many spice blends.

**Coconut:** Coconut is a fruit of a coconut palm tree. Essential to many south Indian dishes, especially in Kerala cooking.

**Coconut milk:** You can make fresh milk by soaking the ground coconut paste in hot water and straining the milk. Canned milk is readily available. Use canned or fresh interchangeably.

**Cumin seeds:** Jeera, is available whole or ground. To intensify flavor, roast the whole seeds and grind them into a powder.

**Curry leaves:** The curry leaf plant is indigenous to India and Sri Lanka. These aromatic leaves are essential to South Indian food. Fresh or dried curry leaves available at Indian stores.

**Dry whole red chilies:** Commonly used as part of the seasoning. Ground fried chilies are used to make chutneys. Whole chilies are added to flavor the food, but not meant to be eaten.

**Dals:** Dal is the term used to describe an ingredient as well as a cooked dish. Dal is technically dried, split peas. Most dals are available skinned or unskinned. Dal is an ultimate comfort food, when served with rice or roti. Indian menus always include some form of dal or the other. Dals play a vital role in providing the primary source of protein for the vast population of vegetarians in India.

**Drumsticks:** Most popular vegetable to use in sambar. They are long, green pods available fresh or frozen at Indian stores. Only the inner pulp is eaten by scraping with the teeth. The fibrous outer shell is discarded.

**Fennel seeds:** Saunf, are long green yellow seeds. To intensify flavor, you can dry-roast them before grinding. Usually eaten raw, after meals as a mouth freshener.

**Fenugreek seeds:** Methi, these yellow square seeds are slightly bitter. You can dry-roast them for few seconds before using for better flavor. If you burn them they turn more bitter.

**Fresh green chilies:** Long, thin variety of green chilies such as green cayenne; they are popular in India. Serrano is a good substitute. If you want just the flavor of the chili and not the heat, cut the chili lengthwise, and remove the membrane and seeds, and use only the skin. If you have sensitive skin, I suggest using kitchen gloves while handling the chilies or washing your hands as soon as you are done with them.

**Garam masala powder:** It is a North Indian spice blend. Usually added as a final seasoning to meat dishes. Main ingredients are black pepper, cardamom, cumin, cloves and cinnamon.

**Garlic:** Garlic is always used fresh and never dried in India. It is a standard ingredient in Indian cooking. When you pair it with ginger, it forms the basis for numerous sauces. Used freshly minced, chopped, made into paste, or sliced.

**Ghee:** Clarified butter is heated until all the milk solids turn golden brown and water evaporates. The leftover fat is strained. It has a high melting point and can be heated to high temperatures without burning.

**Ginger:** Adrak, is a rhizome of a tropical ginger plant. One of the most commonly used spices in Indian cooking. Most important in almost all curries. Choose tender, plump, and shiny pieces that can be easily snapped. A more mature one has lot more fiber. It is highly valued as a stimulant for digestion. Ground ginger is widely available.

**Jaggery:** Gur, it is golden brown dehydrated sugar cane juice. It is sold in big chunks and needs to be grated before use.

**Masoor dal:** Red split lentils, hulled salmon colored split lentils, are very easy to cook and easily digestible. Sold whole and split.

**Methi leaves:** Fresh tender fenugreek leaves are called methi leaves, sold in Indian stores in bunches. Popular to use in breads and meats. Dried fenugreek leaves are called kasuri methi and are used as herbs to flavor the dishes.

**Mint:** Many varieties of mint are available in Indian stores. All of them taste very refreshing. The one that is used in the Indian culinary world is spearmint, used in pulaos, biryanis, chutneys, raitas, drinks and teas.

**Mung dal:** Green gram, hulled split mung beans are a basic dal in North India. Pre-soaking is not necessary to cook. Mung beans are more commonly used for sprouting. Mung dal is very easy to digest.

**Mustard seeds:** Black mustard seeds are popular in Indian cooking. Usually popped in hot oil to bring out their nutty flavor. Commonly used in vegetable dishes and dals. They are ground and used in pickles. Mustard oil is used in pickles. Mustard oil is also popular in Punjabi and Bengali food.

**Nutmeg and Mace:** Jaiphul and Javitri, nutmeg and mace are obtained from the same tropical evergreen tree, which produces apricot-like fruits. The fruits are not edible. The inner part of the seed is the nutmeg. The web-like lacy covering of the seed is the mace. The shell has to be cracked open to harvest nutmeg. I always use freshly grated nutmeg to get maximum flavor. Both nutmeg and mace are used in Moghul cuisine.

**Paprika:** Kashmir mirchi powder, is a ground sweet red pepper grown in Kashmir. Usually added for the color and not for the heat. You can fry in oil to get rid off some of the raw smell. Hungarian or Spanish paprika is a good substitute.

**Pepper corns:** Kaali Mirchi, black pepper is native to India and it is known as the king of spices. It is an essential ingredient in lot of spice blends.

**Poppy seeds:** Khus Khus, black and white ones are available, but only the white ones are commonly used in India. You can roast them at a low temperature to bring out their nutty flavor, grind in a spice mill and use to thicken gravies. Alternately you can soak them in warm water and grind into paste. These tiny seeds can easily go rancid at room temperature. You can store them in the freezer.

**Rajma:** Kidney Beans, belong to the same family as pinto beans. Readily available in Indian and American super markets.

**Rose water and essence:** It is a classic flavoring from the Moghul era for candies and deserts. Rose essence is an extract from intensely flavored roses that are grown especially for culinary purposes. Rose water is a diluted form of the essence. You can dilute a couple of drops of essence with a tablespoon of water to make rose water. Use it sparingly as it has a very strong flavor.

**Saffron:** The dried stamens of the crocus plant. It is the world's most expensive spice. Saffron is grown in Kashmir region. Iranian and Spanish saffron are a good substitute. Only a small amount is used to flavor the dishes. Before using, it is usually soaked in water or milk to extract maximum flavor.

**Silver leaf:** Vark, silver leaf is not a spice but very thin leaves of silver which do not have any flavor or aroma. A signature Moghul garnish. During the Moghul period, elaborate rice dishes, such as pulaos, biryanis and roasts, were garnished with very thin leaves of 24-carat gold and silver and served at banquets. This symbolized the opulence and power of the Moghul court. You can buy them at Indian store as books of thin fragile sheets separated by tissue papers. To use, apply directly onto the food with a tissue paper and peel off the tissue paper.

**Star anise:** Star-shaped fruit from an evergreen tree of the Magnolia family. It has a very strong flavor like licorice and anise seeds, even though it is not related to either one of them. It is not commonly used in India, except as a flavoring in pulaos and biryanis.

**Shea jeera:** Black cumin seeds, are an essential ingredient in Hyderabadi cuisine.

**Tamarind:** Imli, it is also known as Indian dates. The tamarind tree is indigenous to India. It is used as a souring agent in cooking. It has a sweet and sour taste and is indispensable in South Indian cooking. Available as blocks of pods, which need to be soaked to extract the pulp or as ready made paste.

**Toor dal:** Red gram, hulled, split, gold colored disc-shaped dal that is popular all over India, especially in the South. Commonly sold in Indian markets, plain or oiled.

**Turmeric:** Haldi, the bright yellow colored powder is made from a ground rhizome similar to ginger but with smaller fingers. It is the most valuable spice in an Indian pantry, especially in South India. It is used to color the food and flavor dals, meats and vegetables. Commercial curry powders get their rich yellow color from turmeric. It is widely used as an antiseptic. Current research indicates that turmeric works as an anti-cancer agent.

**Urad dal:** Black gram, hulled, split, white, small and similar in shape to mung dal. Sold in Indian stores. Soaked and ground before using in dosas or vadas. In the South, it is also used as a spice. Available whole, split with or without skin. When I call for urad dal in a recipe, I mean skinned urad dal.

**Yellow split peas:** Hulled split dried peas that can be used interchangeably with chena dal. Yellow split peas are made from mature green peas. Available in green and yellow.

# Wine Pairing

Any wine connoisseur would agree that it is difficult to pair wine with Indian food because of the complex use of spice blends in almost all the dishes. In Indian food, the dominant flavor does not come from the meat or the vegetable but rather from the sauces and spices used in the dish. Pairing food with wine is a European concept. In India, tradition and culture prohibit the consumption of alcohol. Even in America, orthodox immigrant Indian homes restrict the use of alcohol in any form. Since the world is becoming smaller, ethnic foods are becoming ever so popular with mainstream Americans as well as the rest of the world; pairing wine with ethnic food types such as Indian is a trend-setting phenomenon in restaurants.

Frank Klein, the current wine director at Mantra restaurant in Northern California recommends wine such as Gewürztraminers, Rieslings and other aromatic varietals with residual sugar with spicier dishes. It is all about low/no oak, high acidity, and clean, crisp flavors to temper the heat. Milder dishes pair best with selections like dry rosés, Gewürztraminers and Sauvignon Blancs. Indian foods prepared with red meats are often complimented by Pinot Noirs/Burgundies, Syrahs and Grenaches. "The spicy earth elements stand up to the food," comments Klein. Soft, lighter reds without excessive tannins shine. Cabernet Sauvignons and Bordeauxs tend to be a little more challenging when pairing with Indian food due to their heavier tannins, as Klein explains.

The new concept of pairing wine with food goes back to the old saying, "Complex wines pair well with simple foods, and simple wines pair well with complex foods." Since Indian food is the most intricately flavored, the wine should be simple, crisp and clean. Most would agree that wines made on the Mediterranean coast are often made to stand up to spicy foods, and they stand a better chance to pair well with Indian food. Avoid any wine with alcohol content above 13-14%. Wines with high alcohol content will intensify the flavor of the spices and give a burning sensation. Gewürztraminers are the popular choice with Indian food because of their sweet flavor with a hint of spice. Here are some suggested wines other than Gewürztraminers that can be paired just as beautifully with Indian food.

1. Examples: Cabbage chena dal fry, carrot salad, beets fry, samosa and naan.
   Suggested wines: Chenin Blanc, Sauvignon, and Syrah.
2. Examples: Mung dal with coconut milk, black eyed peas dal, spinach dal, and khatte chole.
   Suggested wines: Lighter Pinot Noir, aromatic whites such as Pinot Blanc, and harvest Riesling.
3. Examples: Chicken tikka masala, kofta curry, palak gosht and chicken kurma.
   Suggested wines: Pinot Noir, Pinot Blanc, Cabernet Franc, Chenin Blanc, and Cotes du Rhone.
4. Examples: Tandoori chicken, lamb kabobs, and tamarind glazed baby back ribs.
   Suggested wines: Pinot Noir, leaner white wines like Sauvignon Blanc, Muscadet.
5. Examples: Palak paneer, palak gosht.
   Suggested wines: Dry Chenin Blanc, Dry Riesling, unoaked Chardonnay, like Chablis.

Indian foods have several layers of flavor, as do wines. Finding the perfect match is culinary heaven.

# CONVERSION TABLE

Conversions in this book are approximate, rounded to the nearest point. The measurements I have used in this book are imperial. Teaspoon, tablespoon and cup measurements are leveled, unless otherwise stated. Measurements in this book are given in volume, as much as possible. Follow the same set of measurements, either imperial or metric, throughout a recipe.

## OVEN TEMPERATURES

| Fahrenheit | Centigrade/ Celsius | British Gas Mark |
|---|---|---|
| 275ºF | 140ºC | 1 |
| 300 | 150 | 2 |
| 325 | 160 | 3 |
| 350 | 180 | 4 |
| 375 | 190 | 5 |
| 400 | 200 | 6 |
| 425 | 220 | 7 |
| 450 | 230 | 8 |
| 475 | 240 | 9 |

## LIQUID CONVERSIONS

| US cups | Imperial | Metric |
|---|---|---|
| 1 tablespoon | ½ fl oz | 15 ml |
| ⅛ cup | 1 fl oz | 30 ml |
| ¼ cup | 2 fl oz | 60 ml |
| ½ cup | 4 fl oz | 125 ml |
| ⅔ cup | 5 fl oz | 150 ml |
| ¾ cup | 6 fl oz | 175 ml |
| 1 cup | 8 fl oz | 250 ml |
| 1 ½ cup | 12 fl oz | 375 ml |
| 2 cups | 16 fl oz | 500 ml |

Note:
US method
1 tablespoon = 3 teaspoons

## WEIGHT CONVERSIONS

| ½ oz | 15 gms |
|---|---|
| 1 | 25 |
| 1 ½ | 40 |
| 2 | 50 |
| 2 ½ | 65 |
| 3 | 75 |
| 4 | 100 |
| 5 | 150 |
| 6 | 175 |
| 8 | 225 |
| 10 | 275 |
| 1 lb | 450 |
| 1 ½ | 750 |
| 3 | 1.5 |

## MEASUREMENTS

| ⅛ inch | 3mm |
|---|---|
| ¼ | .5cm |
| ½ | 1.0 |
| ¾ | 2 |
| 1 | 2.5 |
| 1 ½ | 4 |
| 2 | 5 |
| 3 | 7.5 |
| 4 | 10 |
| 5 | 13 |
| 6 | 15 |
| 8 | 20 |
| 10 | 25.5 |
| 12 | 30 |

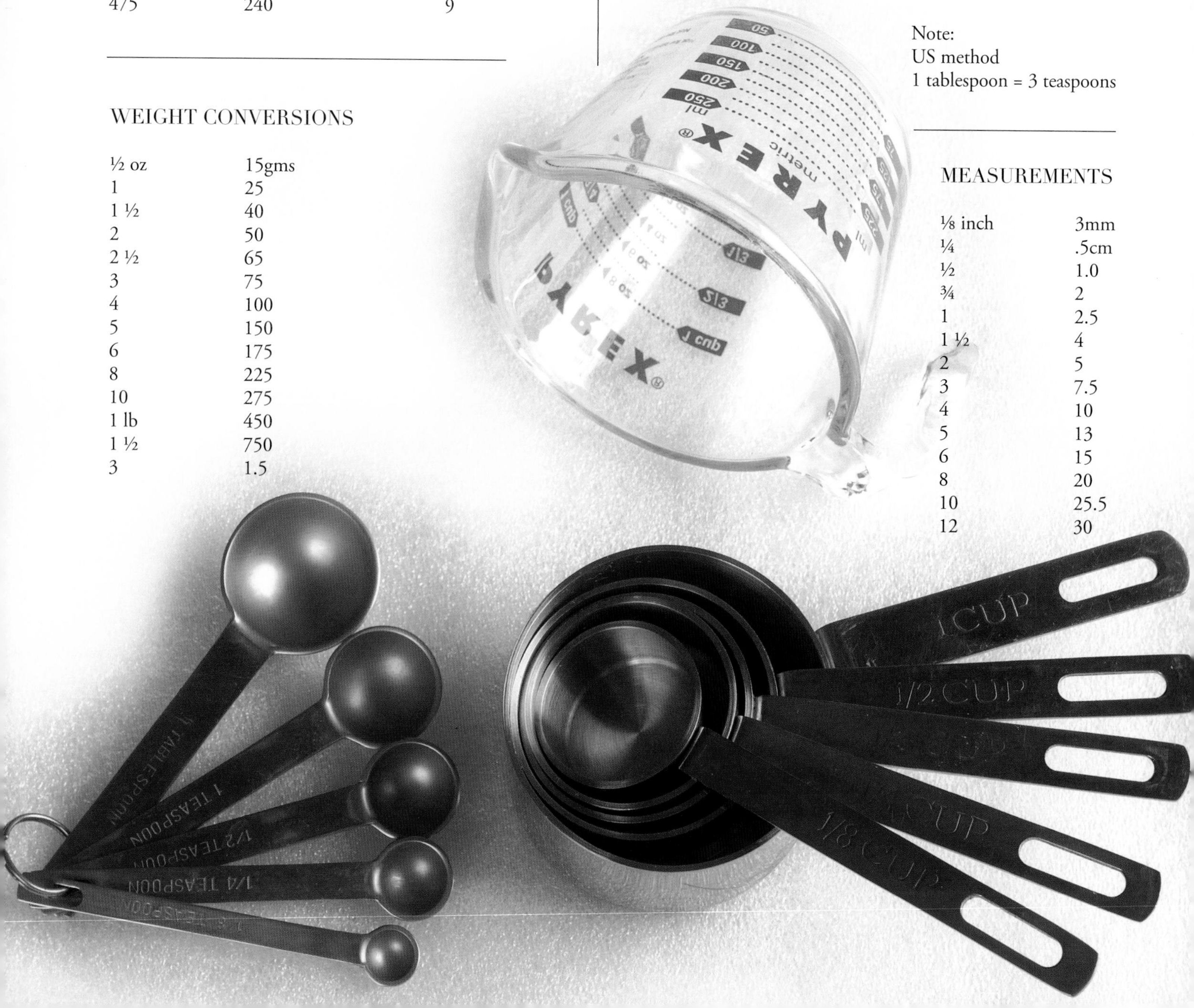

# INDIA
## States and Union Territories

TAJIKISTAN
AFGHANISTAN
PAKISTAN
CHINA
TIBET
NEPAL
BHUTAN
BANGLADESH
MYANMAR

**JAMMU & KASHMIR**
Srinagar

**HIMACHAL PRADESH**
Shimla
*Chandigarh*
**PUNJAB**
Dehradun
**UTTARAKHAND**
**HARYANA**
DELHI

**SIKKIM**
Gangtok
**ARUNACHAL PRADESH**
Itanagar

Jaipur
**UTTAR PRADESH**
Lucknow
**RAJASTHAN**

Dispur
**ASSAM** (Asom)
**NAGALAND**
Kohima
Shillong
**MEGHALAYA**
**BIHAR**
Patna
Imphal
**MANIPUR**

Agartala
**TRIPURA**
Aizawl
**MIZORAM**

Gandhinagar
I
N
• Bhopal
D
**JHARKHAND**
Ranchi
**WEST BENGAL**
A
**GUJARAT**
**MADHYA PRADESH**
Kolkata
**Diu**
Raipur
*Daman*
*Silvassa*
**CHHATTISGARH**
**DADRA & NAGAR HAVELI**
Bhubaneshwar
Mumbai
**ORISSA**

*ARABIAN SEA*
**MAHARASHTRA**
*BAY OF BENGAL*

• Hyderabad
*Yanam (Puducherry)*
**ANDHRA PRADESH**
Panaji
**GOA**
**KARNATAKA**

### LEGEND
–··–··– International Boundary
– – – – State Boundary
☐ National Capital
• State & U.T. Capital

Bengaluru
Chennai
**ANDAMAN & NICOBAR ISLANDS (INDIA)**
Port Blair
*Mahe (Puducherry)*
*Puducherry*
**LAKSHADWEEP (INDIA)**
• Kavaratti
*Karaikal (Puducherry)*
**KERALA**
**TAMIL NADU**

Map not to Scale
Copyright © 2007 www.mapsofindia.com

Thiruvananthapuram
**SRI LANKA**
I N D I A N   O C E A N

# RECIPE INDEX

# ACKNOWLEDGEMENTS

I want to thank my family and friends for their encouragement and support for this venture. This book is yours as much as it is mine. My sincere thanks to my friend and photographer Sethu Sethuraman for patiently working with my very difficult schedule. I am extremely grateful to my design team, Deepak Srivastava, Tina Manickam, Saima Haque, Sarbjit Lal and Suchi Gupta who have made this book stunningly beautiful. My heartfelt thanks to my friend Dr. Prithvi Raj Sharma for editing the text, and for his brotherly advice and encouragement. A special thanks to my friend Shobha Kumar for her recipe contribution, support, and advice from the very beginning. I thank my friends Vinita Bhushan and Ravi Govil for their technical support. My sincere thanks to Frank Klein, the current wine director at Mantra for wine–pairing. I would like to thank Aparna Prakash for editing the text in its final stages.

I am thankful to my friend Oliver Castilleja for reading and editing the text in its initial stages. I would like to show my gratitude to Lakshmi Shastry for her design contribution to the Thanksgiving and Christmas chapters. I want to thank Karthik Sundaram for his guidance in making this book possible. I thank Karthik Mehra from Sahid Sindh Sultan restaurant in Bangalore for sharing his knowledge of Moghul cuisine and for contributing recipes. My heartfelt thanks to my friend Viji Ananda for her recipes and for always being there with her million dollar smile.

I thank Sadhana Sharma for the Rangoli (page 220) display during Dipawali and my sister Kavitha Katiki for the Sankranti Muggu (page253). My thanks to Mrs. Kowsalya Mohana Krishnan for her beautiful kolu display (page 222) at her Oak Park house. I would like to thank Bernance Terando for the flowers (page 32).

My sincere thanks to my dear friends Drs. Prithvi Raj and Surekha Sharma for letting me use their rose garden for hosting a tea party. I am very grateful to my friends Shalabh and Radhika Puri for allowing me use their home and garden as my own for a Christmas and garden party. I thank my friends and neighbors, Cheri and Glen Griswold, for welcoming me to use their fabulous backyard for a Snack and Chaat party.

I thank my husband Mal for standing by me throughout this venture. I thank my darling daughter Silpa for typing the entire book and for giving me a helping hand whenever I needed it. I thank my children Naveen and Silpa Nunna for the initial editing of the book. My special thanks to my brother, Bhaskar Katiki, for his encouragement all through this journey.

My sincere thanks to my family and friends for letting me use their articles for photography.

**Recipe credits:**

Karthik Mehra: Tomato Soup (page 98), Moghul Dhum Biryani (86), Vegetable Kabobs (page 85), Chicken Kabobs (page85), Roti Pae Boti (page 89), Thadka Dal (page90), Pineapple Ka Panna (page 92).
Shobha Kumar: Loki Kofta (page 135), Gobi Shalgam Gajar Ka Achar (page 213), Kheema Kofta (page212) and Bhatura (page 280).
Viji Ananda : Paalak Paneer (page 214), Appam (page 164), Pineapple Pachadi (page167), Vegetable Kootu (page169), Avial (page 165) and Baby Potato Curry (page 288).
Madhu Patel: Kachori (page 198)

**Photo Credits:**
Sethu Sethuraman: Photography for the entire book except the following:
Symoni Johnson: Carrot Salad (page 36), Muruku (page 39), Spicy Fried Peanuts (page 38), and Buffet (page 41)
Victor Chang: Garba Dance (page 193), Author's photo on the jacket.
Silpa Nunna: Christmas Table Setting (page 273).
Jaz Banga: Punjab Bhangra Dance (page 206)

**Library of Congress Cataloging-in-Publication Data:**
Nunna, Komali.
Entertaining From An Ethnic Indian Kitchen/ Komali Nunna
Includes index.
ISBN 978-1-60585-526-4
1. Cooking 2. Entertaining
LCCN 2008902110